THE LITTLE PROVENCE BOOKSHOP

GILLIAN HARVEY

Boldwood

First published in Great Britain in 2024 by Boldwood Books Ltd.

Copyright © Gillian Harvey, 2024

Cover Design by Alice Moore Design

Cover Photography: Shutterstock and Alamy

A CIP catalogue record for this book is available from the British Library.

Paperback ISBN 978-1-80549-968-8

Large Print ISBN 978-1-80549-969-5

Hardback ISBN 978-1-80549-967-1

Ebook ISBN 978-1-80549-971-8

Kindle ISBN 978-1-80549-970-1

Audio CD ISBN 978-1-80549-962-6

MP3 CD ISBN 978-1-80549-963-3

Digital audio download ISBN 978-1-80549-964-0

Boldwood Books Ltd
23 Bowerdean Street
London SW6 3TN
www.boldwoodbooks.com

for Richer

PROLOGUE

It was the same every morning, even Sundays in the high season. At seven o'clock the bell tower opposite would ring out, rousing Monique from her bed, and she'd wash, dress and make her way to the apartment's small *cuisine,* fill the copper kettle and switch on the gas.

She always took her coffee the same: two teaspoons of ground beans, brewed in a pot, poured into a porcelain cup with gold-embossed edges, with two cubes of sugar from the tin. As the heat forced flavour from the grounds, she'd breathe deeply, the smell of the coffee awaking her senses before even touching her lips.

Once her espresso was made, she'd sit by the window and watch the courtyard, the movement of the morning as familiar to her as the lines in her palm. There was André opening the door of the patisserie and brushing flour from his apron; Theo with his two baguettes in brown paper, walking quickly back home for breakfast; Madame Lenore wheeling her bicycle across the cobbles rather than risk riding. By a quarter to eight, the older children would pass, their backs weighed down by enormous bags stuffed with books, their gait loping and reluctant as they made their way to the bus stop.

She loved this morning tableau, seeing the people who'd become friends and perhaps even family over the years. Seeing them evolve and change, encounter adversity and learn how to rise above it, or at least bear it. Growing up in Paris, she'd never imagined that small town life could be as rich; *Maman*, with her scarlet lips and tailored clothing, had scorned what she called the 'dying countryside', and preferred to be where there was life.

Only there was a difference between being amongst life and living. In Paris they had been surrounded by people but had remained lonely. Here, she had been able to make a difference; to use her talent to change lives – and what else was it for? She longed to tell her mother she was wrong.

But she had not spoken to *Maman* for more than thirty years; perhaps she was already dead? The flash of pain was soon subdued by the memory of what her mother had done to her. Some things could be forgiven; others left deep wounds that never quite closed.

Monique stood and brushed her skirt into place, straightened her blouse, walked to the mirror and adjusted her chignon then tried a smile. Her mother's face – perhaps also her daughter's face? – smiled back at her. She was a single entity but carried with her the women who had gone before and those who had come after.

As she placed her cup in the sink and made her way to the wooden staircase that snaked down onto the shop floor, she reminded herself that this was the day when Adeline would come. Monique could feel things beginning to shift, as if what had once seemed a complete puzzle had moved to make room for a final piece; the air was different and her life was in flux.

She glanced, in passing, at the small jar of earth on the

windowsill; soon perhaps she'd untie the knot, remove the cloth from where she'd buried it a few weeks ago. Perhaps.

She breathed in the scent of the books as she made her way down – the smell of ink and fresh paper, dust and older volumes. The mingling of past and present. She felt it healing her, knew the books were there as they always had been, waiting to excite, terrify, enlighten or restore whoever would be next to turn their pages.

As she crossed the shadowed floor of the bookshop, her skirt brushed softly against her calves. She knew the layout of the shelves, the stands, the tables with their high-stacked popular volumes. That knowledge and the tiny amount of light allowed by breaches in the wooden shutters meant there was no need for the electric light. She reached up for the window catch and opened the wooden frame, unfastening the shutters and at last folding them back.

The April sunlight fell into the room, alighting on her face like a theatre spotlight, illuminating her nut-brown skin, her eyes that sparkled like jewels. Her dress turned from grey to a vibrant yellow, her gold hoop earrings shone like stars. Her crystal – a moonstone – glowed against the soft skin at her throat. She fingered it briefly.

Then she continued to work her way around the windows, as if she were Mother Nature herself, calling time on the drawn-out night and allowing the spring day to finally burst into being.

1

From the back of the taxi, Adeline stared out at the darkened streets; the houses shrouded by deep shadows barely pierced by the dull glow of scattered orange street lamps. Lili was curled up, snuggled under her favourite blanket and nestled into her side, her long, dark lashes stark against her pale skin. That side of Adeline's body was warm, a little sticky with sweat. The other remained cold. Adeline had not expected to be so late; she had only worn a light jumper.

Through the tinted window she tried to make out the shapes of things, the size of buildings; to imagine what her surroundings would look like once the sun rose. But the stark gleam of the taxi's headlights was edged with a cloak of blackness that restricted her view and simply showed an empty, uneven and expressionless road ahead.

She had wanted to arrive in the daytime. Delays at the airport, and an interminable wait for first their luggage, then the taxi, had shattered this hope and now she simply hoped that she would be able to find the cottage; that the key would be in the lockbox as promised and that the electricity would have been switched on for their arrival.

It would be different if she was alone, she thought, lightly rubbing Lili's arm as her child slept. Alone, she could let herself in and simply collapse on a settee or mattress or whatever sparse furniture might be in place. But with Lili only five years old, she knew she had to find the right spot, to make sure there were blankets, that her child would be safe and warm. And God forbid she hadn't packed 'Bunny.'

The driver was silent; he'd started with platitudes – asking about their holiday, the reason for their travels, complimenting her on her French. Her responses had disappointed him, she knew, but she was too tired to explain her life to a stranger and had kept her replies monosyllabic at best. In the end, the conversation had petered out – perhaps he thought her French wasn't as fluent as he'd believed at first. She felt a little rude – but actually it was a blessing in disguise for the driver. If she unloaded all her angst, her reason for being here, her worries, onto him, he'd probably wind up thoroughly depressed.

She glimpsed herself occasionally in the blackened glass of the back seat window, a white face hovering against the dark, her shadowed eyes and straight mouth, her forehead creased with worry.

Eventually the taxi bumped to a halt and she stepped out, a half-woken Lili leaning heavily against her. The driver placed their cases by her feet and she thanked him, then turned towards the green front door.

As promised, the little lockbox was there and she punched in the code, relieved when it dropped open to reveal a key. She slipped it into the lock and pushed the door open to their new life.

* * *

It had taken her a while to sink into sleep last night, so when she woke, Lili standing mischievously refreshed and bright-eyed next to her, she felt sluggish and weighed down. But she tried to smile at the indignant little girl at her side. 'Morning, precious,' she said.

'It's dirty.'

'What's dirty?'

The light which fell through the unshuttered windows revealed a whitewashed room with elegant – if a little dated – furnishings, including the antique bed she'd fallen into, with its starched sheet and silk counterpane, and an ornate washbasin at the edge of the room with a rusty smudge of age-old water. Spiders had woven webs in the corners and dust particles, displaced by the new inhabitants, danced and sparkled. Even so, the sudden dislike of dirt was pretty rich coming from a girl who did everything she could to avoid having to clean her teeth each night.

'Everything,' Lili said, screwing up her face in a way meant to show distaste but that instead made her look even more adorable than usual.

Adeline smiled and propped herself up on her elbows. 'Well, the house has been empty for a while, that's all,' she said. 'We can soon clean it. There's some beautiful furniture in here!'

Lili looked doubtful but gave a small, brief nod.

Unlike her daughter, Adeline had been pleasantly surprised at the house; had worried it might be damp or dingy or unin-habitable in a number of different ways, despite assurances on the phone from the landlady. Yet it was light and, while rudi-mentary, freshly painted and more than adequate for the two of them. Lili was used to the straight lines, fresh plaster and the kind of order that comes with a newly decorated house in England. It would take her some time to get used to the exposed stone, the gaping fireplace, the wooden stairs with their worn treads. But Adeline already saw the beauty in all of it – perhaps she had been right to come.

'Come on,' she said, suddenly throwing the covers back and swinging her legs around. 'Get dressed and we'll get croissants for breakfast.'

Her daughter's nose screwed up again. 'Frosties?' she asked.

Adeline laughed. 'I'm sure we can get some later. For tomorrow. But we'll have to make do with fresh pastries from the boulangerie for breakfast I'm afraid.' It was tongue-in-cheek but Lili, used to sugary cereal and cold milk, sighed and nodded her head.

'OK, Mum,' she said, resigned.

Minutes later, they were crossing the narrow road outside their house in hurriedly pulled on clothing, standing in the queue outside the boulangerie behind an elderly man in a blue jacket who turned and gave them a brief *bonjour*. Behind the counter, a young man with sandy brown hair and impressive biceps was wrapping a baguette expertly in a sheet of thin, brown paper. He wore a white apron over blue jeans and a black T-shirt, slightly dusted with flour. As he turned the baguette over with a flourish, his tongue hovered at the side of his mouth. He was almost too good-looking and Adeline's longing, hungry gaze soon grew tired of pains au chocolat and rested instead on the tasty morsel serving them.

'Mummy,' said Lili quietly, tugging at Adeline's hand and interrupting her thoughts.

'What is it?' she said, looking at the little, inquisitive eyes fixed on hers.

'Why are you staring at that man?'

Adeline felt her neck get hot. Had she been? 'I wasn't, silly,' she said, hoping any anglophones eavesdropping would hear her denial. 'I was looking at the croissants. Don't they look tasty!'

There was a slight snort behind her and she turned, her brow furrowed, to meet the sparkling black eyes of an old lady in a green coat. The woman gave a small shrug and winked, her mouth stretched in a delighted smile.

Was she laughing at Adeline? It was true, she *had* been staring at the man behind the counter, but in her defence, he *was* extremely good-looking. Adeline gave a reciprocal shrug of her shoulders and smiled, hoping that covered all eventualities.

The man handed the baguette to the woman at the front of the queue, looking up briefly. His eyes alighted on Adeline and they exchanged a smile.

Adeline had been aware of people watching her and Lili on their way across the courtyard and now in the queue. St Vianne was small and she'd expected to be noticed. Most people she passed nodded or smiled, although one or two affected not to have seen them at all. The patissier had acknowledged her as a stranger, but his smile – albeit brief – had been welcoming.

Another woman joined the queue behind them and soon began talking to the man in front, over the head of Lili and past Adeline whom she apparently assumed couldn't understand.

'It is early in the season for tourists.'

'Yes, but they come earlier each year. It's good for the businesses.'

'But not for the town.'

'Perhaps.'

Adeline felt her cheeks flush as she realised they were discussing her and was tempted to say something sharp. Luckily, she was able to hold her tongue – it wouldn't do to get off to a bad start when she'd yet to even meet Monique. 'Actually, I'm here to work,' she said instead, in perfect French.

The conversation stopped, both participants wrong-footed by her understanding of their conversation; her flawless French spoken with only a hint of a British accent.

'Sorry, *Madame*,' the man said. 'It was rude of us.'

'No matter,' she said and smiled.

He returned her smile and held out his hand. 'Patrick Delage.'

'Adeline Townsend.' She gave him her hand for a small shake, then turned to the woman whose face still seemed fixed. 'And you are...?'

'Eva Lenore.' The woman nodded but didn't hold her hand out for a shake.

'Nice to meet you,' Adeline said, as if Eva's greeting had been perfectly civil.

'And where is it you'll be working?' Patrick enquired.

'La Petite Librairie – the bookshop.'

His eyes widened slightly. 'Oh!' He glanced quickly across at Eva, a momentary shadow seeming to cross his face. 'I see.'

'Oh, and this is Lili, my daughter. Say *bonjour*, Lili!' Adeline added.

Lili, who had a rudimentary grasp of French (Adeline had read *T'Choupi* and *Lili* books to her on alternate nights to *Peter Rabbit* and *Peppa Pig*, and her daughter had followed the stories fascinated, her young malleable brain taking in the fricative 'r's and the absent 'h's and picking up the language with ease) hid behind her mother's legs and remained silent. When Adeline told people that Lili was bilingual, they'd make remarks like 'amazing' and 'wow' – and marvel that Adeline, as a single mum, had the time to tutor her. And they were right – it was difficult to fit it all in, to find energy to do all the things she did for Lili. But that was the point, wasn't it? When people are expecting you to fail, you have to work twice as hard to prove that you can rise to the challenge.

When her ex-love rat boyfriend, Colin, had baulked at the idea of being a father and even suggested an abortion six years ago when Adeline had fallen pregnant, she'd known she'd be doing this alone. She'd been warned by so many people how hard it was going to be. But easier to parent single than parent with someone who doesn't care, she'd thought, as she'd released Colin from all his obligations – telling him that she didn't need a penny from him and that as far as she was concerned, he was better off out of the picture – an option he'd taken with great relief.

'She's shy,' Adeline said, but Patrick had already reached the front of the queue and was ordering his *pain*. Eva nodded once in response and gave a tight smile. 'Well, nice to meet you!' Adeline stroked Lili's hair reassuringly. It was difficult in this unfamiliar place; she shouldn't expect her daughter to suddenly start chatting to strangers in their native tongue.

In the end, she selected a *pain aux raisins* and a *chocolatine*, hoping they'd be more palatable for Lili than croissants. The man gave her the briefest of *mercis* as she handed over the last of her euros – she'd have to withdraw more cash later, perhaps there was a bank in the centre? – and took the proffered paper bag with its buttery contents back across the road and back through the green door. Inside, she laid two plates on the table and split the pastries in half so Lili could taste each one.

It was an hour before she had to be at the bookshop and she felt a flutter of nerves as she sank her teeth into the *pain aux raisins.* But they were good nerves, she decided. Because perhaps now she would find her true home. And if not, judging by the delicious treats produced over the road, she could easily drown any sorrows she experienced in butter, chocolate and flaky pastry.

2

Holding Lili's cold little hand in hers, Adeline stepped forward and pushed open the glass checked door, nudging the little brass bell that hung on a spring attached to the frame, tinkling their welcome.

The smell of ink on paper was unmistakable; reminding her of libraries, the scent of newsprint as she'd packed newspapers in a bag for her paper-round in her early teens, the fragrance of dusty volumes piled high on her desk in the university before she'd left that life behind. There was nobody behind the counter and for a moment she was glad – it gave her a chance to get her bearings, take a measure of the place.

She heard his voice again in her head saying she was crazy – taking a job in a place she'd never been to. But something about the shop already said 'home' to her. Its shelf-lined walls with books spine-out displaying their titles, the tables stacked with volumes of various genres. It was ramshackle, a mixture of old and new. Needed a tidy as well as a dust, but it was a pleasant chaos. Something that spoke of a love of books, a need to over-stock the shelves and pile the flat surfaces high rather than deny any volume its place. She hoped Lili wouldn't remark on the need for a good old-fashioned clean here too.

'*Coucou!*' she called. 'Is anyone here?'

Her voice sounded loud on the empty shop floor – but surely if someone was here, they would have heard the bell? Should she have come in at all? Perhaps she'd missed a notice on the door – 'Back in ten minutes', or 'Closed for the morning'. But surely Monique was expecting them?

Then there was a sound of high heels on wood and a woman's legs became visible descending the wooden staircase at the back, behind the counter. The movement of colourful fabric, the swing of a skirt, a waist, bodice and finally the whole of her – her slim frame, sun-tarnished skin, hair in a loose chignon. Adeline noticed a pen tucked behind the woman's ear and another in the chignon, and a white-blue stone on a golden thread at her neck.

The woman turned. 'You are here!' she said, sounding delighted as she climbed down the final three steps onto the shop floor. 'I wasn't sure if you would come.'

It was the first time Adeline had seen Monique, but she recognised the voice from the telephone. She smiled, reached out a hand. 'Of course. Why wouldn't I?'

Monique shrugged playfully. 'Not many people from London want to work in St Vianne. I thought you might change your mind.'

'You'd be surprised,' Adeline countered, smiling. 'I think many people in London would dream of living, working in a place like this.'

'Ah, they dream!' Monique said, with a dismissive wave of the hand. 'But they do not come. They are too frightened.'

Her words reminded Adeline of Kevin's words – only his had been said in a derogatory way, trying to dissuade her. 'It's the kind of dream that should stay a dream,' he'd argued. 'People don't actually *do* things like this.'

She smiled. 'Well, I suppose I am a person who does.' She didn't feel brave though.

'Yes, I suppose that you are too,' Monique said, clearly amused. 'And you must be Lili.' She crouched down so she was eye level with the little girl. 'It's nice to meet you, Lili.' She looked up at Adeline. 'Does she understand French? Should I speak in English?'

'No, she understands,' Adeline said, feeling a swell of pride. 'I've always used both languages with her.' Adeline tried to move Lili forward, but the little girl remained stubbornly fixed, just behind her legs. 'She'll be going to the school tomorrow, I hope.'

Monique leaned forward, her face playful. 'But there is no rush, Adeline. Your Lili will be happy here too, I think. As we discussed, she's welcome in the shop when you are working.'

Lili's hand tightened in Adeline's as if to suggest anything but.

Straightening and stepping forward, making Lili scuttle even farther behind her mother, Monique passed them, a waft of floral fragrance in her wake, and moved over to a wooden box on wheels filled with picture books. She crouched down, her yellow dress ballooning around her legs, leaving just a sliver of heel visible, and rifled through the content. 'Ah!' she said. 'Here!' She lifted out a book with a picture of a cat on the front. 'For the girl who loves kittens,' she said, straightening and holding it out.

Adeline felt herself tense as she willed Lili to reach forward and take the book, not to snub Monique's gesture of friendship. But she needn't have worried. Lili dropped her hand and reached shyly for the volume; as soon as she gained purchase, she hugged it to herself as if frightened Monique might change her mind and take it back. 'You can sit,' Monique said, gesturing to a small table with chairs in the corner, its surface covered in stumpy wax crayons and discarded paper. 'Read, if you want.'

Lili gave a short, curt nod, a half-smile and made her way over, still clutching the book to her chest. She sank into the chair and began turning the pages, her blonde hair falling slightly over her face as she dipped her head to read.

'Thank you,' Adeline said. 'You're right. She does love kittens.'

Monique shrugged. 'It is nothing. She will be happy for a little while with the book I think.'

Adeline nodded. 'So,' she began, gesturing with her arms.

'Yes. So,' Monique replied, a smile playing on her lips. 'Perhaps we should start.'

Adeline nodded. In all honesty, she hadn't asked much about what the job would entail when she'd answered the advert; had expected an interview, a discussion before taking it on rather than just the acceptance she'd received. But she assumed she'd need to be able to operate the till, become familiar with the stock, hopefully learn how to order books for those who couldn't find what they were looking for. Monique would need to train her, but she'd soon get up to speed.

'Yes,' she said. 'Like I mentioned on the phone, I've worked in a shop before. But not for a good few years.' And a world away from this place, she thought – remembering the bright, stark shop floor lights, the bar-code scanner and the ill-fitting uniform she'd squeezed into for her Saturday job as a teen.

Monique gave another dismissive wave. 'I think you will find things a bit different here.'

'No doubt.'

'And certainly worlds away from being a teacher,' she said, referencing Adeline's most recent job.

Adeline laughed. 'Do you promise?' she joked.

Monique looked at her askance. '*Oui*, it is sure,' she said, all seriousness.

Adeline's smile faltered. She nodded. 'Well, great,' she said, weakly. Perhaps in France, teachers weren't quite as maligned as they were back home – whenever she made a chance remark about leaving the profession in London, people would roll their eyes and drop anecdotes about young people today, or remark that they'd never be a teacher, or tell her 'hilarious' stories about the awful things they'd done in their own schooldays. The more daring of them sometimes commented on the long holidays and be much closer to a knuckle sandwich than they might imagine.

'Come. I will make us coffee. We should talk,' Monique said, gesturing to the stairs.

Adeline shot a look at Lili.

'Ah, she will be fine. The bell will tell us if someone comes. And we will be able to hear if she calls.'

'OK,' Adeline replied doubtfully, hoping they wouldn't come back to find half the stock sold to the next customer for a couple of coins or a handful of sweets. 'Mummy's just popping upstairs,' she said to her daughter who nodded her head, eyes still fixed on a picture of a white kitten playing with a ball of wool.

Adeline followed her new boss up the wooden stairs into a small corridor and then into a pretty room that opened out to reveal a glossy rosewood table with carved wooden seats, a faded chaise longue stacked with books, an armchair with a floral cover. Light from the large windows streamed across the worn wood of the table's surface, highlighting its uneven patina, brushing the upholstered backs of the chairs with a pinkish light.

'Espresso?'

'*Oui, merci*,' Adeline said, although she wasn't really a fan of the strong, bitter and all-too-short beverage. It just felt right to agree.

'Because I have tea also?' Monique called, her voice more distant. Adeline turned and realised she must have slipped from the room to prepare the drinks. There was a laugh in her voice again, as if she realised that Adeline had agreed to espresso out of politeness.

'No, thank you,' Adeline doubled down. 'Espresso will be lovely.'

Her eye alighted on a shelf, on which there stood a collection of jars filled with coloured powders – perhaps bath salts? But no. Now, looking closer, she saw one had a leaf curling around the glass of its interior, another contained a coin resting on a dark powder.

Moments later her host returned with a tray on which sat a large, porcelain coffee pot and two tiny cups. Little biscuits wrapped in twists of paper garnished the saucers and she placed a delicate cup in front of Adeline with a smile. 'I have some juice for your Lili when she wants,' she said.

'Thank you.' Adeline lifted the cup to her lips and was surprised by the mild, rich taste. 'I like your jars,' she said, nodding at the shelf.

'*Merci*,' Monique answered. 'They are pretty, *non*?' Her eyes searched Adeline's face for a moment, before she looked away and took a sip from her cup.

Adeline longed to ask more, but couldn't quite find the words. 'So, I meant to check what my hours will be? And do you use Excel or another programme for the accounts?' she said instead.

To her surprise, Monique laughed – throatily – reaching a

hand forward to steady herself against the table. 'I am sorry,' she said. 'It is rude of me. It's just... you are so very British.'

'I am?'

'Yes. Or perhaps I should say, so very *métropolitaine,*' Monique continued. 'Ah, it is not an insult,' she added quickly. 'It is just that we do things very differently in St Vianne.'

'You don't... have set hours?'

'*Non, mon coeur,* it is not that. What I mean is that your question is so very practical. And this is not a practical shop. It is a shop that sells stories.' Monique swept her arms out wide as if to indicate the enormity of this task. 'Stories do not fit neatly into a spreadsheet. They fill the space they need, in our hearts, our heads, our imaginations. Yes, of course, we must deal with money and opening hours and all the things like taxes that are necessary. But what is necessary is not always important. When you prepare for a role in my store, the first thing I want to learn about you is the content of your heart.'

'My heart?'

'Yes. Why do you love books? Why do you choose to come here to work? What makes your heart beat faster?'

'I... well, I like books, I guess. Love them, I mean.'

This too seemed to amuse Monique. 'But of course. But what is your *passion*?'

'Well, I'm here to improve my French. To... I started a Master's years ago and... well, it didn't work out,' Adeline felt herself stumble over the words. 'I did teacher training though, then taught French...' she trailed off.

Monique was silent for a moment, studying Adeline's face. Then she nodded as if coming to a decision. 'Well, this is a start. A purpose. We can talk more in the future. When you are ready. Or perhaps when you know yourself a little better.' She sipped her espresso. 'And you can recommend books to people?'

'Yes, of course. And I'll try to read more while I'm here. I'd like to...' Adeline wanted to ask Monique what she meant about *knowing herself better*. Was it a slight? Or had she misunderstood Monique's rapid French?

Monique leaned towards her, the moonstone swinging on its delicate chain. 'Yes, yes, this is all good,' she said. 'But what I hope you will learn is not simply to fulfil orders for people or to find – perhaps – the latest crime thriller or a book they must read at school. I hope you will start to find out how to select the right book for customers,' she patted her bosom with the flat of her hand. 'From here. From the heart.'

'Oh. Well. I mean. Of course. I'll try to...'

'*Non*,' Monique said firmly. 'You must not *try*. You must *feel*.' She looked at Adeline's face, a little mischief in her eyes. 'I can see that you try, that you want so much for things. It is an effort, yes? But here, I hope you will learn *not* to try, to *force*, but to *live*, to *be*, to tune in.' She tapped a finger against her head to emphasise the point, found one of the tucked-in pens, removed it.

'OK...?' Adeline began to wonder whether she might have made a bit of a mistake. Clearly, she knew the little independent bookshop in an obscure French village wasn't going to operate like Waterstones. But she had thought she would understand what was expected of her.

Monique was delighted by her hesitant response. 'Ah, you are like the others! When I first came here, many years ago, they called me a witch. Said I was crazy. But they have come to understand that the right book is more than just a tale to entertain, *non*? The right book can heal us, can speak to us and help us to be well.'

'It can? I mean, yes, I'm sure,' Adeline stuttered.

They both sipped their coffee, eyeing each other over the porcelain. 'And they said,' Adeline added, rather nervously, 'that you were a witch?' She tried to laugh, but the sound that came out was more like a monosyllabic whimper. 'Why... why would they think that?'

Monique's eyes sparkled. 'People think what they wish. It is their right.'

'Of course, but...'

'Ah, you will see.' Monique stood and Adeline followed suit. 'Some of my methods are perhaps a little unusual. But they work. Maybe some people would call them spiritual, unusual, even strange,' she leaned forward a little. 'And yes, sometimes there is a little magic involved. But eventually people have come to realise that whatever I do, it is good, it comes from a place of love. Because in La Petite Librairie we do not always give our customers what they want. But we always find them what they need.'

Dear Addy,

I'm not sure when you'll be able to pick up your emails, but hopefully this will reach you OK. Your mobile phone isn't working – I assume you need to get a French one? Please let me have the new number as soon as you do. We really need to talk. Chris has been asking about you – she was really worried. Well, we all are.

I've been thinking about what you said. About needing more from life. About the fact you've never fit in. But don't you think it might just be finding those papers that has made you feel that way? You never seemed unhappy before.

I get that you need to 'find yourself.' But do you really think moving to a French backwater is going to do that for you?

You need to come home. Not for me. But for YOU. I get it, why you did what you did. You want answers. But Addy, there won't be any answers there.

You're in shock, maybe. But the last thing you should be

right now is alone. You're grieving – we both are... Just please get on a plane and we'll sort this out together.

Kev

Standing behind the counter, Adeline ran her hands over the worn wood, feeling the grooves left by years of customers and servers, passing goods, taking money. Monique had said that before she'd arrived, the shop had been a clothing store – and Adeline tried to imagine what it might have looked like. But it was impossible. Surrounded by books – almost bathing in their smell, texture and the colour radiating from their leather- or paper-bound spines, it was impossible to imagine that La Petite Librairie had had a life before Monique. Sometimes, too, only two days in, Adeline felt so divorced from her own life back in England that it was hard to picture what London was like without her. Her flat, sublet to a friend of her cousin. Her favourite cafe, missing a regular customer – although of course, with the constant stream of trade, she wouldn't be missed.

Yesterday, she'd gone with Lili to the *mairie to* register her for school and had been surprised at the ease of the process. A small form to complete, information to provide – a copy of Lili's passport and some health information – and she was told her daughter could start the next day. 'Isn't that wonderful!' she'd said to Lili, feeling something inside her crack at the thought of their imminent separation, but displaying only a smile on the outside. It wouldn't help Lili to show she was afraid for her.

In the end she needn't have been, she thought now, looking out over the empty courtyard with its rather forlorn fountain, and beyond to the little Café des Sports where several locals moved beyond the glass. Lili had dropped her hand the minute they'd entered the playground and rushed ahead. Adeline had lingered at the edge of the tarmacked surface, not sure exactly what to do, until a woman in jeans with a wide smile had told her she'd take it from here. It was exactly what she'd hoped – Lili was unafraid, rushing towards the opportunity to lose herself with other youngsters. But it was a bit insulting, too, to be dumped so readily. One tear, or a small backward glance, would have been nice, she'd thought, shaking her head, amused.

The bell tinkling broke her train of thought and she stretched her lips into a smile as an old woman made her way into the store. '*Bonjour, Madame.*'

'*Bonjour.*' The woman looked at Adeline with interest, her brown eyes sharp and youthful within the walnut grooves of her face. She was wearing a scarf tied around her head, a little like women had worn in the fifties back in England, and a long navy raincoat. She carried an empty canvas bag, which sported a picture of oranges and apples. Adeline watched as the woman eyed the new releases on one of the front tables, before making her way to the counter. 'You're new,' she said simply.

'Yes.'

The woman nodded. 'Madame Dupont,' she said. 'Monique has a book for me?'

'Of course.' Monique had given her a list before leaving, with scrawled names of customers who'd made orders in the preceding days. Adeline looked at the paper-wrapped parcels under the counter, each one inscribed in a looping hand. She found one labelled Dupont and picked it up, feeling the weight of the hard-covered volume inside.

The woman nodded and slipped the parcel into her bag. 'So you are British,' she said, more of a statement than a question.

'Yes,' Adeline replied, hoping that this was something Madame Dupont had learned from Monique rather than worked out from her ropey accent or very 'British' appearance. It wasn't as if she were wearing union flag clothing or sporting a bowler hat, after all.

'And you are here for...?'

'Three months. Maybe more.'

Another nod and the ghost of a smile flickered across the woman's face. 'So you are Monique's new project,' she said.

'A project?' Perhaps she had misunderstood.

The woman barked a laugh. 'Ah, don't be offended. Monique likes to fix people. Situations. I expect she has plans for you!'

'Really?'

The woman leaned forward, conspiratorially. 'She has magic about her, Monique. Mark my words, she'll have you married off within the year.' She nodded, her eyes scanning Adeline's face, perhaps looking for a flash of pleasure at the idea.

'Married? Oh, no. I'm just... I'm here to improve my French. Get to know the country a little.'

Another laugh. 'Ah, but you will see,' the woman said delightedly. 'I am sure Monique has more in store for you. I saw her with her pot of earth and knew that someone would be coming.' She chuckled again. 'Tell her I will pay her tomorrow,' she added, turning from the counter, the book in the canvas bag knocking lightly against her leg.

Was that OK? Monique hadn't mentioned that customers

could delay payment, but Adeline didn't feel comfortable asking. Madame Dupont seemed to be familiar with the shop, with Monique. So she simply smiled and nodded, hoping it was the right call.

The woman left and the shop settled into quietness again; it was a peaceful rather than an oppressive hush – outside she could still hear the growl of an odd passing car, the steps of people out walking, the noise of occasional snatched conversation. She wondered what Madame Dupont had meant by the pot of earth. Perhaps it was better not to know.

A man was next, browsing the shelves and refusing any assistance. He disappeared without making a purchase. Then a woman came in with a small child and chose one of the books from the wooden box of children's titles. She paid her ten euros and said something about the weather. Her child – a boy of about three years – looked at Adeline with interest, his eyes brown pools of wonder. Perhaps it was rare to see new people in the village?

'Don't stare, Louis!' his mother admonished him.

Adeline smiled at him as he peeped at her from behind his mother. When the woman wasn't looking, she made a silly face and saw pleasure spread across his features at their shared joke.

When she'd first seen the shop, Adeline had worried a little that it might be a bit too quiet, a bit too tucked away – what would they do all day if just one or two customers came in? But La Petite Librairie seemed to have a steady stream of visitors. An older woman asked for Monique, but wouldn't accept help from Adeline, saying it was personal. 'I do know about books!' Adeline found herself crying after her. But the woman raised a hand dismissively and continued her walk across the cobbled courtyard.

It was bound to be difficult at first, Adeline reasoned. People had known Monique and her shop for years – they weren't expecting someone new. All the same, she hoped it wasn't her accent, her 'otherness' that was putting them off.

Before she could think further, an older man entered the shop. He was dressed in a long, brown coat which hung misshapenly around his frame, and corduroy trousers in a khaki green, ending in a pair of slightly battered leather shoes. He stopped when he saw her, rather than Monique, behind the counter and Adeline prepared herself for another snub. Instead, he doffed an imaginary cap and wished her a good morning.

'Good morning,' she replied, smiling. 'I'm Adeline. Monique's new assistant.'

He nodded, his blue, slightly watery eyes taking her in. 'Welcome,' he said, at last.

'Thank you. Can I help you?'

'Perhaps.'

A silence settled around them.

'What can I do for you?' she asked, slightly confused.

'Maybe a book?'

She flushed. 'Of course! But, um, what sort of book are you looking for?'

'I think, *Madame*,' he replied, 'the question should be, what book is waiting for me?'

'Um,' her eyes scanned the beige-wrapped packaging. 'Have you ordered something?'

He laughed, softly. Once. 'Ah, no matter,' he said. 'It will arrive when it arrives, *non*?'

'But your name?'

'Claude,' he said, simply.

He was right, she realised; none of the packages read Claude. 'I'm sorry,' she said. 'Monique will be back soon.'

'Tell her I will come again tomorrow. Tell her that Claude still has the heaviness.'

'Oh. Yes. Of course.' She jotted it on the little notebook kept on the counter for that purpose. *Claude. Heaviness.*

The man nodded kindly, then turned towards the door. As he lifted his hand towards the handle he asked, 'But for you... Did you find what you are looking for yet?'

'Oh, no!' she said, quickly. 'I'm... well, I work here. I'm just serving.'

He shook his head, almost fondly. 'But you are looking too. For something. We all are,' he said. 'Sometimes we don't even know it. That's what I learned from Monique over the years, and perhaps you will learn too.'

It was such a strange thing to say that she ended up simply smiling and nodding as if she understood. The shop bell tinkled his departure and she felt quite relieved, inspecting the packages once more for his name, but finding it absent.

There was something quite unsettling about the encounter, but by the time Monique returned from her errands, she'd served two further locals – quite pleased with herself that she'd been able to recommend a book she recognised in the new releases pile – and more or less forgotten about it. Her language, although perhaps a little rusty, had held up well and she'd begun to feel more at home already.

'*Rebonjour,*' her new boss said, breezing in with a basket of fruit. 'Everything all right?'

'Yes, fine, thank you.' She told Monique about Madame Dupont and the book she'd taken.

Monique nodded. 'So all was good?'

'Well, yes. Except...'

'Except?' Monique raised an amused eyebrow. 'Something has happened?'

'Not exactly. Just... it's a little odd, but a couple of people have suggested that you had plans to marry me off or fix me in some way!' she said, half laughing, half serious. 'I'm guessing it's a joke of some sort?'

Monique laughed, throwing her head back with abandon. She set the basket down on the counter; the bright clementines and oranges smelt fresh and sweet; suddenly Adeline remembered she hadn't eaten breakfast. 'They say this?' Monique asked, amused.

Adeline nodded.

'Well, yes. I mean, sometimes I have introduced people if I feel... you know, that they will get along. Perhaps they mean this? But it is rare, don't worry!' she chuckled affectionately, shaking her head at the idea.

'Well,' said Adeline, finding herself smiling. 'Tell you what. If Mr Right walks in through the door, I'll let you know.'

At that exact moment, André from the patisserie – this time without his apron or flour dust – pushed open the door and Monique gave her a pointed eyebrow raise.

'You have to pluck the apple from the tree while it is ripe!' she said, tipping her head slightly in André's direction. Flushing, Adeline turned and busied herself with a pile of books that she'd already sorted, hoping Monique would deal with whatever he wanted and she could hide her embarrassment.

She'd have to be made of stone not to notice how gorgeous André was. But after Colin, she'd learned that whatever the exterior, it was better not to come to rely on a man. Better to look from afar but keep herself safe.

Moments later, they were alone again. 'Do not worry,' Monique said. 'People like to talk, but...! I will tell my friend Cupid to fly off to somewhere else!'

Adeline grinned. 'Thank you.' She almost added that she'd

make an exception for André, if Cupid asked very nicely, but wasn't sure if Monique would get the joke. Instead, she moved the conversation on. 'Oh, and a man, Claude, came in. He seemed to be looking for something but,' she shrugged, 'he said to tell you he'd be in tomorrow. That he still had... heaviness? I'm sorry, I couldn't quite work out what he wanted.'

Monique shook her head. 'Yes, he has some problems right now. It is hard to know what he needs. But we can only try.' She nodded so earnestly, and seemed so sure that Adeline would understand, that Adeline felt compelled to nod along as if she did. In truth she was completely confused and for the first time since she'd arrived in St Vianne, she wondered whether Kev – recently so wrong about so many things – had had a point. What was she doing here?

'Thank you for this,' Adeline said, sitting back in her chair and sighing.

'It's nothing.' Monique turned from the fridge with three glasses of cinnamon-topped chocolate mousse on a tray. They both looked at the little nest Lili had made on the armchair in the corner, her tucked-in legs and arms, her tousled hair, her closed eyes.

'Perhaps we will save hers for tomorrow,' Monique said.

'Yes, I think so!' Adeline replied, draining the last drops of her red wine. It was a heavy blend, rather bitter, but had gone well with Monique's mushroom quiche and green vegetables.

The meal had been Monique's idea – a way to mark the end of Adeline's first week at La Petite Librairie. 'We can go to the cafe, or perhaps to my place?' she'd suggested.

They'd opted for Monique's flat above the shop in the end; Adeline had felt it would be easier with Lili – her little girl seemed exhausted by her first week of schooling. Not weighed down as much as spent – she'd run and coloured and sung and created to her heart's content, and bedtime stories at their little house had turned into relayed events from each of their days. After nibbling the crust of her quiche, she'd quietly gone to the armchair and curled up and they hadn't had the heart to admonish her.

'I'm sorry,' Adeline had said, looking at the wasted food.

'No, it is fine. She needs to sleep; it's important.'

It was half past eight and the April sun had just begun to set, spilling orange rays across the roofs in the square, dusting the buildings with a warm, fading light. The courtyard was dark, the fountain silent, the patisserie closed. Downstairs, the books were neatly arranged on shelves, new releases filed, packages wrapped for the Saturday morning, but for now everything was silent there too.

Monique placed the cold mousse in front of Adeline and sat in the chair opposite. They both dipped their spoons in and, almost as if it had been synchronised, closed their eyes as the rich chocolate flavour flooded their mouths. 'This is delicious!' Adeline said.

'*Merci*; it was my mother's recipe.' A shadow of sadness flitted across Monique's face – the kind that, if you weren't familiar with her habitual expressions, you might not notice at all. Adeline wondered, not for the first time, how old Monique might be. Sometimes she estimated her at fifty, other times closer to sixty. Was it rude to ask someone's age in France? Possibly. 'I added the cinnamon for protection and good fortune.'

'And flavour?' Adeline joked, feeling slightly uncomfortable.

'Perhaps its scent,' Monique said thoughtfully. She looked at Adeline. 'You are uncomfortable. But people have used cinnamon for centuries for warding off bad luck, encouraging good luck and healing. I have cinnamon sticks close to the door.'

'And do they work?'

Monique shrugged. 'Perhaps. But what I do know is, they cannot harm me.'

Adeline nodded; it was a good point. She wasn't sure about some of Monique's ideas, but they were harmless if nothing else. 'Plus, handy to have plenty to sprinkle on mousse!' she joked, taking another spoonful of the delicious dessert. 'How long have you lived in St Vianne?' she asked.

'Oh, many, many years,' Monique said, flicking her hand dismissively as if the effort of counting would be far too much. 'I was quite young when I arrived, and I had been travelling. I had no thoughts to stay. Yet here I am.' She laughed. 'Sometimes life makes the decisions for us.' She touched the stone around her neck.

'So you'd been travelling?'

Monique shrugged. 'Yes, perhaps you could call it this. But I was not one of those children who go on to a gap year, a break in studies. It was not pleasant like that. I was running away, trying to find somewhere to make a new start. I stayed in some places where I felt lost or afraid. Then I came to St Vianne and in time I was made to feel welcome – at least most of the time.'

'So you stayed.'

'So I stayed.' Monique looked at Adeline, her pupils rapidly moving as if she were studying her face closely. Adeline felt herself get red.

'You said most of the time?' Adeline prompted.

Monique laughed. 'Ah yes. Well, there were moments. And who can say whether it was my fault. I was impetuous then, hot-headed. I wanted to do things my own way. And not everyone liked this. Some of the people were suspicious of me, a stranger from Paris. People say Paris is the capital of France, but in reality, from here, it feels like another country.'

Adeline nodded. 'I can imagine.'

'Some people – perhaps some of the older people in particular – did not warm to me at first. And when I opened my shop and began to sell books in my own way, not everyone liked this either. But I told myself that this was OK. As long as I was being true to myself and I wasn't hurting anyone, it didn't matter if they liked me.'

'That's amazing; I wish I could feel like that,' Adeline began.

'*Mais attends!*' Monique said. 'This is what I *told* myself. But I did not always *feel* that way. In reality, it took a few years for me to feel that this was my home. And to realise that even though people resist change sometimes, it doesn't mean they won't accept it after a little more time. People don't like to be shaken up; they want the world to stay small, predictable. But what we want and what we need, they are not always the same.'

Adeline grinned. 'Yes. I see that.'

One or two of the customers had been a little perturbed by her presence in the shop this week. Some walked past her as if she were invisible, going straight to Monique. Others had eyed her suspiciously. One or two had opened the door but changed their minds. But most of the people had been friendly, interested. Perhaps, like Monique, in time, she would begin to feel less on edge, more capable.

'What were you running from?' she added.

'What?'

'You said you were running away. What from?' The question felt a little stark, a little rude, spoken aloud like this, but she hadn't been able to stop herself. Monique seemed so self-assured, it was hard to imagine the younger version of her being afraid of anything.

To her relief, Monique laughed. 'What does every young girl run from? Her mother, of course.' She shook her head, her smile fading slightly. '*Non*, that is not it. I was running from being a child, being told what to do. My mother, she... well, perhaps I will tell you one day what she did to me; now is not the time. The point is she took my decisions away from me; she treated me like a child when I needed to be treated like an adult. And I realised: while I am under her roof, I will never be free. I will always be her daughter, her extension. Not my own person at all.'

Adeline nodded. 'That makes sense.' She remembered her own teenage years – that struggle to throw off the shackles of childhood, the restrictions; yet still retain the safety net that childhood afforded. How she and her mother had argued – she felt awful about that now. But things had looked different to her then, her mother constantly pecking away at her, telling her what to do, what she was doing wrong, giving her unsolicited advice about boyfriends and schoolwork and friendships and hemlines. She wondered if Monique missed her mother as much as she missed her own now? Presumably the woman was dead, given Monique's age. She decided not to ask.

'Not looking forward to the teenage years with this one,' she said instead, nodding towards Lili's prone form.

Monique followed her gaze. 'It will be fine.' She finished her mousse and pushed her chair from the table. 'Coffee?'

'Yes, please.'

Monique disappeared from the room, leaving Adeline alone; the sound of Lili's deep breathing audible now their conversation had petered out. Adeline got up and took off her black woollen cardigan, then draped it over Lili's tiny form. Her child snuggled into it gratefully but didn't wake.

She went over to the shelf with the tiny jars, their colourful interiors bright against the mahogany shelf. Each bore a tiny label, 'love', 'prosperity', 'happiness'. She reached and touched one of them gently.

'And you?' Monique asked as she entered the room with a tray, as if there hadn't been a break in conversation. Adeline jumped back. 'Sorry,' she said. 'I was just...'

Monique followed her eye. 'It is OK. You can look, if you want. It is good to be curious.'

'Thank you.' She racked her brain to try to remember what they'd been talking about. Mothers. Running away.

'Me?' she said, finally answering Monique's question.

'Yes. What do you think drew you here? I know you want to improve your French, but I sense there is more?'

Adeline looked at the little cup of black, glistening liquid in front of her. She dropped a sugar lump in it and it broke the surface briefly, and sent a few bubbles in its wake. She stirred carefully.

'Well, perhaps it's also a way of... I don't know. Finding myself? There's French blood in my family – my mother's side; I only found out recently. Hence my name, Adeline. My mother's choice. I wasn't very happy one way or another in London and knew I wanted to do something different. My mother died recently,' she added, as if by way of explanation. 'And there's some inheritance. Not a lot, but enough to take a few risks. I left my teaching job and needed something new. And I have Lili, but nobody else in my life, not really. No husband, no partner. So I thought if not now, when? And then I saw your advert.'

Monique was nodding. 'And do you feel that you have made a good choice?'

'Yes, yes I think so.'

Monique smiled, sipped her coffee, looked out over the quiet square outside the window.

'Can I ask you something?' Adeline said.

'*Oui*, of course.'

'I've watched you recommend books a bit this week. But I'm

not quite sure what you go on. You seem to know what some of the customers want – but I haven't seen anyone talk to you about plot or genre... Is it just that you've been here so long, you know what they might like or...?'

Monique smiled. 'Well, perhaps it is that, a little. But that is only part of it.'

'OK?'

'In truth I am a doctor. I find the cure for people. Ah, not in their bodies, they must go to the medical doctor for that. But I can cure their hearts. Or perhaps not me, perhaps the writers from today or long ago can do this for them.'

'Cure their hearts?'

Monique arched an eyebrow. '*Mais oui*, don't you believe this is possible?'

Adeline thought about the times she'd revisited a book, read a poem that had moved her. The times when the lyrics of a song seemed to speak to her, or when she'd felt affinity with a character in a book. How affirming it had been, how restorative. 'I think it could be,' she said. 'And I've heard of book prescriptions. I think. Bibliotherapists dispensing books for therapy.'

Monique was nodding. '*Oui, oui*, it is like this,' she said. 'Only perhaps I am not talking so much to people but *feeling* them, their hearts, their needs. I have always been able to do this. Not for everyone. But for most. I can find a connection and it helps me,' she shrugged. 'Probably I sound a little mad,' she admitted. She didn't seem too despondent about the idea.

Adeline smiled. 'Not mad. Interesting.'

'And this is good?'

'Yes. Yes of course.' Adeline paused, trying to organise her words. 'And what about me?' she said.

'You?'

'Yes. What book would you recommend for me?'

'Ah, perhaps it will come to me soon.'

'But not yet?'

Monique shook her head. 'Not yet.'

'And will you be able to train me, do you think?'

'With the books?'

'Yes.'

Monique shrugged again. 'I can help you to find that part of yourself if it is there. If you know how to feel the books as well as read them, and to read people as well as feel them, then perhaps.'

A shout outside stole their attention for a moment; a boy chasing a cat across the cobbles. They locked eyes and smiled.

'Thank you, though,' Adeline said.

'For the meal? It is nothing.'

'Yes, for the meal. But also for giving me this chance.'

6

Dear Addy,

I'm not sure whether you're receiving these emails. Please could you at least confirm that you're OK?

I didn't mean to be harsh with you when I last wrote, but I am so worried about you! And I know this isn't what Mum would have wanted. She'd have hated things to come out this way – and for you to just disappear the way you have. You know that, really.

None of us wanted to hurt you – if anything, the opposite! I understand that you feel we kept something important from you, but maybe look at it a different way. We were protecting you. Or at least we thought we were.

Please reply. And please consider coming back. We've got a lot to talk about! And it's better in person.

Kev x

Adeline clicked the tiny cross in the corner of the screen and the email disappeared, replaced with an online order form. Breathing deeply, she stood up, smoothed down the front of her trousers and picked up a pile of books. It was mid-morning, mid-week – her second in St Vianne – and until a moment ago she'd been thinking just how settled and at home she already felt. The staff in the patisserie now smiled and asked how her job was going when she went to buy croissants – something that Lili was now developing a taste for; she'd begun to rearrange the furniture in their tiny house, and had found a set of voiles in a cupboard to hang at her bedroom window. Lili seemed utterly beguiled by her teacher and prattled on about her non-stop.

Things still felt new; she was daunted at times, still found that not all the customers were happy to see her when Monique stepped out and she manned the shop alone. But each day she felt the momentum of settling into place and that she was making progress.

Kevin's email had been sent a few days ago – but she only had Internet access in the shop and hadn't felt inclined to check until now: something that would have felt impossible back home. She resolved to travel to Avignon to sort out a new mobile phone soon. But there was no great hurry.

It had been curiosity that had led her to check – and perhaps a little flicker of homesickness, or guilt or whatever it was that fluttered in her chest from time to time. Once she'd seen that he'd written again, she'd been unable to stop herself clicking and reading.

Scanning the stands of books, searching for the H, she shelved a small volume of poems, then moved to the table to arrange the rest of the new stock. Keeping herself distracted, moving, was the solution.

It was quiet in the shop this morning, typically. A light drizzle saturated the stone walkway outside, runnels of mois-ture ran down the outside awning and dripped onto the window. She could see the grey world outside in a kind of shimmering semi-focus, her vision impaired by water collected on the glass and tumbling from the expressionless sky. One or two locals had braved it to the patisserie, umbrellas held aloft, hoods pulled up; but it seemed nobody was in the mood for buying books this morning.

Most days, the shop had a steady stream of people coming through its door, whether to chat with Monique, to browse the shelves, to pass the remaining ten minutes before the cafe opened, or to seek advice on literature. Adeline's French was already close to fluent, but she had enjoyed challenging herself with new topics, finding the words coming more easily every day.

Yet today of course, when she needed a distraction, the shop was silent. Outside was silent. Her work was nearly done and there were no diversions. Kevin was there, in her inbox, refusing to be ignored just as he had been when they were growing up.

Her fingers itched to reply to him. To tell him that he had no idea what he was talking about. How could he? He'd been in on it from the start. And if she hadn't discovered it for herself, would they ever have told her?

Would he understand that every memory she had now of them as a family was tarnished, touched by the knowledge that the world she'd experienced hadn't been an honest one? That the people with their arms around her, watching her blow out birthday candles, pulling crackers with her at Christmas; the people who'd stood proudly by her hospital bed holding Lili and smiling with what had seemed like genuine affection and pride had all been lying to her for her entire life?

Worst of all, perhaps she'd never be able to explain adequately the fact that when she'd found out the truth, quite by accident, there was a part of her beyond the devastation of the moment that had been relieved. Relieved that the tiny part of her that had felt uneasy, different, her whole life hadn't been a flaw in her own character – a tendency towards anxious thinking – but her own sixth sense that something wasn't quite right.

She'd try. She'd write an email and at least try to explain, she thought suddenly, determinedly. She turned to cross the shop floor, to reboot the rather outdated computer tucked away on a table at the side of the counter. But as she did so, her hip hit the side of a display table, the corner sticking painfully into her thigh.

She swore, loudly, the expletive feeling completely out of place in the quiet, quaint shop. The table wobbled and several books fell to the floor. As she bent to pick them up, her leg still throbbing, Adeline felt the tears finally escape and pool hotly in her eyes.

Shit. She wiped them away as best she could with her sleeve, returned the books to their table and stumbled to the counter, slipping into the chair and trying as best she could to get herself back together. That was the problem with holding it all in; once there was a breach in her defences, it was hard to find the strength to push her emotions back.

She was not a crier. Had never been. Preferred to solve problems rather than wallow in them. She steadied herself. This was not the time nor the place. But at least the shop was empty.

As if malevolent fate had read her mind, at that moment the shop door tinkled its warning and Monique returned, flapping her umbrella outside before propping it in the doorway on the mat to dry. Her neat, red raincoat was covered with droplets; the back of her hair slightly damp where the wind had blown moisture under the umbrella.

She turned, and Adeline stood up, smiling widely. '*Bonjour!*'

she said, in what she hoped was an upbeat tone. 'Hope you didn't get too wet.'

Monique turned towards her, smiling, but one glance at her employee's face had her forehead crinkling with concern. 'But Adeline, you have been crying?'

Adeline shook her head dismissively. 'It's nothing. Just feeling a bit emotional, is all.'

Monique walked towards her, brow still furrowed. 'But it is not nothing,' she said. 'We do not cry for nothing usually.'

'I just read an email from home.' Adeline shrugged.

'And it upset you? It is bad news?'

'No, nothing like that. Just...' She opened her mouth to lie – trying to find a plausible excuse for her tears. That she missed her brother, perhaps. It wasn't completely untrue, after all. That she was a little homesick? Also a little bit true, at times. But Monique was closer now, her eyes seeming to burn right into Adeline, and she felt suddenly that there was no point in trying to hide – because Monique would know. She could read people; she was reading her.

Adeline took a big, shuddering breath. 'My brother, Kevin, wrote to me. He's not happy about me being here.'

'But why?'

'Oh, he's just worried about me. He knows... well, when I decided to come, I was upset. With him. With my whole family really, only he's the only one who's still here. My parents... Dad died years ago when I was small and my mum died recently. So it's just him.'

Monique nodded towards the stool and Adeline sat on it; she realised she was shaking.

'And he thinks you are running away?'

'Maybe.'

'And are you?'

Adeline smiled through the tears. 'Maybe. A little.'

Monique nodded. 'It was a big argument?' she probed.

Adeline shook her head. 'Not an argument, as such. More...'
She wondered how much she should say, how much she was
ready to say. 'I found something. In my mother's things. And I
realised that my parents had been keeping a secret from me, my
whole life. Mum isn't here, I can't ask her about it. But I asked
Kevin – my brother. And I could hear it!' Her voice became
slightly hoarse. 'I could hear in his voice that he already knew.
That I'd been the only one in the dark!'

Monique's hand reached out, touched her shoulder. 'That
must have been very difficult,' she said. 'And this is why you
came?'

Adeline shook her head, both smiling and crying. 'It's why I
left. But not why I chose to come here. Living in France, really
immersing myself, is something I've always wanted to do. I just
never had a reason before. I never... And when I saw the advert,
it was like fate, I...' She let her sentence trail off.

Monique was nodding. 'Well, I am not glad that this
happened to you. But I am glad that you came here.' She paused
a little, her eyes clouding slightly. 'And I want to let you know
that I understand, perhaps, what you have gone through with
your family. Because of my mother.'

'She lied to you?'

'*Non*, she did not lie. But I know what it is like when
someone you trust, you love, who is meant to love you too, does
something terrible. Something that makes you feel broken,' she
tapped her chest briefly. 'I know it can make you feel very
alone.'

Adeline nodded. 'And you couldn't forgive your mother?'

One short shake of the head. '*Non*, never. One day I will tell
you everything and you will understand. And this broke things

between my sister and me, too – she couldn't stand the way I was treating our mother; forced me to choose.'

'That's awful.'

Monique shrugged. 'It is life.'

There was a brief ebb in the conversation, then, 'What about Kevin?' Adeline asked.

'What about him?'

'Do you think I should forgive him?'

Monique's mouth flickered towards a smile. 'Only you know that. But I would say it depends what he did, exactly, and why. And who for. It seems that he loves you, that he is worried.' She shrugged. 'That is something.'

'Yes.'

It was. And he'd done what he'd done for their mother; had been a child when he'd made his promise. Would she have been any different in his situation?

She wiped her hands across her cheeks, drying any stray tears. 'Thank you,' she said.

Monique smiled, stood back from the counter where she'd been leaning, looking at Adeline intently. 'I have just the thing,' she said. She walked to one of the corner shelves, mouthing words silently to herself as her finger traced the writers' names. At last, she stopped and gently pulled out a thin volume. 'This... If you have time, I think it would be good for you to read.'

Adeline drew the book to her, curiously. It was a small volume, thin with an orange cover. She read the title: *The Collected Poems of Emily Dickinson*. She looked up, a question on her face.

'Read it, when you can. When you want. You will see,' Monique said.

'To... to fix me?' she asked. Suddenly, forcefully, she wanted to believe that it was possible for a book to do this, for Monique to know exactly the remedy she needed.

'To speak to you.'

'I...'

The bell tinkled and suddenly there were three others in the shop bringing with them a flood of reality that tore her away from her problems for an instant. Adeline tucked the book out of sight; she'd look at it properly later.

7

'And then we painted animals and Maîtresse Caroline said mine was the best,' Lili finished triumphantly. She was propped up against the soft, square pillows Adeline had bought for her single bed, having just listened to a couple of chapters of *The Faraway Tree*, a favourite book they must have read at least five times together. She was sleepy; her eyelids blinking closed for a few seconds at a time. But her eyes, when visible, were sparkling.

'What animal did you paint?'

'Duh. A cat of course!' came the response.

Adeline brushed the soft curls that had fallen forward out of her daughter's eyes and kissed her forehead. 'Of course,' she said. 'And I am so glad you've had a good day. I'm really proud of you.'

'Mummy, can we make pop cakes, like Moonface does?' her daughter asked then.

For a moment Adeline was disorientated, then she remembered the lovely honey cookies from the chapter they'd just read. Cookies that melted in the mouth of whomever was lucky enough to eat them. 'Well, we can try,' she said, 'if you want.'

'I told my teacher we might bring her some.'

Adeline laughed at the thought of it – trying to fashion biscuits described only in a book. The delight Lili might feel bringing such things to school. 'Well, let's see.' It was a parental cop-out phrase, she knew, but sometimes the only words that would both soothe her child and keep her from making a promise she couldn't necessarily fulfil. 'Love you, baby.'

Her daughter didn't respond, but turned over on her side, suddenly too overcome with tiredness to interact. Moments later, her breathing took on the familiar rhythm of sleep.

Adeline got up to leave, but stood for a moment in the door-way, feeling a sense of peace that comes with knowing your child is happy, safe and sleeping. The magical moment when all the stress of feeding, entertaining, worrying about them falls away and your heart swells with love – and a little relief that the rest of the evening is your own.

She pulled the door towards her, leaving a gap to allow a sliver of light into the dark bedroom, and made her way down the small staircase to the ground floor.

She would get a phone soon, she decided, and maybe a TV. Perhaps that didn't fit with the idea she'd had of living a simpler life here; but she missed her home comforts – missed the easy distraction of instant entertainment. As it was, of course, she had access to plenty of books – and was already reading her sixth novel in two weeks.

And the poems. Of course. She wasn't someone who read poems often – certainly not collections of them. But she loved coming across them in books, or reading a poignant verse online. She was curious as to why Monique had felt it important she read Emily Dickinson's work. Adeline knew a little about the poet: she'd lived in nineteenth-century America; that her poems were considered the work of an early feminist voice. But beyond that, her mind was blank.

Moving to the kitchen at the back of the property, Adeline cleared the few plates from the table and stacked them by the sink. She opened the fridge and pulled out a half-consumed bottle of wine and poured herself a small glass. Then she rummaged in her bag for the volume, curious to see what insight it might offer – or at least try to work out what Monique felt she'd gain from reading it. 'Damn,' she said aloud, when she realised she'd forgotten to take it with her when she'd locked the shop earlier.

She could leave it. She'd be back in tomorrow morning. She pulled her well-thumbed copy of *Chocolat* from her bag – a favourite that had helped to ignite her curiosity about France – and settled down to read.

But her mind kept buzzing.

It was only a five-minute walk to the shop. Lili would be safe, tucked up in her room behind a locked front door. And she'd be able to dash there and back without her daughter ever knowing.

She slipped on her coat and walked out into the early evening. It was eight thirty, and the air was in a state of flux somewhere between day and night. The sky was murky, unde-fined; a sliver of moon glowed in the sky, and she could make out the whole of it, three quarters in shadow; a black ball of rock with its edge dipped in gold.

Her footsteps sounded loud on the stone pathway as, head down, she passed a few locals meandering home; a group of children out past their bedtime; a man walking his dog. At last, her heart thundering, she reached the bookshop and drew the large metal key from her bag.

She rattled it slightly in the lock to find purchase then

turned it and pushed the door gently, making sure to stop it short before it nudged the bell; she didn't want to disturb Monique in the flat above – she'd only be a moment. The few street lamps and the cool moonlight gave her enough to see by. She stepped inside and there it was, the orange volume, still tucked under the stool near the counter.

She felt the pull of Lili, back in her bed, and felt her stomach twist at having left her; what had she been thinking? She'd never have done this in London, no matter the number of dead-locks and bolts their home had had in its armoury. It was this place, its charm, friendliness. The fact that people all seemed to know one another; people didn't always lock their cars or their doors for that matter.

But people were still people. She shouldn't be lulled by the simplicity of life here. She had to get back.

She was halfway across the room when she sensed it; a shift in the air or atmosphere that made her freeze. Someone was there. Sure enough, as she looked to the wooden stairs that disappeared to the top floor and Monique's flat, she could see movement in the shadows. A figure. A man.

She managed to repress a scream, instead letting out a small squeak of surprise. 'What are... Who are you?' she asked, still keeping her voice soft; still, for some reason, hoping she could retrieve her book and get home without disturbing anyone.

The man stepped forward into the cool, stark light. He was young, his skin smooth and pale, his hair curly and thick, falling forward a little over his forehead. Something about the way he was standing revealed an unexpected ease, a comfortableness at being seen. Not an intruder then. But who else would be there in the little bookshop after closing time?

'I am sorry,' he said. 'I didn't mean to frighten you.' He smiled, the action somehow taking over his entire face – eyes shining, lips stretching, dimples forming in his cheeks. And although her heart had still not slowed from the shock of him, she almost felt her mouth want to smile back. 'I am sorry I made you... squeak.'

Was he laughing at her? 'Who are you?' she asked. 'The shop's closed.'

He laughed, a slightly suppressed sound; perhaps conscious that Monique would be upstairs. 'Don't worry, I am not a customer,' he said, 'but then I think you might be Adeline, *non*?'

'Yes.' She looked at him, still suspicious. 'And you are...?'

'Michel.' He said his name as if she should know it and she racked her brain for any memory of Monique mentioning him. He looked far too young to be her partner, and anyway she was sure Monique was single.

He laughed again at her incredulous face. 'I'm sorry,' he said. 'I thought my aunt would have spoken about me. I'm Monique's nephew. Michel Chambon.' He held out his hand as if expecting her to move forward and shake it.

'OK,' she said, still annoyed at his 'squeak' comment. He was lucky she hadn't used some of her slightly dormant self-defence moves she'd learned in a course at uni... 'Look, I have to get back. I just wanted to grab this book.' She stepped forward and slipped the small volume out from under the stool, holding it towards him as if proving her point.

'There is no rush,' he smiled. 'We have just eaten, but I'm sure Monique...'

'No. I really have to go.' She wanted to tell him her child was at home on her own, but it suddenly seemed horribly neglectful. She didn't want him to know. 'I'll see you tomorrow perhaps?' she said.

'Yes. I will be here tomorrow,' he smiled. 'And I know that Monique would like us to meet.'

She nodded, briefly, and raced across the shop, her heart suddenly full of terror at the thought of Lili in that dark house alone. What if she woke up? She'd be scared. And would she trust Adeline again when she next lay down in bed and closed her eyes?

'Well. Bye,' she said as she closed the door, noticing the curiosity in his eyes. She must have looked strange, she reflected, racing from the shop so quickly – as if collecting the poetry book had been some sort of emergency. But it didn't matter. She had to get home.

She was crossing the courtyard, just a couple of hundred metres from her front door and head down, when it happened. She felt a sudden resistance as she collided with someone. There was a ripping sound, and the drumming of objects; a bag had spilt oranges and coffee and a bag of sugar onto the pavement. Looking up, she saw a familiar person. André, his usually open face furrowed to a frown.

'Sorry,' she said, turning as she continued to race past. 'I can't... I'm sorry.'

He glowered at her, reaching down to pick the box of coffee and the bag of sugar from where they'd tipped into the road.

'Sorry!' she said again, holding her hands up briefly and almost running backwards in an attempt to make eye contact. 'It's just...' But André, crouching in the street to gather his things, didn't look up.

When she reached her front door, her hand was shaking and she had to steady herself before inserting the key. Then she let herself into the silent house and raced up the stairs to the open bedroom door.

Inside, Lili was in a deep slumber, her arms flung above her head, her face smooth and serene. Adeline felt a rush of love that almost catapulted her across the room to take her daughter in her arms. But she managed to resist it, leaning back on the frame and feeling her heart rate settle.

She thought about André, his bag of oranges, and cringed inwardly. What sort of person rushes past someone, knocks their bag flying and disappears into the night? She'd been working so hard to make a good impression on everyone. It wasn't a great look.

Michel probably thought she was rude or abrupt. She thought about his relaxed attitude, the lazy smile, his joke at her expense. She must have seemed frantic and unkempt.

She reminded herself that it didn't matter. Nothing else did, really, when it came down to it. Just her and her daughter – her little family.

But her cheeks still burned whenever she thought of the events of the last half hour. 'Idiot,' she said under her breath.

Downstairs, she picked up her neglected glass of wine and made her way to the small armchair in the corner of the sitting room. It smelled old, musty – like an antique shop – but she curled into it and took a sip from her wine, trying to recover the equilibrium she'd felt earlier.

She opened the orange book on a random page and read the opening lines:

> *I'm nobody! Who are you?*
> *Are you nobody too?*

She felt herself laugh at the witty lines written almost two hundred years earlier. Was Monique trying to offend her? But then she looked again – recognised the sense of not being someone, but yearning for contact. And she realised that the poem did, in some way, speak to her.

8

The next morning dawned bright – the darkness and cloudy skies of yesterday seemed like a distant memory as Adeline threw open the shutters and found light flooding in. Lili was up, playing in her room with her stuffed rabbit; Adeline could hear her prattling away in French and smiled to herself that the language came so naturally to her young child. She thought of her own struggle with the language: the verbs, the conjugations, the grammatical errors, and felt proud that she'd given her daughter the opportunity to acquire the cadences and rhythms of another language at a time when it came so easily.

The tree just outside their house had begun to flower, its pink blooms promising cherries later in the season. And the birds, delighted too at the sunny morning, chirped enthusiastically from their various perches in its branches, on the roofs of the buildings opposite, on windowsills, and flew rapidly through the clear morning air.

'Hope is the thing with feathers,' Adeline thought to herself, remembering a line from an Emily Dickinson poem she'd read last night. She thought of how birdsong had always lifted her –

the promise of spring in its melody – and felt new meaning in the centuries-old words. She smiled, then wandered to the bathroom to get ready for another day.

This morning, she'd gone to the patisserie to buy breakfast, hoping to see André and apologise for her rudeness last night. But he hadn't been there. A woman had served her instead, with a cheery grin and a *Bonne journée!* as she left. Part of her was relieved that she didn't have to stumble out an explanation in the busy queue, part of her wished she'd been able to get it out of the way. She wondered what André made of it all.

Just over an hour later, with Lili despatched happily to school, she was in the bookshop, a pile of orders in front of her and her mind elsewhere. Monique was across the shop floor, in the middle of rearranging the vintage novels, dusting each shelf with a rather extravagant-looking feather duster and talking softly to each book as if they were old friends. Adeline watched with a combination of amusement and fascination. 'What are you saying to them?' she asked from where she was arranging an order for a new customer.

'To the books? Ah, nothing much,' Monique laughed. 'I am so used to being here alone, I have started to talk a little out loud. You must think I am crazy.'

'Not at all,' Adeline said, thinking of how only last night she'd told the wine bottle that she'd better just stick to one, as she had work the next day. 'I think we all do that sometimes.'

'Anyway, it is not as if I am talking to just *anything*,' Monique said, her expression light. 'I am talking to my friends. These books, these older books, they have seen some history. They have stories inside, yes, but I wish they could tell me their own story too. Sometimes, I think of all the people who have read this one book,' she said, brandishing a green, leather-bound volume with embossed gold lettering, 'and how perhaps they have never met, but have this connection. And I think of the next person the book will go to and wonder about their story too.'

'I like that,' Adeline said. 'The idea of books having stories of their own.'

Monique nodded. 'Perhaps that is why I am always recommending the older books,' she said thoughtfully. 'They carry so many spirits with them.' She smoothed her skirt – today a vibrant blue – and reached up to return the book to its rightful place.

Adeline wasn't sure she liked the idea of spirits. But perhaps Monique was being metaphorical. She smiled and turned back to her work.

She'd begun to admire Monique's style – although the woman was much older than her, she always dressed in vibrant colours, patterns, silk scarves, swishing skirts. She always wore lipstick and earrings and necklaces which sparkled with colour and caught the light. Often, she'd wear a crystal around her neck – usually the moonstone, but sometimes another, a pink stone that radiated a kind of gentle warmth.

Over the years, since becoming Lili's mum, Adeline had faded. She'd adopted a style that was unconfrontational, dull. Jeans and T-shirts and the occasional summer dress in a nondescript fabric. Modest. Boring. She saw how Monique's clothes, worn with confidence, added to her boss's vibrancy and wondered which came first. Did you have to be confident, assured, to wear bright colours and ambitious styles, or did the clothes themselves imbue you with the confidence once you slipped them on?

Just as she was considering whether a trip to the larger town of Avignon was needed to freshen up her wardrobe, the bell made its habitual clinking and the main door of the shop slowly opened. For a moment she wondered if it was Michel, whom she'd learned had an apartment at the end of the high street. Monique had filled in the details of her nephew – he was a professor in Avignon and rented a room in an apartment there during term time. But at weekends and holidays he'd be back in the space he owned, popping in to see his aunt and catching up with local friends. 'He likes to look out for me, I think,' Monique had said.

'That's lovely of him,' Adeline had replied.

'Yes,' Monique had said fondly. 'I suppose he is my only family,' her expression had darkened briefly, 'or the only family that I see. He feels responsible for me, I think.'

'I'm sure he enjoys seeing you though,' Adeline had said quickly.

'*Mais oui*, he is a good boy. A little lonely too, I think.' Adeline hadn't been sure whether the look Monique gave her after she'd said those words was pointed, but she'd looked away, studiously *not noticing* if there was any hint being dropped.

But this wasn't Michel, it was an older man. One she recognised from her first day in the shop. She reached for his name in her memory and it came to her once he closed the door behind him and stood in the entrance, his gait a slight stoop, as if he were carrying a heavy burden. '*Bonjour,* Claude,' she said, smiling.

His eyes met hers. '*Bonjour,*' he replied with a smile that carried with it more sadness than a frown might have.

'Ah, Claude!' Monique said, putting down the book she was dusting and straightening her skirts as she stood up. 'You have come.'

'*Oui*, you have a book for me?' he said, his voice hopeful.

Monique nodded and lifted out a box from behind the

counter. In it there were several books they'd ordered in. She picked out one with a burgundy cover and handed it to him.

He took it gratefully, turning it over in his hand. '*Merci.* Thank you for not giving up on me.'

Monique walked closer to him, put her hand on his shoulder. 'But Claude, we will never do that. You know this.'

He smiled. 'How much...'

'It's nothing. A gift.'

'Thank you.' He slipped the book into the pocket of his large overcoat – surely too warm a thing to be wearing on this clement spring day – and nodded. 'I am sorry to be such a difficulty for you,' he said.

Monique laughed. 'It is not a difficulty. It is a challenge perhaps. But it is also a pleasure. I am happy to do it. And it is certainly what Violet would have wanted.'

He nodded, a brief shadow flicking over his features. '*Oui,* I hope so.'

Moments later he shuffled off, his hand hovering over the pocket containing the slim volume. Once the door was closed, Adeline turned to Monique, her head full of questions.

'He seems so sad,' she said.

Monique nodded, a wry smile on her lips. 'Yes, he lost his wife two years ago. They had fifty years together. And he is lost,' she said, shaking her head sadly.

'Oh, poor man.'

'*Oui.* And he says he is too old to start again, to find a new purpose in life. But he is too young to give up too. And I promised him that I would help him to find a way.'

Adeline was silent for a moment, wondering how to phrase the question. 'Sorry,' she said. 'How exactly?'

Monique laughed. 'With books of course. We find the right

book for him, and it will give him hope. Maybe ideas or a purpose.'

'Like a self-help book?'

'*Non*,' Monique shook her head. 'He does not need instructions. He knows how to look after his health. But he needs to find a way to bring his heart back to life. The book I gave him is about another who lost their love – it will call to him. His spirit.'

There it was again. Spirit.

Adeline continued typing the ISBNs from Monique's list into the machine, but she found she couldn't quite let the subject go. 'I'm really sorry,' she said. 'But I don't... I know having a good book can be a distraction. Can be good for our mental health. But I don't quite understand what you are doing for Claude. He seems so very sad, so hopeless. Do you really think that the right book will help him enough? The right story?'

Monique turned, her skirt moving softly around her calves. 'But of course. That is what I do. I find a book that speaks to their situation, their soul.'

Suddenly something struck Adeline: '"He ate and drank the precious words; His spirit grew robust",' she murmured softly to herself, remembering the lines from her Emily Dickinson volume.

'*Exactement*,' Monique said with a nod.

Perhaps she had been going to say more, but they were interrupted by the bell ringing loudly as the door was pushed open with more force than Claude had mustered earlier. And there he was, Michel, smiling, tousled, somehow bringing with him a sense of lightness – flooding the room with optimism.

Adeline shook her head. She was thinking lyrically now. She had to get her head out of the clouds. He'd let in a little more sunlight, was all; he was wearing a light yellow shirt. He wasn't bloody *Apollo*.

'*Bonjour,* ladies!' he said, stepping fully into the shop.

Monique turned, lining the last volume on the shelf she was working on. '*Bonjour,* Michel. I am surprised you are so happy this morning after so much wine last night.'

He smiled mischievously. 'Perhaps I am still young enough to get away with it.'

'Ah, you are not so very young. He is thirty-five,' she said, turning to Adeline. 'But he still thinks he is a boy.'

'A boy with great taste in wine,' he reminded her.

'Ha! Not as good as perhaps he thinks,' she said, and he laughed delightedly.

'My aunt likes to make sure I know my place.'

Adeline smiled. 'I can see that.'

'Anyway, it is a glorious day, but I am alone, and Monique said I must come to take her for coffee.'

'Ah, I am sorry,' Monique said. 'I am so busy now! Perhaps you could take Adeline – it would be nice for you to get to know each other?'

Adeline shot a look at Monique who seemed once again preoccupied with her shelves. 'Thank you,' she said. 'But no. I think I'd better get on.'

'Ah, is my aunt such a hard taskmaster?'

'It's not that,' she said hurriedly, feeling her face get hot. 'It's just...'

He nodded, his smile remaining but perhaps not quite as brightly as before. 'Monique has told me a lot about you. I am keen to learn a bit more about England,' he said hopefully.

'Perhaps another time?'

He nodded. 'As you wish.' He glanced over at Monique. 'And I suppose I can't tempt you, Monique, for a coffee either?'

Monique shook her head. 'Sorry. But I have to go soon. To

see the bank.' She shrugged. 'But you know, someone will talk to you in the cafe. You will not be alone.'

He smiled. '*C'est vrai*. And you have my books?'

'Soon. And take this.' She rummaged momentarily in a drawer and extracted a purple stone, walking forward and pushing it into his hand. 'It will help with your hangover.'

Michel looked at the stone doubtfully. 'I don't have to eat it, do I?' he asked teasingly.

'Ha. Not if you want to keep your teeth. Just slip it into your pocket, you will see.'

'OK, well, I will go and enjoy the morning alone with only my little rock for company,' he said with mock sadness. 'And I will see you both soon.'

'Sorry,' Adeline found herself saying guiltily.

'Don't worry,' he said. Then, moving towards her, he added under his breath, 'Don't tell my aunt, but my head is quite sore this morning. So perhaps it's better for me to be quiet.'

She laughed softly. 'Good idea.'

Then he was gone and the shop seemed slightly duller without his presence.

'He is a nice boy,' Monique said to her.

'Yes, he seems lovely.'

'And his aura – it is so yellow, *n'est-ce pas*?'

'His... aura?'

'Yes. We all have one. A colour that surrounds us. And his is bright. Perhaps you noticed.'

'No. Not really,' Adeline said, trying not to think of the way the light had changed when he'd entered.

Monique smiled, her gaze resting on Adeline's face for a moment. 'You do not like when I talk of auras?'

Adeline grimaced slightly. 'It's just not my thing,' she said apologetically. 'It's fine though. Interesting even.'

'OK,' Monique said thoughtfully.

'And the stone you gave him – the crystal?'

'An amethyst – for healing.' Monique smiled. 'But I expect you do not believe in this either?' She seemed amused rather than insulted.

Adeline shrugged. 'I know people use them. But I've never...' She let her words drift off, not wanting to offend her boss.

'Don't worry. We are all different. And some can see, and some cannot. And others, they sense, but cannot let themselves see,' she said, almost to herself. 'Ourself behind ourself concealed.'

The words seemed familiar, but Adeline couldn't place them. Luckily at that moment, a woman she hadn't seen before walked in and asked whether they had the latest Stephen King.

That, at least, Adeline knew how to deal with.

9

A few days later when Adeline left the shop to pick Lili up from the after-school *garderie*, her daughter was less chatty than usual. She walked home quietly, holding her mother's hand and responding to questions with short, basic answers rather than her usual meandering prattle. Adeline felt her forehead once they were home, but it felt soft and cool. She crouched down, taking herself to eye level, and looked at her daughter's face. 'Are you OK, *mon coeur*?' she asked. 'Has something happened?'

Lili shook her head from side to side in response.

'Are you feeling poorly?'

Another shake.

'Just tired?'

Another shake.

Adeline sighed and lifted her daughter onto the armchair. 'I'll get you some juice,' she said. 'And a biscuit?'

This time there was a nod. Lili was no doubt weary from the day rather than anything else, Adeline reassured herself as she poured *jus de pomme* into a small glass and grabbed a couple of butter biscuits. No doubt after this pick-me-up she'd be back to her usual self.

It was after she'd arranged Lili's snack on a small side table and given her one of her favourite books to flick through that the words came. 'Mummy,' her daughter said, just as Adeline was returning to the kitchen to make herself a cup of tea. 'Why are we always alone?'

She turned, looked at her daughter's earnest eyes, the crumbs at her mouth that made her look adorable and so very young. 'We're not alone,' she said. 'We're new here. But we have our friends already. You've met Monique – she's Mummy's friend, and yours. And you have Alice and Manon in your class – you told me you played skipping with them yesterday in the playground.'

Lili shook her head.

'You've had a fight with them?'

Another no.

'But today Alice's *mamie* picked her up from school, and her *papi* was there too,' Lili said sadly. 'And Manon says she can't play on Saturday because she is going to her aunt. And I know my granny has gone to heaven. But I had Uncle Kevin once and now he's gone too.'

'Oh, Lili.' Adeline walked back over to her daughter and sat on the arm of her chair, reaching out to stroke her tousled curls. 'Uncle Kevin isn't gone. He's still in England, just where he always was. But we've come for an adventure!' she said as brightly as she could. 'We're far from him at the moment, but it won't always be that way.'

Another sad little nod.

'But at *le weekend*, everyone says they see their families, but we haven't got a family, have we? I don't have a *papa*, and I only have one *oncle* and I don't know if I had another *grand-mère*, some people have two,' she said, looking at her mother accusingly. 'Why don't I have anyone, Mummy?'

Adeline tried to keep her mouth from wobbling. Instead, she leaned and kissed her daughter's head. 'Lili, you do have Uncle Kevin, and one day perhaps he'll get married and there'll be an auntie. Maybe cousins. And I know you miss Granny – I do too.'

'When will I see Uncle Kevin?'

'Soon, my darling. Soon,' she said, feeling a prickle of guilt at her own words. Because she'd cut Kevin out, at least for now, while she healed, but hadn't stopped to think how she was denying her daughter pretty much her only other family member in the process.

Her words seemed to appease Lili though, who began to munch on a biscuit thoughtfully. 'OK,' she said.

But as Adeline walked again towards the kitchen, a little voice asked her, 'And Mummy, why don't you have any friends? The other mummies talk to one another. But you don't talk to anyone, do you?' This was asked in the way that many children's questions are asked: in complete innocence of their impact.

Adeline felt herself pause at the doorway. She breathed deeply. 'Well, Mummy had friends in England,' she said – although had they been friends? Were they still friends now they were no longer colleagues, now she'd disappeared from their daily lives? Even Chris, whom she'd thought of as a best friend, hadn't been in touch. 'And I have Monique here now. And there's Michel,' she added, 'Monique's nephew. He's nice.'

Lili nodded. 'So you're not lonely?' she asked.

'No poppet, I'm not lonely.'

Once in the kitchen, she boiled the kettle and leaned on the counter watching it rattle into life. It was funny how children could cut through to the heart of things without realising. She'd read the odd clickbait article about the funny things children say or the difficult questions children ask. And they'd often seemed amusing. But Lili's questions had cut her to the quick – the way her five-year-old was able to see things that perhaps she'd been denying herself. That she was lonely, and it was essentially her own fault.

The day she'd found the papers amongst Mum's things, she'd felt her entire world shudder. And now everything in her life seemed divided into before and after. Before, she'd been relatively sure of who she was, what she was. After, she'd found herself freefalling; her memories tainted, her sense of who she was, altered. Her reaction had been to try to start again. Create a new her with the new knowledge she had of herself.

Colleagues who'd signed her leaving card had called her brave when she'd told them she was going to France.

But was she brave? Had she been running towards a new future – a future she could create for this new Adeline, the one she'd discovered under the lies? Or had she been running away; had she cut everyone out because she didn't want to have the conversations about it all, didn't feel ready to face the truth properly?

It had been the timing of everything, she thought. The fact that she'd thrown her phone across the room after the call with Kevin, shattering its touch screen so it was no longer usable. And then the advert she'd stumbled across online when she'd been looking up this area of Provence just to see what it looked like. She'd made an abrupt decision in a heated moment, had come across with her passport and her daughter and not a lot else. She didn't know anyone's phone number, couldn't remember her passwords for social media; but if she was honest with herself, she could have made more effort to get back online. To get a phone. To, at least, answer her brother who was perhaps a little at fault, but didn't deserve the worry she'd no doubt piled onto him.

Here, everything was new. Her job, the people, the house, Lili's school. And so different from everything that had come before. And she'd created a partition in her brain; allowed herself to step forward and done everything she could to avoid looking back. It had felt good; she'd convinced herself nothing was wrong. The only things that sometimes pierced her denial had been the emails from Kevin – and she'd stopped checking even those.

Looking at it rationally as she poured boiling water onto a teabag and watched the water stain copper-brown, her actions had been far from proportionate. She'd raced to this other version of her, as if by living the life that perhaps she should have had from the start would erase the lies and the pain. Instead, she'd isolated herself, made herself lonely. And confused her daughter.

She fished out the teabag with a spoon, added milk to the amber liquid and watched it swirl and combine as she stirred. She would get herself back on track. Buy a phone and re-establish old connections. Force herself to read Kevin's emails and respond. She'd ask Monique whether she could finish early a couple of times a week and try to chat with the other mums, rather than race to the *garderie* after the shop closed; and she'd accept any invitations for coffee or any gestures of friendship that were offered, without suspicion. Michel had seemed nice, there was no reason to believe he had any ulterior motive in asking her for coffee. Even if, as she suspected, Monique had put him up to it.

She took her tea through to the living room where Lili was

working on her second biscuit, spraying crumbs on the page as she looked at the pictures of a little, lost chick trying to find its family. It was a French book, borrowed from the school, but they'd read it almost every night recently.

Adeline smiled at Lili's earnest face and messy eating, then picked up her volume of poems. Turning to the next one, she read:

Tell the truth but tell it slant

Reading the short verse, the end lines stood out most for her:

The truth must dazzle gradually
Or every man be blind.

A memory flashed in her mind – Kevin, his face red with frustration or anger or some other mixed-up emotion, saying to her again and again, 'She was always going to tell you. But it was never the right time. She was scared.'

'Scared of what? That I'd reject her?'

'No, Addy. Scared of breaking you.'

Tell the truth but tell it slant – the idea of gradually revealing truth rather than letting it hit others with its starkness out of nowhere. Wasn't that a kind sentiment rather than something malicious? Mum had been sick for several years – maybe she'd put off telling Adeline because of this thing, or that thing, or Lili's birth, her illness; perhaps she was always waiting for the right time and was never given the chance. Adeline would never know. But she had to believe her mum's intentions were good – she owed her that, at least.

Perhaps, even now, she'd have been better off not knowing.

Adeline had lied too – to Lili, she realised. About Kevin. About being lonely – because if she was honest with herself, she *was* a little lonely. A little lost. She'd lied to protect her child's feelings. Because that's what you do when you're a mother.

'Are you crying, Mummy?' a little voice piped up. Lili had left her chair and was standing next to her, looking worried.

Adeline realised her cheeks were damp. 'It's just this poem,' she said. 'It made Mummy feel sad for a moment, that's all.'

And she missed her mother, she realised. Despite it all, she'd do anything to have her mother back.

'Stupid poem,' Lili said crossly.

Adeline found a laugh breaking through her sadness. 'Oh, no, it's a lovely poem. It just made me feel sad for a moment, that's all.'

Lili reached for her hand and pushed something into her palm.

Adeline looked. It was a small, blue stone. 'What's this?' she asked.

'Monique gave it to me. To help me make friends. But maybe you need it too. She said it's magic. And it worked! I've got lots of friends already.'

Adeline felt a shiver of unease. 'That's kind of her,' she said. She turned the stone over in her hand. 'You know it's only pretend, though, don't you? You make friends because of who you are, not because of a crystal.'

Lili shrugged dismissively.

'But maybe it helps,' Adeline added. Because if there was a time to believe in a little magic, childhood was certainly it.

She took a big sip from her tea and shuffled a little so that Lili could climb onto her lap. Dickinson's poems were replaced with the chick story, the blue stone was laid carefully on the table, and she read to Lili as her girl snuggled in and gave her the comfort she'd instinctively known she needed.

Tomorrow, she decided, it would be a new start. She'd start being honest with herself about who she was. She'd accept her past and work towards a better future. And this time, there would be no more lies.

10

It was absolutely typical, of course, she thought the following morning after dropping Lili off at school, that she'd bump into Michel straightaway – the moment she'd decided to be more open, to accept invitations and make friends as and when the opportunities struck. Mornings were often slow and today Monique had called to say she didn't need her to be in situ until 10 a.m., and suggested she treat herself to a coffee. 'You have worked so hard,' she'd said. 'Why not go to the Café des Sports – they make the best coffee.'

The moment she'd walked into the cafe, she'd seen Michel sitting at one of the small, round tables, his head buried in a book. He'd clearly been there a little while, as his cup was empty, but he looked in no rush to leave.

Rather than interrupt him, she made her way to the counter and ordered her coffee, which came with a small chocolate on the side, but when she turned, she found that he had lowered his book and was looking at her with a smile.

She walked over. '*Salut.*'

'Sit down, join me,' he said, gesturing at the chair opposite.

'Oh, no. You're reading. I don't want to interrupt,' she replied hurriedly.

He laughed. 'You are *rescuing* me. My aunt gave me this book and I simply can't get on with it.'

She glanced at the title – it wasn't one she recognised. All out of excuses, she set her cup down and slid into the wooden chair opposite him. 'I take it I should keep this information from Monique,' she grinned.

'Yes, perhaps, although she is used to me and my terrible taste!' he smiled. 'I might be a professor, but my subject is *mathématiques*, much to her dismay. She is trying to educate me with fine literature, but I still prefer modern thrillers.' He shrugged. 'So there we have it. I am beyond help.'

Adeline chuckled. 'I'm partial to a thriller once in a while myself.'

He grinned and signalled to the man behind the counter that he wanted another coffee.

'Don't feel you have to stay for me,' she said, sipping her drink and deciding that after all, she'd need to add both the sugar cubes proffered.

'Ah, not at all. I am on leave for a few days – I have nothing to do!' He seemed delighted by this.

'It'll be nice for Monique to see a bit more of you,' Adeline said. 'I don't think she has anyone else. Family, I mean.'

He shook his head. 'No. Or not family she will talk to.'

'What about your mother? Her sister, I presume?'

Another shake. 'Yes, she talks to my mother. But they are not actually true family. Not related. Monique is my aunt because she has been best friends with my mother for many years, since before I was born. So yes, we are family, but not by blood.'

'Oh, I see.'

Adeline was itching to ask him why Monique had cut her

mother out of her life – to find out more about her mysterious boss. She took a sip of her coffee instead and began to unwrap the foil-wrapped square of dark chocolate at its side.

'And you want to ask me – *why does Monique not speak to her mother?* But you are too polite,' he said, his eyes mischievous.

She felt herself getting hot. 'It's fine. It's none of my business.' Could everyone in this place actually read minds?

'Well, I will tell you anyway. Because it is not a secret. She had an enormous row with her mother when she was very young – perhaps not even twenty.'

'Do you know what it was about?'

'Yes. My mother tells me it was something to do with a baby.'

Adeline lifted her head. 'A baby?'

'Yes. My mother told me Monique had a baby. She was very young and it was quite a scandal at the time. And of course, Monique's mother was horrified. She wouldn't let her keep the baby, and Monique could not forgive her.'

'Oh.' Adeline felt a question rise up in her that she couldn't silence. 'Michel, how long ago was this? When she gave her baby up?'

Michel shrugged, not realising the importance of his answer. 'Perhaps forty years, or more. Before I was born, for sure.'

Adeline felt whatever had welled inside her snap; a strange cocktail of disappointment and relief washed over her. She thought then of Lili. She'd been in her mid-twenties when her daughter had been born, so it hadn't been a scandalous age. But she had been single. At least once she'd told Colin she was pregnant. She tried to imagine how it would have been if she'd been forced to give Lili up. But her mother would never have done that to her. Mum had been with her from her first contraction to the final push.

'Yes. It was the times, I think. Her mother... her mother

regretted it later. But it was too late. It was done,' Michel continued, seemingly oblivious.

They were silent for a moment. Adeline feeling a surprise of tears prick at her eyes. 'And she came here because of that?'

'I think so. She went to a few different places. She was a bit lost, I think. Then here. She said it felt like home.'

'I can understand that. It's a nice place.'

'*Oui*. Although not much happens here. Except where Monique is involved.'

'Really?'

'Yes.' His coffee arrived and he thanked Marcel, the server, and began to stir sugar into the tiny cup. 'Monique always seems to be where the adventures are.'

There were two people at the counter now. Adeline recognised one as André, his back to her. She felt herself stiffen. He looked around, almost as if he could sense her gaze, his eyes meeting hers then moving away as if something beyond, through the window, had caught his eye. Should she get up? Take the opportunity to apologise? She felt rooted to the spot; embarrassed that she'd left it so long, not sure how to bring it up.

'And you?' Michel asked, after a pause.

'Me?'

'Yes. What brings you to St Vianne?'

'Oh.' She felt suddenly shy. 'Well, it was chance really,' she said. 'I... well, I had a falling out, with family. And I'd been working as a teacher for so many years. I'd had enough. I'd got a bit of inheritance. It was as if everything came together at once.'

'But France? And here? In this tiny place?'

She smiled. 'Well, why not? I got my degree in French, and I was teaching the subject to bored teenagers. I'd kind of lost my way, my love of language. My school realised it didn't need such a big French department.' She smiled ruefully. 'Someone was going to be made redundant. I volunteered. I was caring for my mum – both me and Kevin, my brother, were living with her by the end so that someone would always be there. Nights were terrible and I was exhausted. And I had a little saved. It seemed right.'

He nodded. 'That was brave.'

'It didn't feel brave,' she said simply. 'Just... as if it were something that was right at the time. Then Mum... well she died before I'd even finished my contract. More quickly than they expected at the end. And I had all this time on my hands and absolutely nothing to do.'

Michel nodded quietly. 'I am sorry to hear about your mother. It must have been very hard.'

She nodded. 'Very. But then I found something. A family connection to this area. It seemed almost as if fate were propelling me.' She stopped, surprised at her own words. 'Not that I really... I don't believe in things like that.'

'At least you chose to come here,' he said, clearly trying to inject some positivity back into the conversation. 'It is a friendly place – welcoming.'

'Most of the time,' she said. 'One or two people seemed less than thrilled at first.'

'C'est vrai?' Michel raised an eyebrow.

'Yes. I think some – well, not everyone likes newcomers,' she shrugged.

Michel was watching André now, as he opened the door and exited into the sunlight, giving Michel a nod but avoiding Adeline's eye. 'And him? He is one of these people who don't like newcomers?' he asked, noting how Adeline studiously stirred her coffee during the brief encounter.

She made a face. 'Not exactly. No. André was quite friendly

until...' She told him about knocking into him in the street, rushing away as his food rolled across the pavement. 'I'm so embarrassed,' she said.

Michel laughed. 'I don't think André would hold a grudge for this. He's very easy-going. I will talk to him, don't worry.'

'Oh, you don't need to do that!'

'It is nothing. I am sure he has barely remembered anyway.'

She hoped not. André was one of the people who made the village what it was; someone she encountered almost every day. And someone, if she was honest with herself, she felt drawn to. It would be nice to clear the air at least.

'And your job,' he said, returning to their conversation. 'You did not enjoy teaching the children?'

She thought of her unruly Year 11s and smiled. 'Oh, I did. They were great. But in England, there isn't as much interest in foreign languages as you might think. People aren't always that motivated. I'd love to be able to really share my passion for it all – and I think choosing to teach students who have decided to specialise could be really fulfilling.'

'I understand this,' he smiled. 'Teaching *mathématiques* has taught me that it is certainly not the subject for everyone.'

She laughed. 'It never was my favourite subject at school.'

He clutched his heart in mock horror. '*Mon dieu!*' he said. 'How could you say this! Maths is a beautiful language of its own.'

'I'll take your word for it.' She finally popped the chocolate in her mouth. It was bitter, soft on her tongue and she closed her eyes momentarily.

'And the job?' he said.

'Sorry?'

'How did you find it? I don't think many people have even heard of St Vianne.'

She shook her head. 'It was strange. I was online. And fed up. And it was just by chance, really, that I did a few Internet searches. You know: *Jobs in France* and *Teaching in France* and *Positions vacant* – that kind of thing. Looking for something in the *département* – it's where my family connection is. Most of what came up was a lot of nonsense. And then I found that I can't teach here without doing a whole new qualification. I was about to give it all up, but suddenly I found this little ad for the job, tucked in the website of a local paper. And it seemed perfect.'

Michel's eyes studied her face. 'Yes, it is strange that you should stumble across this. Just by chance.'

'Very,' she agreed.

'I would not be surprised if...' he began. Then he shook his head. 'No matter.'

'No. Go on. What?'

He laughed. 'No, I am starting to think like my aunt. I do not believe in her charms, her magic. But sometimes things happen around her,' he shrugged, 'well, they are hard to explain.'

She nodded in agreement, feeling something stir inside her. 'Yes, I know what you mean.'

'And did you come over for an interview and then...'

'That was the strange thing. I rang the number on the ad, all ready to explain that I'd need a visa, and why I'd be coming, and hoping to convince someone that I could do a good job even if I wasn't local, and Monique simply said she was glad I'd called and that I could start as soon as I wanted!' Adeline still remembered the stunned silence she'd sat in after making the call, somehow having secured herself a job when all she'd meant to do was enquire. 'I thought about changing my mind, but it all seemed so serendipitous...' she shrugged. 'So here I am.'

Michel laughed, shaking his head. 'This is typical of my

aunt. She believes in fate, believes that the right things will come to the right people. I can imagine that she simply felt you would be right, and didn't need any more proof.'

'Risky strategy.'

'Perhaps. But it worked this time, *non*?'

'Well, yes.' Adeline drained the last of her coffee; it was almost time to go. To her surprise, she'd really enjoyed speaking to Michel. There was something open, easy about his manner. 'Can I ask you something?' she said.

'*Oui*, of course.'

'Is... I mean I'm not even sure if I believe in this stuff. But... is Monique psychic?'

He smiled, shook his head. 'I am not sure if I believe in *this stuff* either,' he admitted. 'But I would say she is intuitive. She senses things. And sometimes things happen for her that I cannot explain.'

'Oh.'

'And some people – when she first came, many years ago – they said she was a witch. It was hard for her.'

'Yes, she mentioned that. But why did they think that?'

'Well, they said that she does magic. Perhaps she does. She likes crystals, charms. Nothing terrible. The kind of things perhaps all of our great-grandmothers did. She helps people – or tries to. And heals them too – with the books. Some people felt suspicious of her.'

'Oh, wow.'

He shrugged. 'People are often suspicious of new people, of strangers, at first, but after a time, they began to accept her. And they stopped saying she was a witch, and realised that she was a friend.'

'She could be both, of course,' Adeline said with a smile.

'*Oui*. She has something, some skill we do not understand.

But when I asked my mother, she said she does not believe in anything like this. She says that Monique is simply a reader of people.'

'A reader of people?' Adeline tried the phrase. 'I like that. We can read books, can't we? And some people find more meaning – like reading between the lines. Perhaps Monique does this.'

'She reads between the lines of people,' Michel laughed. 'Yes. I think she would like that description.'

The conversation petered out, a man walked through the door and went to the counter. Adeline glanced at her watch. An hour had passed. 'Oh!' she said. 'It's almost ten.'

He nodded. 'Time to go.'

'Yep. But thank you. It's been nice. And you won't mention to Monique about…'

'That we talked about her magic powers? That you are a sceptic? That you think maybe she goes home on a broom with a cat?'

'Well, yes.' She felt herself get hot. 'Some of it, anyway.'

'Of course. It is between us. Although she would not mind. Monique, if nothing else, she is a character. And individual. And when we are a little bit different, people talk. She knows that. It is not always a bad thing.'

'No, I suppose not.' Adeline put her chair under the table and smiled at Michel again.

'But your secret is safe with me. As long as you keep my secret too.'

'Which is?'

'That I think this book she has given me is terrible!' he said, looking at the volume again. 'She may be able to work magic, but I don't think she will ever give me her love of literature.'

11

Dear Kev,

I'm sorry that I haven't been in touch. It wasn't fair of me to just disappear. But I had so much to process and I was SO angry – I just didn't know what to do.

Finding the papers was hard, but then finding out that you'd known all along felt like a betrayal. But I've had a lot of time to think about it since. And I'm starting to understand that you were put in an impossible situation. I know you were just a child when I came along – I honestly can't blame you. I was just angry and confused and the anger had nowhere else to go. I am really sorry.

I've ordered a new mobile phone and I will give you the number as soon as I have it. And I'm going to get back online properly, rather than just on this work PC. I'm actually meant to be looking up books right now, so have to be quick!

Please don't worry about me. Lili and I are having a lovely time in St Vianne; my French is really starting to feel fluent and we've made some new friends.

Thank you for not giving up on me!

Addy

She was going to close the screen down after sending the email, but almost instantly a reply appeared.

Addy! Thank God you're OK. Hang on a mo… Kev

She sat for a minute waiting for another message. Kevin, she knew, was not the fastest typist in the world. She flicked to the other screen and continued searching ISBN numbers for books, checking back every few minutes to see if anything else arrived. At last, there it was.

Hi Addy,

I am so pleased to hear from you!

And please don't feel too bad for how you acted. I'm not sure I'd have been much different! Please believe me that I wanted to tell you so many times. But there was always this voice in my head telling me it wasn't the right time – that you simply didn't need more stress dumped on you. I guess that's probably what Mum felt too. I hope you can forgive her and Dad too, in time?

And Addy, if you ever want to look for, well, anyone, I can help. Your birth mum, I think people tend to say. I'm happy to support you in finding answers. I know that our mum would want you to do what felt right.

I'm off to work now, but I'll write more later.

Glad you're OK, sis.

Kev xx

Alone in the shop, Adeline shut down the computer and stared at the blank screen. Her reflection, greyed out in the dark surface, wobbled in front of her. And she was struck again by the knowledge that the woman she'd thought she was didn't really exist. That in some ways the reflection in front of her was of a stranger.

She closed her eyes and remembered pulling out the box from the pile and beginning to sort through its contents. It had been one of several boxes left over from sorting Mum's stuff; part of the painful process of post-death admin.

When Mum had died, she'd left everything so organised for them. Adeline had been in awe of the way she'd set out the right papers, made everything straightforward. The rest of her things, she'd said, just take to the dump: recycle, give away.

Of course, that part hadn't been as easy as their mother had imagined. Clearing old furniture and sending it to a charity, putting Mum's clothes in bags ready to donate. Easy on the face of it, in a practical sense. But every item they'd dispatched had felt like a bereavement in itself. They'd each kept one or two of Mum's things and the rest had needed to be disposed of before the house sale could go through. Adeline felt her eyes well, remembering how she'd had to hold her emotions in when bagging up Mum's jumpers and T-shirts. So familiar that she'd wanted to simply wrap herself in them and sob.

Then suddenly – a month ago – it had been done. Except for a few boxes of photos and keepsakes that neither she nor Kevin had had the heart to throw away, and neither had had the strength to go through. They'd gone, instead, to the loft in Adeline's tiny, terraced house. They'd get to them eventually, they'd told themselves.

She still wasn't sure what had led her to opening the box that day. She'd returned to work a few days earlier after compassionate leave, with her redundancy date looming, filled with a kind of restless energy. It had made sense to occupy herself with something, and for some reason she'd chosen the box at the back of the stack to open first.

She'd almost not reached the certificate. It had been buried under piles of baby photos – faded pictures of her in Kevin's arms as a baby; of her mum pushing her in a pram. Sporting the kind of clothing styles that made her feel ancient, as if she were part of history.

Then she'd pulled it out – noticing her name – and had read the words 'Adoption Birth Certificate.' She'd got her own, shorter, birth certificate at home. The one that she'd always used for identification. But this one she'd never seen. And there she'd learned that a week after her birth, in the London High Court of Justice Family Division, the strangers she'd called Mum and Dad her whole life had adopted her as their own.

Her first instinct had been to call Kevin. He'd answered at work, his conversation limited by the fact that he had to keep his voice low. She'd gabbled out the information, feeling almost high on adrenaline. And when he'd finally responded, his voice hesitant, she'd suddenly realised that what she'd told him wasn't news to him at all.

That's when she'd thrown the phone in a sudden fit of rage, and seen it shatter against the wall.

She'd been stupid – hot-headed, her mum had used to say when she'd get in a temper as a child. She'd always had this explosive force inside her, one she'd learned to tame over the years. She wasn't often impulsive, impetuous now. But the news had been too much, too shocking. That the mother she'd mourned hadn't really been her mother. That the childhood she remembered had, in part at least, been a lie.

Kevin had come around later, dishevelled in his work suit. She'd let him in, warning him that Lili was asleep upstairs, that they had to be quiet. They'd had a whispered argument in which he'd confessed he'd always known. After all, he'd been four when they'd adopted her. 'Mum developed some health problems after having me. The doctor said she couldn't have any more kids. She always said she'd tell you when the time was right,' he said. 'We spoke about it, you know. Towards the end. But she was scared and I just couldn't force her, not then.'

'I wish you had, or you'd told me or something. There are things I would have asked her. I...'

'I know. But I felt it was her decision; her thing to tell. She was dying; you know what it was like in those last weeks. I couldn't think about anything else. And I'll be honest, Adeline. I didn't think it mattered that much. You were – are – my sister and I love you and it didn't seem important.'

'Not important!'

'I don't mean it that way. I realise it's... Information about your past is really important. But it didn't affect how I felt, how we were as a family. We were – we are – just *us*.'

'But you don't understand,' she'd whispered as loudly as she'd dared. 'Everything about my life I'd thought was true, isn't. I don't know who I am any more.'

'You do. You are the same person, Adeline. Just more... well, maybe with a bit more of a back story than you'd thought,' he'd said, trying to smile.

But it wasn't the time for smiles. 'This isn't a joke to me, Kevin. It's my life.'

He'd told her what little they knew. That her mother had been French, had come over with her family to London for a year. She and her British father had been teenagers. And the pregnancy had been unplanned. They'd arranged the adoption before she'd even been born.

'That's all you know?'

'Sorry. It was a closed adoption. We didn't get any real information.'

'So my dad's from London, and my mum's from...'

'Provence,' Kevin had said. 'I'm sure they said Provence, in France.'

Over the days that followed she'd withdrawn from her life. Finished her time at school, signed off her social media accounts on her laptop, ignored Kevin's calls to the landline. Avoided him as much as possible. In the evenings, she'd googled Provence, thought about taking a holiday there. Then she'd started to wonder whether she could take a year out – get away from it all.

She still couldn't quite understand how she'd managed to stumble across the advert. She'd clicked on a link about English teaching abroad, then followed a train of links and found herself on the site of a local French newspaper. It was when she'd pressed the 'back' button that the advert had sort of popped up and filled her screen.

In French, it had said:

BILINGUAL BOOKSELLER WANTED. Must be passionate about books.

And a phone number. And things had snowballed. She was in St Vianne before she'd really had time to think it through.

Adeline breathed deeply, feeling relieved that she'd finally made peace with her brother.

She brought up the orders page for their supplier and was about to start entering titles they wanted to stock to try to distract herself with something ordinary when there was a loud thud upstairs in the flat. She stood, ears pricked, unsure whether to call out. But then she heard the rumble of voices; angry voices, shouting.

Only the odd word was audible. The shrill sound of Monique's voice – raised in a way she'd never heard it, telling someone it was none of his business.

Then another voice – a man's – yelling that she was crazy, that she was going to hurt people. There was the grumbling of more angry conversation, voices slightly lowered – she couldn't pick out the words. Then another crash.

She rushed to the bottom of the stairs, ready to race up and help Monique if needed, but before she could, the door at the top opened and Michel stood there, his expression thunderous.

He looked at her, his eyes unreadable, and then began to walk quickly down the stairs. Instinctively, she stood to one side to let him pass, and he stormed towards the exit almost as if she weren't there.

Reaching it, he turned, and his eyes seemed to alight on her for a moment, and he looked as if he wanted to say something. Instead, nodding curtly, he pulled open the door, jarring the bell, and disappeared into the street.

Her heart thumping, she turned back towards the stairs and made her way up to the flat. 'Monique?' she said softly, knocking on the door.

It wasn't locked and pushing it open, she could detect a little movement in the small kitchen, so she carefully made her way there. Inside, Monique was picking up the shattered pieces of a plate that had obviously been thrown.

'Oh my God,' Adeline cried, rushing to help. 'What happened?'

Monique turned her slightly tear-stained face towards her, and instead of sorrow in her eyes, Adeline saw they were shining with anger and spirit. 'My nephew, he is a pig.'

'He threw this?'

'*Non*,' Monique admitted. 'This was me. Because I got so angry. I am hot-tempered. But I regret this,' she sighed, holding a piece of shattered porcelain. 'It was a lovely platter.'

'You argued?' Adeline prompted.

'*Oui*. Oh, do not worry,' Monique sighed and straightened up. 'It is not so bad. We had a disagreement. And it got a bit crazy, but we will be OK.'

Adeline longed to ask what it had been about, but couldn't help but feel it was none of her business.

'Can I get you anything?'

Monique looked at her, her face softened as if the anger was falling away. '*Oui*, thank you. A coffee.'

'Why don't I go and get us some pastries too?' Adeline suggested. 'A bit of sugar always helps.'

Monique smiled. '*Oui*, a good idea. When life is bitter, you need to add some sweetness.' She put her hand on Adeline's shoulder. 'Thank you.'

They'd touched before. Exchanged brief *bisous* and shaken hands when she'd arrived. But it was the first time Monique had put her hand on Adeline for any length of time. It was strange, how warm her hand felt on Adeline's shoulder and how, as she looked at the older woman standing in front of her, she could feel almost an electrical charge.

They stood like this for a moment before Adeline nodded and moved away. 'Pastries,' she said. 'Coffee.'

And the moment was broken.

But as she exited the shop into the sunshine, hoping not to run into Michel, it was hard not to wonder whether Monique really did have some sort of magic about her.

12

———

'Are you OK, Mummy?' Lili asked the following morning on the way to school.

Adeline looked down at her daughter's face, tilted up towards her, brow furrowed with concern.

'Yes, of course!' she said brightly. 'Why do you ask?'

Lili shrugged. 'You aren't talking.'

Adeline laughed. 'You should be grateful for that!' she joked. Then, 'Sorry, I'm just thinking about a few things.'

'Like the bookshop?'

'Yes, like the bookshop.' Or to be more precise, she thought, as she waved her little daughter off at the edge of the playground a few minutes later, the bookshop owner. She had been aching to ask Monique more about her past, ever since she'd spoken to Michel. What happened with her baby? Had she ever thought about tracing her? She longed to know what it was like for a mother in that situation – what it might be like for *her* birth mother if she was still out there somewhere. Monique had clearly been forced into having her baby adopted – and although her story would have taken place some time before

Adeline's own birth, it would be interesting to know how it had unfolded. Just to imagine, for a moment, what things might have been like for her own mother.

But how could she? It had been Michel who'd told her about Monique's past; she wasn't even sure if she was meant to know. Still, she had watched Monique since – wondered about whether the thought of her baby ever crossed her mind, or whether she'd been able to truly move on.

The morning air was warm, with a breeze that felt fresh and cleansing, and she slipped off her cardigan to let the air play on her bare arms for a moment as she made her way to the shop. She'd decided to go in early – there was nothing much to do at home and she wanted to avoid the cafe just in case Michel was there – the last thing she wanted to do was bump into him after his thunderous outburst yesterday. Monique had been subdued afterwards and Adeline had become angry at his ability to simply upset her and walk off.

But today, in the shop, everything was light. Monique was standing on a small stool, cleaning the windows with a vinegar solution that made the air smell tangy and, teamed with the aroma of some of the older paperbacks, reminded Adeline a little of the newspaper-wrapped fish and chips of her childhood.

'*Bonjour*,' she said. '*Ça va?*'

'*Oui*,' Monique smiled down at her from her slightly taller position. 'You are early.' Her smile seemed wide and genuine, and she had her usual happy air. Hopefully she'd recovered from whatever had occurred the day before.

'Yes,' Adeline gave a shrug. 'It was a lovely day and I just found myself walking here after dropping Lili at school.'

Monique stepped down from her stool, spray bottle in hand. 'Well, thank you. And actually, it could be a favour for me.

Would it be OK for you to mind the shop while I pop to the *pharmacie*?'

'Of course!' Adeline said. 'I'll keep the crowds at bay.' She laughed, but Monique looked confused: 'I think it will be quiet.'

'Yes,' Adeline acquiesced, embarrassed that her joke had fallen flat. After Monique tidied away the stool and exited into the street with a cheery wave, Adeline sat behind the counter, looking through the names on the paperbound books and the scribbled notes of orders on the notepad Monique kept for the purpose. It was hard to read Monique's handwriting in some places and many of the titles she hadn't heard of – she'd highlight any queries and wait until her boss came back before ordering something completely wrong.

She could make out the name Claude on one of the papers, and the thought of him made sadness well in her chest. He'd been in again yesterday, with his timid smile and anxious eyes. Monique had slipped him another book – a slim volume of poems – and he'd taken it gratefully. 'We will find it, Claude,' she'd said. 'I promise.'

Adeline wondered what book Monique was going to try with him next. She liked the idea of bibliotherapy and – despite Monique's allusions to magic and psychic insight – liked to think of what Monique did in this practical, ordinary way. But could it really be enough for Claude, who was clearly so steeped in grief he could barely move? Surely a trip to his doctor might do better for him? Perhaps she'd suggest it if he ever came in when Monique wasn't around.

She did believe in the healing power of books, in the way that words could find places in the heart and soul that even medicine couldn't always reach. But she was also practical – sometimes it took a little more science to get someone back on track.

When the bell jangled, she looked up to see a woman in jeans and a sweatshirt walking in, a large handbag over her shoulder and a shopping bag straining with vegetables in her hand. 'Morning!' the woman said in English.

Adeline had been speaking French with everyone but Lili for so long, the familiar greeting startled her a little. She replied, on autopilot, with a friendly 'Bonjour.'

The woman coloured. 'Oh,' she said. Then peered at her a little, walking forward. 'Desolée, j'ai pensé... j'ai pensé... I thought you were English,' she finished, lapsing away from her attempt to speak French.

'Oh, I am,' Adeline replied. 'Sorry. Force of habit.'

The woman grinned and stuck out a hand for a shake. Adeline's hand met hers and she gave it a firm up and down. 'Stacey.' She wore her blonde hair tied in a scrappy ponytail, bits escaping to frame her face. Her complexion was red and rather blotchy, possibly from too much sun over the years, and she looked to be in her forties.

'Adeline.'

Stacey nodded. 'Pretty name.'

'So do you live locally?' Adeline asked.

'Not far. In one of the hamlets. My youngest goes to the *maternelle* here, so I have a wander round sometimes after dropping her off.' She held a bag of chocolate up. 'Always get my fix of this stuff too from the patisserie. Have you tasted it yet?'

'No. Well, only the pastries from there. Not the chocolate.'

'You're missing out. It's divine. As is the guy who makes it!'

'André?'

The woman shrugged. 'The tall guy, you know. Good-looking.'

Adeline smiled. 'That's the one.'

'Yep. His chocolate costs a fortune, but talk about tasty!'

Adeline wasn't sure if Stacey was alluding to André's looks or the deliciousness of the chocolate, but decided to move the conversation on, either way. Michel had hopefully spoken to André by now, smoothed things over after her collision and rude departure. But thinking about how she'd barged into him always made her prickle with residual embarrassment.

'Hey, you've gone red!' Stacey seemed delighted. 'Don't fancy him, do you?'

'Don't be ridiculous!' she said, perhaps a little too sharply.

Stacey looked at her knowingly. 'Well, can't say I blame you!'

'I don't... it's not...'

But Stacey smiled at her, clearly convinced. It made more sense to change the subject.

'So, are you looking for anything in particular?'

'Just thought I'd have a browse. Don't often come in here.'

'Not a reader?'

'Nah. It's not that,' Stacey said, looking furtive. 'It's just the other woman that's normally here... Sometimes she gives me the creeps.'

Adeline found herself stiffen as her body went into defence mode. 'The creeps?'

'Ah, she's nice enough. It's just someone told me once that she used to do witchcraft. You know, spells and that. Fortune telling. I just...' Stacey shuddered. 'That sort of stuff gives me the chills.' She grinned, as if to make light of her words. 'I know lots of people believe in it,' she added with a shrug.

Adeline laughed. 'Oh, Monique's lovely! Yes, maybe a little eccentric, but you definitely don't need to worry about coming in. She's not going to cast a spell on you.'

Stacey nodded and gave a self-conscious grin. 'That's good to know. I like bookshops, it's just people talk and...' She trailed off.

She picked up a book, almost at random, and thrust it at Adeline. 'I'll take this one.'

Adeline looked at it. It was a recent release from an American crime writer. 'Oh, this is a great book,' she said. 'Had me up half the night afterwards though.' She rang the purchase up on the till, then made change from a twenty euro note.

'Thanks, love. And look,' Stacey jotted a number on the back of her receipt and handed it back to Adeline. 'Let me know if you want to grab a coffee sometime, see the lie of the land. It can be hard here, on your tod.'

'Oh. Thank you.' Adeline tucked the receipt into her pocket and smiled. 'It's really kind of you.'

Stacey shrugged. 'People always say to integrate, and I do try. But it's hard – always nice to have someone to talk to who gets it,' she said. 'Have a proper natter about things back home, that kind of thing.'

Adeline nodded. 'Well, thanks.'

The bell rang to signal the door had opened and they both looked up to see Monique, carrying a paper bag with a green *pharmacie* logo on it. She looked at Stacey. '*Bonjour,*' she said with a smile.

'*Bonjour,*' Stacey nodded. Her shoulders seemed to stiffen.

Adeline handed her the book she'd purchased. 'There you go. Let me know if you enjoy it.'

'Will do.' Stacey turned and made her way to the door, giving Monique a rather wide berth, but smiling at her as if not wanting to cause offence.

Once she'd exited, Monique came over and set the *pharmacie* bag down on the stairs, then looked at Adeline quizzically. 'She was a little strange, *non*? I have not seen her here before.'

'Oh, yes. She's English. I think someone had told her I was here and she was curious,' said Adeline with a shrug.

'OK,' Monique made to pick up her purchases and take them to the flat and then stopped. 'But she seemed strange with me. She made a big circle to get around me, as if I was an elephant!'

Adeline laughed, then felt herself begin to go a little red. 'She's a bit... nervous, I think.'

'Of me? But why?'

'Perhaps...' Adeline thought of Stacey's stumbled attempt at French then felt Monique's knowing eyes on her and realised that only the truth would do. 'She heard some rumours about you. About you doing some magic and things like that.'

Monique shook her head. 'Ah yes, because I am a witch.' She rolled her eyes, then shook her head and laughed – such a joyful noise usually, but this time tinged with sadness. 'Some people have no imagination,' she said. 'You are either a doctor with a medical diploma, or you are a witch. They cannot conceive of anything else. Anything in between. It is all black and white. And of course if you are a witch, then you must be dangerous, perhaps evil. They cannot imagine that some people use magic for good.'

'People can be narrow-minded,' Adeline said, feeling a little hypocritical.

'*Oui*. When I first arrived, I was so young. And people were suspicious of me. But I thought...' Monique shrugged. 'Ah, it does not matter.'

'I honestly think she's an exception. I haven't heard anyone else say anything, I think perhaps it's an old rumour – and maybe if she doesn't mix much with local people she hasn't been corrected.'

Monique fiddled with the paper bag in her hands, worrying its edges. 'It is just the word "witch". It makes me feel like an old woman on a broom,' she said, half amused. 'But why is it that people need to label everything? *Non*, I am not a doctor. I do not ride a broom like a witch. But I do use magic and I do heal people.'

Adeline felt a shiver, thinking about the strange charge she'd felt when Monique's hand had rested on her shoulder the day before; the way in which the Dickinson poems seemed almost to have been written about her at times.

'Ah, but not hocus-pocus, no cauldrons,' Monique said, gathering the bag to her and smiling again. She looked, suddenly, more like her usual self. 'Perhaps crystals. Maybe spells. A little intuition. Jars for luck and love and fortune. And stories of course. They are magic, *non*? Poems.'

'Yes. I suppose.'

'Pah! There is no "suppose". I gave you a book from a woman who is dead many years, yet you hear her voice. You feel what she feels. You sense it. There is a connection. What is that if it is not magic?'

Adeline felt a shiver of recognition.

'Stories, they are human souls trapped in words. One soul calling to another, across pages, miles, sometimes centuries. And they tell us the thing we need to know more than anything. That we are not alone. That we can connect. Maybe the writer and the reader will never meet. Maybe the writer has been dead many years. But there is a voice saying "We have the same mind, the same thoughts. Do not worry. You are heard. You are understood." It is this.' Monique said, tapping her chest. 'This is what heals us.'

13

It was her first time in Avignon. It was only twenty kilometres from St Vianne, but with so much to do and find out about and settle into, she hadn't had a chance to visit. But she'd received notification that her mobile had arrived at the local phone shop, so had to make the journey.

It had been more difficult than she might have imagined. Without a car, and with no local bus service, she hadn't been quite sure what to do. A taxi to the town was a possibility, but she'd baulked when she'd enquired about the price. Thirty euros each way was far more than she was willing to fork out for such a short journey.

Adeline wished she'd thought it through more before she'd ordered the phone. Everything on the website had seemed so straightforward – until she'd got to creating a contract for herself. Then she'd needed ID and address details. As she was so new to her rental, she hadn't yet received a bill addressed to her, so in the end she'd had to go to the *mairie* where a local official had printed out a proof of residence with painstaking slowness, and stamped it with an official-looking stamp. Now she had to take it to the shop to prove her existence and collect her phone.

Living in London, she'd been so used to stepping out of her house and getting on public transport; and although she'd been under no illusion that St Vianne was anything like London, she'd assumed there'd be some way of getting from A to B. A rickety bus or a local station she could walk to. But clearly not.

She'd just hung the phone up to the taxi service when she heard a cough behind her and jumped. 'I'm sorry,' Monique said. 'I didn't mean to scare you. But if you're looking for a way to get to Avignon, I can arrange something.'

'You can?'

The result had been a ride in a van with a ninety-year-old farmer in blue overalls called Grégoire who'd regaled her with graphic stories about birthing lambs that would have made James Herriot turn pale. But somehow, she'd managed to cope and – when he'd dispatched her in the town centre – she'd waved him off, grateful both for the lift and for the fact that it was over.

Then she was alone, standing on an unfamiliar street and somehow back in the heart of things. She'd only lived in sleepy St Vianne for a few weeks but it had lulled her into a different rhythm. It was a shock to see people walking briskly, cars driving past, the number of shops and boutiques that garnished the high street. After a moment, though, she realised she was enjoying being around a little more hustle and bustle – she drew energy from the other people passing and, as she searched for rue de Combles, began to enjoy peeping into artisan boutiques, chocolate shops and shoe stores and doing a little window-shopping.

She'd loved living in London. Loved the vibrancy of the city, the fact that whatever time it was, whatever season, there would be something going on if you wanted to join in. More often than not, especially since Lili had been born, she'd opted to stay at home instead and indulge in her secret passion for reality shows, but had known that London was waiting, ready to welcome her back whenever she was ready.

Since arriving here, she'd come to appreciate the slower pace of St Vianne, the fact that the locals, even those who'd seemed a little suspicious of her at first, were friendly and always exchanged *bonjour*s. The fact that Lili was now thriving in a class of just eight pupils rather than being lost in a class of thirty or more.

But that didn't mean she had to hide from everything, she realised, looking at an enamelled bracelet in the window of a jewellery store and wondering whether to treat herself.

Deciding against it, she moved forward again and made her way to the shiny glass front of the Internet shop. Inside, a boy who looked sixteen at most explained the features of her new phone to her as if she was ancient and out of touch – she wasn't sure whether it was because she seemed decrepit to him, or because she'd told him she didn't currently have a phone at all – something that was apparently astonishing.

She had to admit it felt nice to slip the new mobile into her handbag and know that she was once more 'back on the grid'. She'd pass her number to Kevin later, and reset her logins for social media. Get in touch. Share her journey, see what others were up to.

It was cooler today, and as she exited onto the pavement, she pulled her cardigan more closely around her and wondered how she was going to spend the next two hours before her ride home was due. A cafe seemed her best bet, and she took a moment to peruse the few along the street she was on before selecting one with a burgundy awning and outside tables with a few scattered customers inside.

She was just walking towards the door when a woman came up to her, smiling in recognition. '*Bonjour!*' she said.

'*Bonjour,*' Adeline replied uncertainly.

'You do not recognise me!' The woman seemed unfazed. 'I'm Catherine. Catherine Dupont. You served me in the shop.'

'Oh, sorry.' Adeline felt a prickle of heat in her cheeks. 'It's been so busy... I...'

'No matter. I just wanted to say, I'm just so pleased that you've come.'

'You are?'

'Yes. I couldn't say it in the shop, with Monique there. But she has been lonely.'

'Oh, poor Monique.'

'Yes. Of course she has friends, but family is so important. I heard that Monique had a daughter and I always wanted to meet you.' Catherine smiled widely. 'It's nice for Monique to have you here, I'm sure.'

'Oh,' Adeline said. 'I'm not... I just work for her. I'm not Monique's daughter.'

Catherine's kohl-framed eyes registered confusion. 'Oh. But I was so sure. And... well, you seem so alike...' she trailed off, her cheeks flushing a little.

'Don't worry. An easy mistake to make.'

'Yes. Perhaps. Maybe I've been reading too many books! But I could have sworn Monique said...' She put a finger to her lips. 'Ah, no matter. I'm sorry to disturb you.'

'Not at all.'

Once Catherine had turned and continued along the pavement, Adeline walked into the cafe, breathing the scent of freshly ground coffee, and feeling the warmth of the interior begin to penetrate her thin cardigan. Her hands felt slightly shaky – something about the encounter with Catherine had upset her.

Stepping past the counter with an apologetic wave, she slipped into the toilet and locked the door. Inside was a fairly large, tiled room with a loo, sink and a large mirror. She leaned on the sink and looked at herself in the glass. Her hair hung as always, straight and neat, a few inches above her shoulders. Nothing like Monique's curls. Dark eyes, but without that extraordinary depth that Monique's seemed to have. Her face – all she could see was Adeline. She couldn't make out a shadow of Monique.

So why had Catherine been so sure?

As far as she knew, Monique didn't have any relatives other than her sister, her mother, and the baby she'd given away all those years ago. A baby who would be decades older than Adeline. There was no way they were related. She rinsed her hands and splashed a little water on her face then made her way back to the counter. She ordered a *chocolat chaud* and took the tall glass balanced on a small saucer to one of the empty tables towards the back of the seating area to finally begin the arduous process of resetting her social media passwords.

Two hours later Grégoire picked her up, and after another conversation about livestock, she was dispatched close to the shop and, with a thankful wave, watched him disappear around the corner. Then she pushed the door of the bookshop open, inhaling its familiar scent and feeling that she was absolutely in the right place; it had started to feel like home.

Monique wasn't behind the counter, but on hearing the bell, began to come down from her flat, her small heels clicking on the wooden stairs.

'It's only me, Monique!'

'Ah, *bonjour!*' came the reply. Monique appeared bit by bit: shoes, ankles, the folds of her skirt, until she emerged whole onto the shop floor. She came over and greeted Adeline with a kiss on each cheek. 'I hope you have your phone?'

'Yes, back on the grid.' Adeline grinned.

'And that you did not hear too much about sheep and cows,' Monique added with a mischievous look.

Adeline laughed. 'Well, put it this way, I know more than I'll ever need to. But thank you, too, for arranging the lift. It saved me a fortune, and a bit of rural conversation was a small price to pay.'

Monique smiled. '*Bon,*' she said. She began to tell Adeline about an order that had come in, and how she was thinking of investing in a new, spinning book stand for the centre of the shop – one to contain new arrivals to catch the eye of customers.

Adeline couldn't help looking at Monique's face as she spoke, trying to see any similarity with her own. Something about the lips, perhaps? The eyebrows? But nothing that seemed overtly like a shared feature. She wondered again about Catherine, what had made her jump to the conclusion she had.

'...in the catalogue,' Monique finished. Then her brow furrowed. 'But you are not listening!'

Adeline shook herself slightly. 'I am!' she said. 'I'm sorry. Just a bit distracted. But I got the gist...' She felt herself flush.

'Are you OK?'

'*Oui.* Just thinking.'

Monique gave her such a quizzical look at this that she felt she had to say something. 'It was just I bumped into a friend of yours – Catherine. She seemed to think I was your daughter!'

Monique laughed. 'Ah, people see what they want to see. Many businesses here have family members working for them. She made a false connection.'

'Yes. I mean, I don't think we look alike, do you?'

'*Non*. I do not see it,' said Monique dismissively. She seemed to lean forward then, studying Adeline's features, her eyes darting this way and that as she took in her skin, eyes, nose, lips. She opened her mouth briefly, almost as if she were about to say something. Then clamped it shut.

'*Non*,' she agreed. '*Rien*, nothing.'

A silence settled over them as they carried on with their tasks, interrupted by the occasional customer or browser. But once in a while, when she glanced over at Monique, she saw her looking back at her, a thoughtful expression on her face.

14

Adeline posted a picture of herself standing outside the bookshop the following morning, smiling, and wrote underneath 'Taking some time out in France.' Almost immediately the likes and comments began – many from people she only half knew, whom she'd followed in another life.

There were several messages in her inbox that her best friend Chris had sent over the past few weeks – hoping she was all right, asking why she hadn't replied. Then one saying she'd spoken to Kevin, and that Adeline must call her as soon as she had a new mobile phone. Adeline felt guilty; with her new surroundings, new job, it had been easy to push thoughts of home to the back of her mind. But she ought to have kept in touch with Chris who had clearly been worried.

A couple of other messages from friends had arrived – one fairly generic catch-up mail from a university friend, another saying that she hadn't heard much from Adeline and wondered what she was up to. But that was it. When she'd first signed back onto Facebook, she'd thought she might have a barrage of concerned messages from people who'd noticed her absence. But of course, it had only been a few weeks. People did disappear from the platform; and she didn't really have daily contact with anyone except Lili and the school she'd attended in the UK.

It was amazing how she could slide out of her own life, do something so momentous to her and have nobody really notice other than Kevin. What did that say about her? Or perhaps it wasn't her at all, but just the way that life was. The illusion of communication through likes and GIFs, but no real connection at all.

She slid the phone back into her handbag and resolved to check her messages just a couple of times a day from now on; she'd got used to a life without a phone and in many ways it made her feel freer.

It was market day and there were more people browsing in the shop than usual. Some simply looking around, others flicking through volumes and smiling at the odd word or page. One or two simply there to pick up orders. Monique was deep in earnest conversation with a woman by one of the contemporary fiction stands, and a little child was rifling through the books in the wooden box. The little girl must have been three at most – almost on the cusp of going to school here. Adeline thought of Lili then, how her child skipped off from her today, already seeming so happy and settled; it made her wonder about the future – she'd intended to go back to England after a year at most. But whose future was it, really? Hers or Lili's, and what would Lili choose?

'...can never seem to find the right one!' Adeline realised with a start that a woman was talking to her, just beyond the counter.

She smiled. 'Sorry, I was on the moon,' she explained, using a French saying that she thought was particularly apt. 'What were you asking?'

'It's OK,' the woman replied. She was about the same age as Adeline and dressed in floral yoga pants and a white T-shirt. Her neck was draped with multiple necklaces and her hair twisted up on top of her head with a large clip. 'I was just saying how I never seem to find the right book. I want one that really grips me.' She put a hand to her heart. 'And I have read many beautiful books recently, but not one that has swept me away.'

Adeline nodded. A line from Dickinson came to her: 'There is no frigate like a book to take us lands away.' She loved the image of a boat; the way that the poem had made her remember the best novels – the ones that had enabled her to disappear into their pages. She almost said the words out loud, but then wondered if it would seem pretentious, and the moment passed. 'Let me have a think.' She mentally rifled through the list of books she'd recently catalogued and those she'd read over the past few weeks.

Then she found herself looking up at the woman again. Their eyes locked and suddenly she felt something, like a tingle, in her hands. And the image of a book came to mind. She darted from behind the counter. 'Hang on a moment,' she said, and went over to the stand of contemporary fiction, passing her finger over the volumes to find the right surname. Then she slipped out a work by Virginie Grimaldie – described by some as the French Marian Keyes. *Il est grand temps de rallumer les étoiles*. A book about chasing the stars, finding new light. The kind of book that would lift someone's spirits.

'Here,' she said, almost breathless back at the counter. 'Try this one.'

The woman looked at her. 'What's it about?' She sounded a little dubious.

'Oh, it's wonderful! I think you're going to love it.'

Catching her enthusiasm, the woman smiled. 'OK, why not?' and passed over a twenty euro note in payment. Adeline slipped the book into a paper bag, adding a bookmark and a flyer about the shop, then passed it to the woman, who slipped it into a raffia bag already filled with apples.

'Thank you!' Adeline said as the woman turned to go. 'Let me know if you enjoy it.'

'I will.'

The woman disappeared through the door and Adeline turned to serve another customer who was buying something for his granddaughter. It was only later, when the clock in the square had chimed for midday and Monique was locking the shop for lunch, that she thought again about what had happened. On the face of it, she'd simply suggested a book that met with the woman's requirements. But it had been her heart – her emotions – that had led her to it; she'd just had a strong, overwhelming sense that the woman and the book belonged together.

Across the shop, she saw Monique looking at her, her hand on the bolt that would secure the door for the two hours they took for lunch. 'Are you all right?' Monique asked.

'Yes. Yes, fine,' Adeline replied. She didn't feel like sharing what had happened with Monique; imagined their interpretations would be entirely different. She stretched and yawned. 'Just a bit tired. Could do with a coffee.'

'Amen to that,' Monique said with a smile. A shadow fell over her face as the glass of the door was blocked by a figure, and she looked up to indicate to the would-be customer that they were closed until two o'clock. Then her face changed.

It was Michel.

Monique unbolted the door and he entered, his mouth

somewhere between a straight line and a smile. '*Bonjour*,' he said, leaning down and kissing her lightly on each cheek.

'*Bonjour*,' she replied, her tone guarded.

Adeline felt uncomfortable, as if she were witnessing a private moment. She'd brought some food from home to eat in the shop today; the small cafe was always heaving after the market had packed away. But perhaps she ought to make herself scarce – go home and eat something there. 'Shall I...?' she said, and both of them looked at her.

'*Non*, don't be silly. You stay. Perhaps Michel will come up to my apartment?' Monique said, nodding towards the stairs.

He nodded in return, smiling more broadly at Adeline as he passed her, and was it her imagination or did he give her a wink? She hoped he was here to make amends. Something about his presence always seemed to light Monique from the inside, and she'd started to worry about her friend – Adeline didn't have much family, but she couldn't imagine what it might be like to have none at all.

The shop fell silent, the only noise coming from people passing by on their way to lunch, the traders packing their stalls, and the odd customer who tried the door before noticing the 'Closed for lunch' sign in the window.

Adeline munched on her rather dry ham baguette and tried to resist the urge to draw out her phone and distract herself. Instead, she pulled a book off a nearby shelf and tried to engage with that. But it was impossible to stop her attention from wandering upstairs and wondering exactly what might be happening there. Would there be another argument? Would Michel apologise? What had they fought about in the first place?

Monique had been vague whenever she'd mentioned their fight, saying they'd had a difference of opinion. But it was hard to believe that anything ordinary could have caused such a violent response in Monique, who seemed so calm most of the time.

Then there was a click that sent a thump of surprise through Adeline. The door at the top of the stairs opened and Michel jogged down them, barely making a sound. He stopped at the bottom and grinned. '*Ça va?*' he asked.

'Yes, I'm fine, thank you. Everything OK?' she added, raising an eyebrow.

'*Oui*,' he nodded. 'We have made things good again between us.' He smiled and leaned against the wall.

'That's good,' she smiled back, feeling herself relax.

'And don't worry, I am also hoping to speak to André today, to make things good there too.'

'Thank you.'

'It's fine. I can see that you are worried about it.'

She laughed. 'Don't tell me you're a *reader of people* too?'

'Who knows?' he said. 'Maybe sometimes we all are.'

He left with a cheery goodbye, but once the door closed his words remained. He'd been joking, but in some way perhaps he was right.

15

Sunday had become her favourite day. Not because she didn't enjoy her time at the shop, but because it was the only time she had just for her and Lili. On Saturdays, when Adeline was working, Lili would come to the shop and sit quietly, reading or colouring before, more often than not, venturing up to Monique's flat to watch TV. Monday afternoons and Wednesdays, Adeline would have time off, but often Lili was at school or Adeline was too tired to play.

So Sunday had become *their* day – and Adeline found that she looked forward to it each week.

This morning, they were lying together in Adeline's double bed – Lili had joined her under the soft, feather eiderdown sometime during the night and was snuggled up against the pillow, lost to sleep. Adeline lay on her back and looked at the patterns the sunlight made on the ceiling, thought to the day ahead and what they might do.

When she heard the car, she didn't think much of it. The road through St Vianne was often quiet, especially on a Sunday morning, but there was always the odd car, the odd motorbike, making its way past. In London, the traffic had been a constant backdrop to their lives – the peal of a siren, the persistent trundle of buses and cars – and she'd blocked the noise out as best she could. Here she liked the sound of tyres on cobble, reminding her that, although she was tucked away, there was still life out there.

The car engine stopped and there was the slam of a door, the murmur of voices, then the sound as a car drove off. She stretched luxuriously in her warm bed, wondering whether it might be time to get up and make a coffee.

The knock on the door downstairs startled her and she sat up, suddenly alert. She called out a loud *'J'arrive!'* and swung her legs out from under the covers, feeling the cool of the room on her skin. She grabbed her towelling robe and wrapped it around herself as she raced down the stairs, stopping briefly to smooth her hair – but really there was no hope – before reaching the front door and opening it onto the street.

She'd barely had time to consider who might be on the other side. It was Sunday, so it wouldn't be the postwoman, or any sort of delivery. Perhaps Monique – although surely she'd have called? Adeline didn't really know anyone else well enough for them to call on her. Perhaps it was a neighbour with a question, or someone who'd knocked on the wrong door entirely.

She gasped when she saw the man standing outside, looking uncertainly around him. His light brown hair and well-groomed beard, sweatshirt and jeans, looked incongruous in this setting. As if he'd been taken out of a completely different picture and dropped into her world from somewhere else entirely. The little yellow man on Google Maps placed in her French town and looking around, trying to establish where he was.

Their eyes met and her hands flew to her face. Then instinctively, she rushed forward and wrapped her arms around him, not caring that she was in the street with bed hair and wearing a dressing gown.

'Kevin!' she exclaimed. 'What are you doing here?'

He laughed, and squeezed her back. 'I wouldn't be much of a big brother if I never visited my sister, would I?'

Moments later, he was installed in the armchair in the living room and the kettle was on. She brought one of the wooden chairs through from the kitchen and pulled it close to him so they could talk.

'Where's Lili?' he asked.

'Asleep, upstairs.'

'Wow. At eight thirty?'

'I know. Don't knock it. Once she's up and sees you, you won't stand a chance!'

They smiled at each other; Adeline felt the mood shift as if they were both allowing for a more serious topic.

'Thanks for coming,' she said, more quietly.

'It's OK. I just...' He looked at his hands, turning them over as if he were an ill-prepared actor and might find the right words scribbled on them. 'I had to see for myself that you were OK. That we were OK.'

'I'm sorry.'

'Don't be.' He looked at her, their eyes meeting, all serious-ness. 'You'd had a shock. I get it. And there's no one else there to...'

'To blame?' she said softly.

'Well, yeah,' he said with a shrug. 'I'm it, I'm afraid.'

'Still,' she said, reaching out and touching his hand. 'It wasn't your fault and it wasn't fair of me to act as if it was.'

He nodded, once, apology accepted, subject closed. 'Anyway, I'd be mad not to take advantage of the chance of a free holiday in France.'

'Free?' she joked. 'The rooms are very expensive in this hotel, I'm afraid.'

'Is that so?' He cocked an eyebrow and they both laughed.

It was wonderful how easily their relationship settled back into its habitual groove. She'd missed him more than she'd realised.

'Still,' she said, patting his knee.

'I just asked myself what Mum would have done,' he said. 'She would have come.'

'She would have,' Adeline replied, her voice suddenly thick, her throat feeling restricted.

She excused herself and went to make coffee, pouring hot water into her steel coffee pot, then waiting before she pushed the plunger down to remove the grounds from the water. Then she brought him back a steaming mug, a couple of yesterday's pastries on a tray, and a little jug of milk.

'Thank you. How the other half live, eh!' He nodded at the pastries.

'They're a bit dry,' she said apologetically. 'Try dipping them in the coffee.'

'Seriously?' He seemed dubious.

'It's the done thing around these parts.'

He looked at her, then dipped the very end of a croissant into his drink, watching as the hot coffee flooded into the parched pastry. Then he bit it, chewing thoughtfully. 'Not bad,' he said. 'Could get used to this.'

She smiled and a comfortable silence settled around them as he sipped his drink and took a few more bites.

Then: 'I wanted to ask—' he began.

'Uncle Kevin!' a little voice shrieked from the doorway, and he was hit full-on by a tiny girl in a nightie, almost upsetting his coffee and very nearly causing him to tip sideways as she flung herself into his arms.

He laughed, passed his coffee to Adeline with one hand, then wrapped his arms tightly around his niece. 'Hello to you too!' he said.

She pulled back. 'Why are you here?'

'Your mum was just asking me the same thing,' he said, grinning. 'I guess I just missed you both too much.'

Lili giggled and cuddled into him again, planting an enormous kiss on his cheek. 'Do you want to see my bedroom? And I go to school here. They all talk French! I can show you my books. And I'm reading bigger books now – did Mum tell you? And here we eat chocolate for breakfast, and I read books after school and Mum lets me sit in her shop and draw on Saturdays. And there's a market and the people are lovely and I have a best friend...' she rattled, barely stopping for breath.

'Come on, let Uncle Kevin drink his coffee,' Adeline laughed, peeling her daughter from her brother and sitting her on her lap instead. 'I expect he's tired after his journey.'

Kevin looked grateful. 'Why don't you go get your schoolbooks and you can show me once I've finished my breakfast?' he suggested.

Lili didn't need telling twice. She raced from the room and they chuckled together at the sound of her little feet pounding up the stairs.

Silence descended around them, broken only by Kevin slurping his coffee in the way he always had done. It was funny, the sound had used to annoy her as a child and teen, but now, far away from home, there was something comforting about his inability to consume a hot drink without making a ridiculous amount of noise. Adeline found herself smiling at him.

'What?' he asked.

'Oh, nothing. Just missed you, I suppose. And you were right. What I found out. It doesn't change anything. Not between us. You'll always be my weird, disgusting big brother.'

'Glad to hear it.' He gave her a grin. 'And on that note, I wondered whether... well, I kind of hoped that I might persuade you to come home.'

'Come home?' Something dipped inside her chest.

He shrugged. 'This seems lovely, for a break. But you rushed here without a thought. Ran away, kind of. You're so far away from your family – well, me – and your old life. Lili's friends. I wondered if maybe it was time to knock this French thing on the head; to come back to reality.'

It was like a slap. 'This *is* reality!' Adeline said, her voice sounding sharper than she'd intended.

'I know, sorry, this is coming out all wrong.' He pulled his backpack towards him and began to open the zip one-handed, before setting his coffee down and opening it properly, rummaging through. 'What I meant was, you found this shocking, awful information. This job came up... somehow. You rushed off. And I completely understand you wanting to find out more about this area, about your... well, your roots. I'm all for it. But is tucking yourself away here... Well, you're not going to find any answers working in a little backstreet bookshop are you, Addy?'

She opened her mouth to say something, but closed it again.

Kevin was still intent on his bag. 'I get it,' he said, glancing up before returning to the messy interior of his backpack. 'I understand that you want to find out who you are. Well, who *else* you are. I thought about it a lot over the last few weeks and I reckon I'd be the same. But I hate thinking of you living alone here, trying to find that missing part of you.' He was gabbling slightly and her anger subsided; she felt his discomfort and was sorry for him.

'Spit it out, bro,' she said lightly. 'I can handle it.'

He grinned as he finally found what he was looking for and drew a white envelope out of the bag.

'Anyway, I was racking my brains, because I knew it was a closed adoption. I mean, I think there are ways of finding things out these days; but the French element, well, it makes it all so complicated. And then I thought "Ha! Science".' He handed her the envelope.

She turned it over, confused, then opened it, drawing out the papers inside, the tiny plastic vial. A DNA test.

'Oh,' she said.

'If your birth mother's out there, it could be a way of actually finding her. Your birth mother. Answering some of the questions.' He shrugged. 'I think Mum would have been all for it. If she'd had time to... well, if she were here.'

They looked at each other in mutual grief.

'Thank you,' she said, looking at the little container, the instructions written on glossy paper – the words 'Priority processing' in French showing that he'd paid for a rapid test and even gone to the French website on her behalf. 'But Kevin, do you really think she's going to have put herself on this DNA database? The adoption was closed; everything was secretive. Signed. Sealed. Why would someone in that situation risk putting herself out there?'

He shrugged. 'I thought of that,' he admitted. 'But there might be other relatives... other routes of finding out. And I thought...'

'Thought what?'

'Well, you're right. She might not be on the database. But...'

'But...?'

'What if she *is*? What if she *wants* to be found?'

16

Last night, alone in the bathroom, she'd felt a little self-conscious as she'd taken a saliva sample, completed the form and sealed the plastic bag then the envelope. She'd looked at the package on her bedside table the moment she'd woken up this morning and her heart had thundered with a mixture of fear and excitement.

Twenty-nine years ago, when her adoption had been finalised, they wouldn't have dreamt that it would be so easy for people to trace their own DNA by the time she was an adult. And Kevin was right – even if her birth mother hadn't taken the plunge, any one of her blood relatives might have. If she managed to make that connection, surely she'd get closer to the truth.

The problem was, now faced with the prospect, she wasn't sure how much of the truth she really wanted. Mum and Dad had given her a wonderful childhood; after Dad had died, Mum had been the centre of their world. Kevin had been a ridiculous, funny, annoying big brother and had become a great friend too. The discovery she'd made had rocked all that, and she was only just coming to terms with everything. Part of her was desperate to know; but another part wished she'd never found out about the adoption at all.

But she'd decided to force herself to do it. Partly because Kevin had bought the test, and partly because it was a chance to settle down some of the questions that raced through her mind when she tried to get to sleep, or when she sat in the empty shop waiting for the next customer. She'd drop it in the postbox on the way to the shop, then try to put it out of her head until the results arrived. The 'priority payment' Kevin had made and the fact he'd bought the test from the French website meant this might be just a few days' time.

She stretched her arms, pleased that the sun appeared to be shining outside the window, making the thin curtains glow with yellow light. She wanted Kevin to have a good time while he was here – he'd just booked a couple of days and would be back to London before they knew it. At least he'd see a bit of sunshine; see St Vianne at its best.

She'd offered to ask Monique for a day off, but he'd insisted she carry on as usual. 'I don't expect you to drop everything for me,' he'd said. 'Besides, it means I get to spend the morning with this one,' he'd added, tickling Lili who'd giggled delightedly. Adeline had phoned the school at eight o'clock, and Lili's teacher had been more than happy to give her the day off to spend it with family. 'It will do her good,' she'd said.

As for her, it was good, at least, that they only worked a morning on Monday. La Petite Librairie, like the rest of the shops in St Vianne, kept its doors closed for the day – but Monique liked her to come in for a couple of hours to sort through new stock and get things ready for the week. She'd do that, then they could explore later – perhaps get something to eat at a cafe in Avignon or go for a walk into the countryside.

Adeline looked at her daughter now, still completely out of it after her late night yesterday, and smiled. She ached to brush the hair on her head, to lean in and kiss her perfect cheek, but resisted the urge. It would only wake her, and Adeline valued these rare mornings when she had a little time to herself to come around before her whirlwind of a five-year-old was activated. She slipped out of bed, pulled on her dressing gown and made her way to the bathroom to get ready.

When she reached the shop an hour later, her hand aching from the amount of times Lili had insisted she and Kevin swing her as they walked, she gave her brother a peck on the cheek and disappeared through the door. 'Pop in later,' she said. 'When it's tidy – I can give you the tour!' He'd nodded then turned away with Lili who was talking excitedly about the slide in the park and just how brave she was when she climbed it.

Inside, Adeline shut the door and relocked it, making sure the sign read 'Closed' in the window. Then hung her bag on the little hook under the counter. When she straightened, she saw Monique's feet on the stairs behind her. 'So,' her boss said, with a raised eyebrow as she emerged fully onto the shop floor, 'you must tell me everything!'

At first, Adeline wondered whether Monique was talking about the DNA test that she'd shoved – with some difficulty – into the tiny slot in the yellow postbox en route. It would be hard to deny her psychic skills if she'd known about *that*. Instead, she realised when she saw the mischievous look in Monique's eyes that she was referring to the mysterious man who'd dropped her off this morning with a kiss, and strolled off holding Lili's hand.

'You have a new lover?' she asked.

Adeline laughed, shaking her head. 'Definitely not!' She

explained what had happened – how Kevin had surprised her with a visit.

Monique nodded. 'That is nice. He is a kind man.'

'Yes, yes he is,' Adeline agreed. She was quiet for a moment. 'I was worried, actually,' she admitted. 'About whether I'd feel differently now I know he's not my *real* brother.'

Monique's eyebrows furrowed. 'He is not?' and Adeline realised how little she'd confided in Monique about this aspect of her life.

She flushed. 'We grew up as brother and sister,' she said. 'But it turned out that I was adopted – I've only just found out.'

Monique's face seemed to grow paler. 'Adopted? What happened to your mother? Your first mother, I mean.'

'My birth mother? I don't know. All I know is that she was young, and that she came from France originally. From this *département,* actually.'

'From France?' Monique seemed surprised. 'And you are here to find her, perhaps?'

'Not at first,' Adeline admitted. 'Now... well, I don't know.'

'Are you angry with her?'

'It's not that,' Adeline said. 'I'd love to find her, to find out my story – why I was adopted, what happened. And I think my mother – my adoptive mother – wouldn't have minded me doing that. It's just... I don't want to let myself hope. Because it's so unlikely. I can't...' She felt tears and touched her hand to her eye in surprise. 'Sorry,' she said. 'I haven't let myself think about it much.'

'But it is nice that you don't blame your mother. You are not angry about it.'

'Why would I be angry?'

Monique shrugged. 'Sometimes people do not understand.' She seemed to want to say something else, but closed her mouth and shook her head almost imperceptibly. Adeline wanted to say that she knew about Monique's own baby; but wasn't sure whether to. And the moment passed.

'Anyway,' Monique said, breaking the silence that had settled over them. 'There is no doubt that he is your real brother.'

'Sorry?'

'It is not blood always that binds us. That man, he got on a plane, he came all the way here because he was worried for you. A real brother is not always the man who shares this physical connection. A real brother is a man who comes to you because he loves you and he wants you in his life.'

Adeline nodded, her fingers tracing the outline of some writing on their order book. 'Yes, you're right. And he surprised me really.'

'You didn't think he felt that way?'

'No, not that. He... well, he bought me a DNA test. You know, one of those you send off in the post. And I suppose it surprised me that he could be so... generous. Not feel threatened about my finding out whether I have other relatives. Because I'm all he has.' Hearing the words out loud made her throat feel constricted. Poor Kevin. She'd been so caught up in her own feelings she'd barely thought about him at all.

'Yes, he is a good man for sure,' Monique said, turning back towards the bookshelf she was dusting. 'Not all men are so generous. Michel, he says he is my nephew, but he is very quick to criticise. Very quick to tell me I am doing the wrong thing.'

Adeline laughed. 'Well, Kevin does that too. Definitely. But maybe that's a way of showing love too.'

Monique snorted. 'Perhaps,' she said, not sounding convinced.

They worked silently for a few moments, Adeline ticking off

orders in the well-worn notebook, Monique flicking her rather elaborate feather duster along rows of books.

'This DNA test,' Monique asked then. 'How is it done?'

Adeline explained about the website, the envelope, the little vial of saliva. 'I'm not even sure if I'll find anything,' she admitted. 'It'll only work if my mother – my birth mother – or someone she's related to has done a test herself. And if she doesn't want to be found...' She let the words hang.

Monique continued her dusting, her brow furrowed. 'And they have this in France?' she asked. 'This DNA service.'

'Yes.' Adeline was cautious. 'Do you want me to write down the website for you?'

Monique shrugged. 'If you want.' She continued dusting, but something in her movements was sharper, more pointed.

Smiling, Adeline noted down the address on a scrap of paper. 'And let me know if you need any more help with it,' she said. 'I'm happy to help.' It would be wonderful if Monique could find something out for herself. Despite the fact she'd cut her mother out of her life, and didn't speak to her sister either, Adeline sensed a similar yearning for connection in Monique. She wished she could say more; tell her what she knew, help her to open up. But with Michel clearly still in the doghouse, she didn't want to make things worse for him by admitting she knew about Monique's baby – just in case.

'Well, I might do it,' Monique said. 'It could be interesting.'

'Yes.' Adeline agreed. 'Maybe.' *I am out with lanterns,* she thought, remembering a line from Emily Dickinson, *looking for myself.*

Outside, the square was quiet, save for the odd figure walking past with a baguette. The only place other than the patisserie open this morning was the cafe – she could just make out its windows at this distance, the yellow light emanating from inside. Adeline wondered what Lili and Kevin were doing, hoped the weather would remain bright for the afternoon, and resolved to put all thoughts of blood ties and adoption and saliva tests from her head for a little while. Because Monique was right – whatever she might discover down the line didn't change anything between her and Kevin. He was her brother, and the least important part of that was his DNA.

17

'So,' said Kevin, when she arrived back at her little terraced rental three hours later. 'Are you going to show me the sights and sounds of this big city?' He was relaxed – or perhaps collapsed would be a better way to describe it – on the sofa after taking Lili for a walk, spending half an hour playing hide-and-seek in the house and its small back garden, then being forced to endure what Lili had called 'a makeover', which seemed to have consisted of Lili raiding Adeline's make-up bag and applying liberal amounts of eyeshadow, blusher and lipstick to her uncle's face. He looked exhausted and although he'd clearly tried to clean the make-up off post-glow-up, he still had a smudge of lipstick in the corner of his mouth. Adeline tried not to laugh. She'd wondered why they hadn't come up to the shop to meet her, but looking at her crumpled brother, it was now easy to see.

'Well,' she said, eyeing his slumped form, 'I was thinking of grabbing us a pizza at the Café des Sports if you think you can cope with leaving the house? Or should I call an ambulance?'

'Ha ha.' He sat up with a groan. 'If you think a young man

like me can be worn out by three hours with a five-year-old, you'd... well, you'd be right,' he admitted with an eye-roll and a shake of his head. 'That girl has endless energy!'

'Tell me about it.'

As if to prove them both right, Lili rushed into the room and thrust a picture into Kevin's hand. It was a wobbly oval, coloured in with a multitude of different colours, one or two lines spilling over the edge. 'Wow,' Kevin said obediently. 'This is amazing!'

'It's an Easter egg,' Lili said. 'My class is doing an Easter dance next week. In the square. Are you going to come?'

Kevin looked guilty. 'Well, I have to be back at work by then. But how about your mum films it for me? I'd love to see it.'

Lili looked downcast. 'You have to go?'

Kevin reached forward and pulled her onto his lap. 'Yes, Lili. I do. But you know what? I'll come back. And you can visit me in England. And you can show me your dance and tell me all about it.'

This seemed to appease Lili a little. She gave a small, curt nod, although her mouth remained downturned. Adeline felt a shiver of guilt, watching them together. Both at her past actions and at the fact that she'd chosen to take her daughter so far from her only known family.

'I can get *Mamie* to take pictures too,' Lili said suddenly, her face brightening.

'Yes,' Kevin nodded. 'Mummy will take lots of pictures, I'm sure.'

'No, silly!' she said, smiling. '*Mamie*. At the shop.'

Kevin's brow furrowed. 'Who?'

'That's Monique, sweetheart,' Adeline said.

'But she's my *mamie*?' Lili said, a question in her voice.

'She means grandmother,' Adeline whispered to Kevin. 'No,

Lili,' she said more loudly. 'Monique is kind of like a *mamie,* isn't she. But she's not *your mamie.*'

'Oh,' Lili said, her voice flat. 'OK.'

'But listen, that doesn't matter,' Adeline said. 'She thinks you're amazing! And I know she'll take lots of pictures for you.'

Another curt nod.

Adeline looked at Kevin who raised his eyebrows. 'Anyway!' she said loudly, clapping her hands. 'Who's up for pizza at the cafe?'

Lili nodded and slipped off Kevin's lap. Her uncle stood up and took her hand. 'Of course,' he said, 'you're going to have to show me the way. I don't want to get lost again!'

'Silly Uncle Kevin,' Lili said, in the manner of one whose endless patience was being tested by an adult's incompetence. 'Come on then.'

'Might want to give your face a quick wash first?' Adeline suggested to Kevin, nodding towards the mirror.

He looked, baulked and nodded. 'Yep. Good call.'

The walk to the cafe was quiet. Adeline thinking about the Easter show and the fact that Lili clearly longed to have family there to watch her. One or two locals whom Adeline had seen in the shop but couldn't yet name walked past and gave cheery *bonjour*s, and it was adorable to see Lili greet them back with a *bonjour* of her own.

'Very friendly here,' Kevin remarked once they'd passed a third person who'd nodded and smiled at them.

'Yes,' she said. 'It really is. Maybe it's a French thing. Or a small town thing? It didn't happen at first, not when I was new. But over time I think people have seen me in the shop or the street – they know I'm local. It's nice.'

At that moment, they entered the cafe and almost collided

with André, who was standing just inside the entrance. He looked at them all and gave a curt nod.

Of all the people, why did she keep nearly barging into André? He probably thought she was constantly rude. 'Sorry,' she said quietly.

'It's OK,' he said, opening his mouth to say something else. 'I—'

'*Bonjour!*' Lili said with a smile.

He looked at her and grinned. 'Hello, *petite Lili,*' he said, his voice soft. Lili giggled delightedly. 'Well, I must go,' he said after a further moment's silence, moving off and taking a seat at one of the tables in the far corner.

'One of your *friends?*' Kevin raised an eyebrow.

'Kevin! It's not like that. He's just a nice guy. Runs the bakery.'

Kevin nodded knowingly.

'For god's sake, why does everyone seem to want to set me up with someone?' she said, half exasperated, half laughing.

Kevin smiled. 'Sorry, I should probably sort out my own pathetic love life before trying to set you up.'

She elbowed him discreetly. 'He *is* pretty gorgeous,' she admitted. 'But I very much doubt I'm his type. And besides, I was a bit rude to him one time. Not intentionally. But he probably thinks I'm a bit of a cow.'

'Still,' Kevin said, looking over again. 'He seems to be looking at you a lot.'

'Really?' she glanced over again, but this time André had lifted the menu and seemed to be studying it. She wanted to ask Kevin what he meant. Was André looking at her or *looking* at her? But she shook herself. It didn't matter.

By the time their pizzas had arrived, she'd put André out of her mind. The cafe had filled up and the mixture of noise, the smell of freshly baked pizza, mingled with coffee and wine and various perfumes, created a buffer between his table and theirs. Lili ate with gusto, determined to finish her pizza first and buoyed by the promise of ice cream from her uncle.

'So,' said Kevin carefully. 'Have you thought any more about what I said? About coming back?' His cheeks flushed a little. There was a bit of cheese, Adeline noticed, in his beard.

Adeline looked at him.

'How long is your contract?' he pressed.

'Three months, initially.'

'Oh, that's not too bad!' Kevin looked relieved. 'So maybe finish that up and come home?'

Adeline felt something sink inside her stomach. 'Kevin, I'm not sure I want to. For starters, I'm hoping Monique is going to extend it. And I'm not sure I'm finished with this place yet!'

'Even if you find your birth mum? You still want to stay?'

Adeline set her fork down. 'Well, what's the harm? It's lovely here. Somewhere different. And... I don't know, it's starting to feel like home.'

He made a face. 'But you'll come to your *real* home eventually, right?'

'London? Yes, probably. But I'm not sure when.'

'Just be careful.'

'Careful?' She felt herself stiffen. 'Why?'

'It's a lovely place,' he agreed. 'But it's not *you*, Addy. You're a city girl.'

'Am I though?' she challenged. 'Just because I've never lived somewhere like this doesn't mean I don't love the life here.'

'But have you thought about her?' he said, nodding discreetly at Lili who was chopping up her remaining piece of pizza, creating some sort of elaborate artwork on her plate.

'Yes. She's pretty happy here, Kevin, in case you hadn't

noticed.' She could hear anger in her words when she spoke and tried to lighten her tone. The last thing she wanted to do was argue with him. And it didn't matter really what he thought. She didn't need his or anyone else's approval to live her life the way that was right for her.

He put his hand over hers, gently. She felt her fingers stiffen but kept her hand in place. 'Yes, she is,' he said. 'And that's the problem.'

'What do you mean?'

'What I mean is, maybe you have to make a decision sooner than you think. About whether you want to live here for years. Forever maybe. I can imagine it'll be great to live here for a bit. Get your fix of the French culture – a break from the everyday. But sooner or later you're probably going to want to come home.'

'So then I'll come home.'

'But by then,' he said, '*this* will be Lili's home. It's already becoming her home.'

'But...'

'You've got this feeling of not belonging. Not quite fitting in. That's what you said, isn't it? That's what you told me when you found the papers.'

'Well, yes.'

'But don't you see? You might be fixing your own need to understand yourself, feel part of things. Find your roots. But what are you doing to her? She won't remember London in a few months' time. This will be her home. So when you move back, you'll be making her feel displaced. Torn. She already thinks your boss is her grandmother.'

Adeline drew her hand away. 'Oh, come on, she's just five. Five-year-olds create their own sense of things.'

'We all do. We all try to make sense of things. And I get it. I really do. But just be careful you aren't creating problems for Lili down the line. Her own sense of not fitting in. Displacement,' he said, shrugging and shoving a piece of pizza into his mouth.

Adeline put her fork down. She suddenly didn't feel hungry.

Across the table, Lili was looking at them. 'Stop it,' she said.

'What?'

'Stop fighting, you two,' she said, wagging a finger.

The moment was broken by this little display of defiance and they both laughed. 'We're not fighting, love,' said Adeline. 'Just talking about boring grown-up stuff.'

He waited until they'd eaten dessert, paid the bill and exited into the sunny street before raising it again. Lili was running ahead now, skipping and singing to herself, when Kevin cleared his throat. 'Look, I don't want to fight. But I do know that I want to say this before I go. I wouldn't feel right if I didn't.'

'I get it. I understand what you're saying about France and Lili and London. And I do appreciate it. It's nice you care enough to be a pain in the arse about it,' she said, raising an eyebrow.

'Hey, I'm your brother. It's my job.'

She laughed.

'And I guess I wanted to say you're not the only one who feels lonely.' He shrugged as if it didn't matter. 'Not the only one who wants a connection.'

'Oh, Kevin.' She put her arm around him. 'Come on. It's not like we're so far away.'

'You're in a different world.'

She snorted. 'Kevin, you live in London. There's a different world around every corner. We're just trying something. It'll be OK.'

'Just make sure you think about it,' he said, firmly. 'That you're not being...' He trailed off.

'Not being what?' She took her arm away and stood to face him.

'Selfish.'

She felt heat rise inside her and before she knew what she was doing she shoved him in the chest. 'Selfish! Oh, that's rich.'

He stumbled back slightly, surprised, then stepped towards her again, mouth open as if he wanted to say something. But before he could reach her, there was the sound of running feet and a tall man rushed up and grabbed Kevin's arms, pinning them behind his back.

'What the...?' Kevin turned slightly to see his assailant.

It was André.

'André!' Adeline said, then in French, 'What are you doing?'

'He's hurting you.'

'No. No, he's not.'

He nodded. 'In the cafe. I saw how he spoke to you. And now, you are shoving him away. Your boyfriend, he is not a nice man.'

Adeline felt her cheeks get hot, she gave a little laugh. Kevin looked on, confused and not understanding a word. 'André, he's my brother. Not my boyfriend. And yes, we've argued. But honestly, he'd never hurt me.'

Slowly André released Kevin's arms. Her brother rubbed his wrists, like a prisoner on TV being removed from handcuffs, and glowered at André.

'It's OK,' Adeline said to him. Then to André, 'Thank you,' she found herself saying. 'It was... well, kind of you to try to help.'

André nodded. His face was flushed, and his eyes shining. 'And you are sure you're OK?' He lifted his hand and touched her shoulder lightly, his eyes not wavering.

'Yes,' she said. 'I'm fine.' She felt herself locked for a moment in his gaze. And just for a second she felt as if she knew him, as if André's soul was speaking to hers.

She shook herself. It was the wine talking. Yes, André had deep, beautiful eyes but she was deluding herself by reading anything into the look. He barely liked her.

Ahead of them in the street, Lili had turned and was watching. André nodded, said a gruff *Pardon, Monsieur* to Kevin, then turned and began to walk back to the cafe.

'What the hell was that about?' said Kevin, once André was safely out of earshot.

'I'm not entirely sure.' She watched André as he reached the cafe, looked up briefly then disappeared inside. 'I think he was trying to protect me. He thought you were my boyfriend.'

'Well, you're right about one thing,' Kevin said, regaining his equilibrium.

'What's that?'

'They're *really* friendly around here.'

Then they were both laughing. And Lili, running towards them, laughed too.

Adeline looked at her brother. 'I will think about what you said,' she told him.

And he nodded. The subject closed.

18

The next morning, they walked Lili to school together, each holding a hand. The air was cool, but with the promise of sun later; the clouds glowed golden and once in a while, a ray would emerge through the whiteness and flood the road with light.

The little girl chattered and skipped and swung herself on their arms, making the most of every moment and excited for Kevin to see where she went to school. Once they'd dropped her off and watched her race into the playground, delighted to show them how fast she could run, they turned to each other and smiled.

'It's a shame you can't stay a bit longer,' Adeline said.

'I know,' he agreed. 'It's actually been really nice.'

'Well, don't sound so surprised!'

He grinned. 'Well, you rushed off so quickly, and hadn't seemed to think things through. I had no idea how you'd be living. I imagined you in some derelict farmhouse somewhere.'

She laughed.

'But this place... well, it's a community.'

'It is,' she said, pleased.

They began to walk back towards the house. Monique had told her she needn't come in for a couple of hours this morning, to give her a chance to see Kevin off properly, and she'd accepted gratefully.

'I'm sorry,' he said out of nowhere as they passed the patisserie.

Adeline, looking through the glass, saw André serving a customer. She gave him a nod and he smiled back. 'What for?' she asked, feeling a shiver of pleasure that things were clearly OK with André now.

Kevin kicked a stone, suddenly boyish in his stance. 'I had this idea that I'd come here, give you the DNA test – you know, a way of finding out your roots. And I guess, rescue you from it all. Bring you back to London.' He laughed, lightly, and shook his head. 'I'd been so worried about you, especially with you not answering emails. I just imagined you were in a state.'

'Oh, Kev,' she wrapped an arm around his back.

'What?'

'I'm sorry. For worrying you. It was selfish.'

'It's OK,' he said, giving her a quick squeeze in return. 'I get it. Although don't do that again, will you?'

'Promise.'

'Pinky promise?' he joked and she laughed, remembering little promises they'd made as children not to tell their parents about hidden sweet stashes or midnight feasts, or the fact that one or the other of them had got in trouble at school.

'Pinky promise,' she agreed.

He was silent for a moment, then continued. 'What I'm trying to say is... I was wrong. You're obviously *not* in a state. And you've made a nice life for yourself here – already. Lili seems happy. You seem pretty happy?' He looked at her face as if for confirmation.

She shrugged. 'I'm OK.' She made a face. 'At least I think so.'

He laughed. 'Welcome to the club.'

The silence resumed, but it was companiable and they reached her front door. Just inside, Kevin's suitcase was waiting, leaning against the wall and reminding them how limited their time now was.

'Come back, won't you?' she said.

'You know me. Never say no to a cheap holiday.'

She laughed and gave him a little shove. Kevin, as a pretty successful architect, wasn't short of money, but they often joked about his frugality – the result of their not having much money as they'd grown up.

'Careful. Don't want your burly protector launching himself at me,' he said and they both laughed.

'Sorry about that.'

'It's OK. It's nice to think you have friends looking out for you.'

'He's not really a *friend*.'

'Well, what would you call him?'

'I just...' But it was too complicated; they didn't have time. Kevin's taxi would be here soon. Instead, she offered a cup of tea and they made their way through to the kitchen where he sat waiting patiently, fiddling with the corner of a coaster.

'What's up?' she asked, setting his mug in front of him and wondering at this suddenly silent version of her usually talk-ative brother.

'Just thinking.'

'Careful!' she joked.

'I think I need to do it too,' he said.

'What? Move to France?'

He laughed. 'No, I think I'm a London boy through and through,' he admitted. 'But you know. Find myself. After Mum, after everything. I'm a thirty-three-year-old bloke feeling lonely because his sister's having an adventure. How sad is that!'

'Aw, don't be silly. You just wanted to sort things out. And a lot of that was my fault. I get it.'

'Yeah, but this has all made me realise I've kind of let my life get swallowed up too,' he admitted. 'So much focus on Mum, and of course that's what we both wanted to do. But it made my world shrink. And maybe it's time I think about what *I* want. I was convinced I was trying to fix *your* life, but maybe your going just showed me how small mine's become.'

She slipped into the chair opposite him and grabbed his hand. 'Well,' she said. 'I guess we're both kind of rebuilding things after everything that happened. And maybe that's OK.'

'We're in this together?' he offered.

She laughed. 'Both losers.'

Their eyes met and there he was again, her affable, upbeat big brother. 'Ha. Yes,' he agreed. 'Both complete and utter losers.'

By the time the taxi came the atmosphere between them was upbeat. And as she waved her brother off, she felt a sense of freedom. That she had someone in the world who loved her enough to let her make her choices, mistakes, decisions and support her no matter what. Monique was right – there was no doubt that blood or no blood, Kevin was her *real* brother.

With her late start, her time in the bookshop passed quickly and it was soon four thirty. She slipped out of the shop and took the short walk to the school to pick up Lili. Waiting outside, she exchanged a few words with the other mums and, although she didn't know them very well yet, realised that she felt part of a collective whole; no longer so much on the outside.

Lili raced towards her when she exited the classroom, and flung her backpack at Adeline's feet. Adeline picked it up and slung it over her own shoulder then bent down to smooth Lili's hair back into place. Her daughter often looked adorably rumpled after school – eyes bright, and usually quite well-rested after the afternoon siesta all the children were encouraged to have.

'Good day?' she said.

'Lunch was disgusting,' her daughter told her seriously. 'Too much spinach.'

She nodded. 'Oh dear. What else did you do today?'

Lili shrugged. 'I dunno.'

Her daughter seemed to have a switch that clicked the moment she reached her mother, separating her life at school from her home life. At first, Adeline had thought that maybe Lili was hiding something from her, but she'd come to realise that Lili genuinely couldn't remember. School was compartmentalised in another area of her brain – she'd now tucked it away until tomorrow.

Refusing to hold her hand, Lili skipped ahead on the narrow pavement, Adeline keeping an eye out for cars in case her daughter stepped out into the road. There were never many, but they came up unexpectedly sometimes.

And then they were outside La Petite Librairie, where Lili would draw or snuggle up with a book until it was time to close. 'Can I have my bag?' Lili asked unexpectedly.

Adeline removed it from her shoulder and gave it to her little girl who placed it on the ground outside the shop, unzipped it and began rifling through.

'Can't you do that inside?' Adeline asked, as a couple of pencils fell onto the pavement and rolled away.

'No!' Lili said, still rifling, 'It's a surprise.' Finally, she found what she was looking for and drew out a rather crumpled piece of paper with a drawing of a stick woman wearing a triangular dress.

Underneath, in wavering letters, Lili had written the word *Mamie.*

'Is this for Monique?' Adeline asked, trying to keep her voice light.

'Yes,' Lili replied, snatching the picture back. '*Don't look!*'

'It's a lovely picture,' Adeline said carefully, picking up the pencils for her daughter and slipping them back into the bag. 'And I'm sure she'll love it. But, darling. You know that Monique isn't your granny, your *mamie*, don't you?' She crouched down and looked into her daughter's eyes.

Lili looked away. 'Yes, she is.'

'No, darling. Your granny was in England, remember? She got poorly and she had to go to heaven.'

Lili scowled. 'I know about Granny, but Monique is my *Mamie*. All the children at school drew pictures for their *Papi* and *Mamie* and I wanted to too.' She stamped her foot in its bright white trainer.

'OK,' Adeline said. 'I mean it's OK to call her that sometimes. But Monique is more of a… a *friend* who seems a bit like a *mamie* to you. You do understand that?'

'No, she *is*,' her daughter said again.

Adeline straightened, feeling an ache in her thighs.

'I know. I know you think that,' she said, feeling tired and wondering whether it was worth trying to explain complicated relationships to her daughter.

Then: 'Monique is my *mamie* because I feel it here,' Lili insisted. She patted her hand against her chest and looked at Adeline defiantly.

Feeling a little shiver, Adeline looked at her daughter's fiery eyes. 'OK,' she said. 'Monique hasn't... she's never *told* you she's your *mamie*, has she?'

Lili shrugged, unwilling to say anything else.

'Lili.'

'She's my *mamie*,' her daughter said, stubbornly.

Adeline sighed. She'd talk to her more about it later; she clearly wasn't going to get through to her now.

But as she opened the door and Lili ran forward, flinging herself around Monique's legs and giving the woman a huge squeeze – much to Monique's delight – Adeline thought back to what Kevin had said. Her daughter was already putting down roots, establishing a sense of connection. And if she wasn't careful, soon the decision on their future might become all the more complicated.

As she watched, shutting the door behind her, the bell jangling a warning, she saw Monique bend down and take Lili properly into her arms for an enormous hug, and she felt a tug of unease.

19

The following Friday, the day before Lili was due to finish school for the spring holidays, Adeline asked whether it would be OK to take the afternoon off. 'There's a little concert at the school,' she explained.

Monique had been delighted at the idea. 'Do you think I could come?'

'Are you sure?' Adeline had said. 'I think they're just doing a couple of songs or something, a little dance maybe.'

But Monique was adamant. '*Mais oui*! I'd love to see *ma petite Lili* perform. I can close the shop for a couple of hours.'

Adeline nodded and smiled, but felt something in her stomach tighten. 'Well, that's lovely,' she'd said.

After lunch, they sorted out some new orders, then wrote a note and fixed it to the inside of the glass on the door. Locking the shop behind them, they set out on the short walk to the school.

The late April sun had warmed them, and halfway there, Monique slipped off her cardigan and tied it around her waist.

They passed familiar faces – exchanging nods and smiles and *bonjours*. Adeline, uncomfortable at first with the idea of Monique coming, began to relax. Perhaps it wasn't so terrible that Lili thought of Monique as a grandmother figure. She'd understand more as she got older.

'I can see why you decided to settle here,' she said to Monique as they crossed the road and turned down the narrow strip of tarmac that led to the school.

Monique looked at her with a smile. 'I felt as if it were my home; this strange place I'd stumbled across.'

'Do you ever miss Paris?'

'Ah, a little. Sometimes. But then Paris is always there when I want. The train is perhaps just four or five hours. I used to go often. Not so much now. *Oui*, Paris is wonderful. But I am always happy to come home too.'

Adeline nodded. 'You know, in London, I don't think I knew anyone's name,' she admitted. 'Not even the people in the same apartment building. I used to say hello to one or two people, but they were strangers really.'

'It is like that in Paris too. It can be nice, sometimes, to be private. But I am someone who needs connection. People.'

It was an odd thing to say in some ways, Adeline mused, when she considered how Monique had cut herself off from her family. But then, some things fractured a relationship to the point of no return. It wasn't her place to judge.

They reached the school and joined the stream of parents making their way to the playground, following a series of coloured arrows directing them to where the performance would take place. A set of orange plastic chairs had been laid out in three neat rows to create an audience, leaving the majority of the playground free for the children. Monique and

Adeline sat down in the second row and gradually, the other seats filled up. A teacher was hurriedly arranging some paper flowers and marking out an area with chalk, and when she looked up the stone steps, Adeline could see movement and colour inside, but couldn't make out anything specific. She longed to see what Lili was wearing – her daughter had let something slip about a hat she might be sporting, but otherwise had tried to keep the whole thing a secret.

She turned to Monique and was just about to say something, when the doors opened and another teacher walked out – Adeline recognised her as the head of the school, Maîtresse Fabienne. They'd spoken once or twice in the playground but not in any detail. She was a friendly woman with grey hair tied back in a neat ponytail, and looked to be around sixty years old. The waiting parents settled obediently into silence as if they were pupils at the school themselves; and Adeline wondered if perhaps some of them had been Fabienne's pupils once.

The head teacher read out a brief introduction – how the children had been studying spring and new life as part of their term's work and how the dances and songs they had prepared were all about welcoming in the new season.

The doors opened again and the children came skipping out, dressed in colourful T-shirts and each sporting a paper hat, which they'd clearly made themselves. Adeline spotted Lili, whose hat was decorated with pieces of colourful paper cut into the shapes of butterflies and flowers. As her daughter's eyes met hers, Adeline gave a little grin of pride.

A small speaker began to emit some music and the children joined hands in a circle, skipping around in time and singing along.

It was then that it happened.

Adeline felt something swell inside her as the children began to sing:

> *'Vole, vole, vole papillon au-dessus de mon école*
> *Vole, vole, vole papillon au-dessus de ma maison.'*

It was a simple song about a butterfly, and yet she felt a shiver run through her body at the tune and the words. Something stirred inside her – a feeling of déjà vu, of having experienced this very moment, this very song, this very sound before.

She was about to say something to Monique, but when she turned to look at her friend, she saw that tears were running freely down her face. Her eyes were fixed on the dancing children, her head nodding slightly to the sound of the music. Yet something was clearly very wrong.

Adeline nudged her. 'Are you OK?' she whispered.

Monique looked at her, her face creased with something like grief. '*Oui*,' she said. 'Do not worry.'

But it was hard not to.

Once the performance was over and the children had been herded back into the building, the teachers thanked the parents for turning up. The children would change now, but if their parents could wait, they could take their offspring home with them for an early finish for the holidays.

As soon as people began to stand and stretch and mill about, some disappearing beyond the gates to sit in cars or light cigarettes, others clustering in gossipy groups, Adeline walked to the shade of a large tree that stood proud at the back of the outdoor space, its roots clearly so big that they had grown beyond the patch of earth left between the tarmac for it, and had begun to raise the black surface, sending cracks running along its length.

Monique followed her, quiet now. Her tears had gone and she looked a little more like herself.

'That was so sweet,' Adeline said. 'Did you enjoy it?' She looked at Monique's face and watched a myriad emotions race across it before Monique seemed to gain control.

She fixed her eyes on Adeline's. 'Yes, it was beautiful. Very sweet. And Lili's hat was *vraiment* adorable!'

They were silent for a moment. Adeline leaned on the metal fence that surrounded the playground and looked across at the stone houses, the tiny bend in the road; she could see the spire of the church over the tiled roofs and above it, the wash of blue and white sky. The words came, despite her trying to repress them: 'Why were you crying?'

Monique shrugged. 'It was just the song.'

'The butterfly one.'

'*Oui*. So many memories.'

The silence fell again.

One or two children began to open the door and run into the arms of their waiting parents. A couple raced to the little climbing frame, chattering loudly. Lili had yet to emerge.

'Because you know, one time, I had a baby,' Monique said, almost out of nowhere.

Adeline nodded. 'I do know.' She felt her face get hot. 'Michel told me. I hope that was OK.'

Monique shrugged, her eyes shining. 'I suppose it is not a secret.'

Adeline put her arm out and touched Monique briefly. 'It must be hard, to remember.'

Her friend nodded. 'It is. But then it is also hard when I forget for a time. I don't want to forget her. But I don't want to remember.' She smiled, acknowledging the contradiction. 'It was the song I sang to her, when I held her just that one time. At that moment, I wanted with all my heart to keep her, but I'd finally accepted that I didn't have the strength to defy my parents. I was a child; no more than sixteen. I sang that song because I imagined my baby was a butterfly, and that she would fly and be free and have a good life.' Her mouth twisted. 'And I hoped perhaps one day she might fly back to me.'

'Oh, Monique.'

Monique shrugged, half-heartedly. 'It is long ago. The pain is not normally so raw. It was just the song, it opened up a passage in time for a moment and I was back there, with my lips against the baby's ear, whispering, singing a little. And hoping that my mother might change her mind.'

Adeline felt her eyes moisten. She blinked away the tears. 'It must have been awful.'

Another shrug. 'Yes. It was a terrible time. But it was thirty years ago now.'

'Thirty? Michel said maybe forty or more?'

Monique flapped her hand as if it weren't important. 'Thirty, forty, fifty. It doesn't matter. It was long ago. And I have had to learn to live with the pain. But it is hard sometimes.'

'Of course. It must be awful.' Adeline's mind raced. Because the amount of time did matter. To her, at least. Thirty years – she looked at Monique, studied her face.

'*Oui*, but there have been a lot of days since. And the pain gets less.'

Adeline nodded.

Then, '*Non*, that is not right,' Monique said. 'The pain does not get less. But somehow I grow around it. I find that I can bury it more deeply. And some days I do not even think of her. At least not for many minutes.'

Adeline imagined how she'd have felt if Lili had been taken from her. It sounded impossible; far-fetched. Yet she herself had only been in her twenties, and single, when she'd had Lili. A generation beforehand, or if she'd been a few years younger, the same could easily have happened to her. 'And you were sixteen?' she asked.

'*Oui.*'

'And what year was that? How old are you now?' The questions seemed stark; rude almost, but she couldn't help herself.

Before Monique could answer, something small barrelled into Adeline's legs and she stumbled slightly into the fence. 'Oh!' she exclaimed, then looked down to see Lili, smiling excitedly up at her. 'You scared me half to death!' she said.

Lili's face fell.

'But the dancing, the singing, it was wonderful!' Adeline added quickly. 'We were amazed!'

'You were?'

'Of course,' Monique said, 'and of course you were the best one.'

'I was?'

'*Mais oui*! How can you think otherwise!' Monique exclaimed, putting her hands on Lili's upper arms. 'I am sure everybody thought so.'

Adeline held back her urge to say something a little more measured to Lili about it being a team effort and her classmates shining too. But it was nice to see Monique smile after everything she'd said. And if she inflated Lili's ego a little, well, it wasn't the end of the world.

As they walked back to the shop, with a promise to pop into the patisserie en route, Adeline studied Monique's face, trying to establish her age. She couldn't be as young as forty-six, could she? The age her mother might be? Monique was truly a mystery. Sometimes she looked young, vibrant. Sometimes older. Always beautiful, glamorous and confident. But somehow ageless – her personality shining through and making any wrinkles or grey hairs seem irrelevant.

She wondered, as she paid for three slices of chocolate fondant, as they made their way chattering along the street, as they unlocked the shop and stepped inside, how she might get Monique to open up again. It wasn't fair to interrogate her about something so painful. But there were questions she absolutely had to know the answers to.

20

Saturday morning was a whirlwind of activity. With Easter approaching, and the weather warming up seemingly by the day, more and more traders were arriving: the four or five stalls that had lined the streets on market day had swelled in number to almost twenty. Some traders decked their stall with colourful awning, others simply had put-you-up tables. One or two local producers sold goods through the sliding door of a van, or from wooden boxes full of vegetables laid out on the street.

The atmosphere was infectiously joyous, and despite the fact she'd slept badly, Adeline found herself smiling her *bonjour*s to those she passed, holding tightly onto Lili's hand as her little girl walked quickly beside her.

She arrived on time and, once inside, propped the door open to let fresh air, sunshine and the hustle and bustle of outside seep into the empty shop; she noticed the bright light revealed streaks that Monique had missed in her window cleaning efforts, and that the tops of some of the shelves were dusty despite her own tour yesterday evening with Monique's feather duster.

The minute a few customers came in to browse, her attention was taken up with slipping books into paper bags, making recommendations or tapping in orders on the computer. Monique walked around the shop, today in a blue dress belted tightly at the waist, the moonstone glowing at her neck, and made conversation with a few familiar faces.

A combination of the prospect of a holiday, the new stalls on the market, and the warm spring sun injected the air with a positive vibe, and almost everyone they saw was smiling or chatting happily as they made their purchases or indulged their desire for a browse of the bookshop shelves.

The moment he entered, it was as if something in the atmosphere shifted. Adeline had just served a young boy and his mother who'd spent ten minutes telling her about their plans for the boy's Easter break, and had even invited Lili over to play later in the week – her first official invitation. When the bell rang again, she looked, smiling towards the door, and saw his stooped frame making its way to the counter.

'*Bonjour*, Claude,' she said, trying to keep her face in the same, upbeat position as it had been when serving the previous customer.

He smiled back, but with a combination of such kindness and sorrow it almost made her heart crack. Monique looked over and Adeline thought for a moment she'd come and take Claude under her wing as she usually did; often with the recommendation of a new book or short story, or at least some conversation that seemed to lift him a little. This time, though, Monique returned her attention to the little coloured jar she was arranging on a shelf, leaving Adeline at the helm.

Claude shuffled to the counter and stood for a moment in silence. 'Have you any recommendation?' he asked.

Adeline looked at Monique again, but her boss seemed to be

completely taken with the jar and a crystal she'd placed next to it, and seemed to be mouthing something to herself. Adeline smiled. 'What did you think of the last one?' she asked.

Claude nodded. 'It was beautiful,' he said sadly. 'I read it in three days. And it reminded me of myself, years ago.' He laughed softly. 'So many years.'

Taking a more guarded look at Monique, who was still apparently transfixed, Adeline reached out a hand and touched Claude's outstretched palm. Gently taking hold, she looked at his face, until his eyes moved from their fingers to meet hers. This was her moment. She wanted to tell him that he must see a doctor. Perhaps a counsellor. That reading couldn't do what a professional could. She felt furtive, not knowing how Monique would view her action. But the desire to help Claude was so strong that she couldn't seem to stop herself.

Then, just as she opened her mouth, something happened.

When she looked back later, she found herself unable to explain exactly what came over her. But looking into Claude's eyes and touching his hand, she suddenly saw a series of images flash past her eyes: a young boy running with a puppy; a boy at school, his head bent over his books. The same boy – a young man now – at work in a small office. Then again, this time walking with a beautiful girl. She saw a couple, arm in arm, on their wedding day. A man holding a baby, then the hand of a child. And a woman, her eyes beautiful, her face gaunt, propped on a bed, still smiling. Her hand reaching out.

And suddenly she knew what Claude needed. 'Just a moment,' she said, her voice slightly choked and not sounding like hers, and walking quickly to one of the shelves.

Her fingers felt stiff and clumsy as she ran her hands feverishly over the volumes, trying to hold on to the certainty she felt, keeping in mind the book she was looking for. And there! She found it. *Vivre vite* by Brigitte Giraud, a beautiful story of grief and strength. She handed it to him, and although later she felt almost embarrassed at how she'd felt, in that moment she was completely convinced that this was what Claude needed to read; needed to know. This was the book that would help him to live.

He took it from her, turning it over in his hands, a question in his eyes. But she nodded. 'Try it,' she said.

'Thank you.' He slipped a shaking hand into his pocket, pulling out a tattered wallet, and she found she couldn't bear it.

'No. It's a gift. From me.' And she smiled again, nodding, encouraging him to accept. She reached out to touch his hand again and held his gaze for a moment. 'You need to find joy, Claude, and I think this book might help. But I think maybe it would be good for you to go to the doctor. Just to talk? That might help you too.'

He nodded, just once, and she wasn't sure whether he'd agreed or simply dismissed her. 'Thank you,' he said, holding up the book. 'I will try.'

It wasn't until he'd left the shop and they were alone again that Adeline looked over at Monique.

Her boss was standing, looking almost ethereal in a shaft of sunlight. Dust particles from the shelf she'd set the jar on danced in its glow; the light illuminated her face, but threw her body into darkness. Her eyes were watching Adeline as if she were seeing her for the first time.

'Is everything OK?' Adeline asked, wondering if she'd done something wrong.

Monique walked over to her, her gaze unwavering. '*Oui*,' she said, in a voice that was quieter than usual. 'It's just, I was watching you with Claude.'

Whatever had come over Adeline when she'd served the elderly widower was already fading, and she found herself flushing, embarrassed. 'I hope that was OK? You seemed busy, so...'

'*Mais oui!*' Monique replied, her voice stronger now. 'I am ashamed to say that I feel at a loss with Claude. I wondered... I didn't come over as I thought you might talk to him. That it might help. And I had to finish what I was doing. Once I start, it's important.'

'Oh,' Adeline said. 'Well, I found him a book. Hopefully he'll enjoy it.'

'But you did something else. You read him, didn't you?'

'Read him?' Adeline tried to sound incredulous. She remembered the images, the tingle of something when their fingers had touched. But already the moment had passed; she felt foolish. 'Oh, no. I just thought of a book he might like.'

The lie hung between them. Monique paid no attention to it. '*Non*, Adeline. You saw him. Into him. I watched you. And you gave him *Vivre vite*. And I realised of course that this book would speak to him. Speak to his soul. And you knew, didn't you? You felt it?'

Adeline didn't like to think about what she'd felt. It was both embarrassing and a little terrifying. For the first time in a long while she thought of London, and that although it had been busy and she'd been lonely, at least everything had been familiar. Now, in this new place, stripped of all the sights, sounds, smells she'd known, she was suddenly exposed. 'I just thought he'd like it,' she repeated, her tone not sounding convincing even to her.

'Do not be scared of it,' Monique said. 'It is a gift. It is a wonderful gift. Ah, you can call it bibliotherapy if you want. You can give it a name that you are comfortable with. But I like to think of it as being able to see people, properly: to read them.

This desire to help others.' She shrugged. 'And perhaps we have to admit there is a little magic there too,' she added.

Adeline looked down, still not willing to accept that what had happened was anything but a moment of inspiration. Monique walked forward and touched her hand lightly. 'Whatever it is, it is not a bad thing. It is good,' she said.

Adeline longed for a customer to come in and break the moment; longed for Lili to run down the stairs from the flat where she had gone to play and ask her something ordinary. It was uncomfortable, thinking of things that she couldn't find a rational explanation for.

'No,' she said. 'I don't think it has anything to do with magic. Not for me. Just... perhaps being empathetic.' She turned away, getting her purse from her bag and slipping the payment for Claude's book into the till, her ears burning.

Monique laughed, but kindly. '*Oui, c'est vrai.* We are empathetic booksellers.' She grinned. 'But for me, it was a wonderful moment. I have never met anyone before who can do this, who can see people the way I sometimes do.'

Adeline clenched her fists, digging her nails into her palms. All she needed to do was move past the moment. Then she could pretend nothing out of the ordinary had happened.

'"*If I can ease one life the aching... I shall not live in vain*".' Monique's words sounded familiar.

'I know those lines, don't I?'

'You do if you have been reading your poetry! But these lines, they say everything I believe in. If we can help, we should help. And who cares why or how.' She grabbed Adeline's hand. 'You and me, we read with our hearts. And yes, sometimes we feel things we don't understand. But it is a gift. It is good. We do not have to understand it. Just live it. Use it. Share it.'

Adeline found herself nodding.

And then to her relief she heard the stomping sound of her daughter on the wooden stairs, and Lili pounded down from the flat clutching a scribbled drawing in crayon. 'Look,' she said, holding it out. 'It's you, Mummy.'

On the paper was a scribbled drawing of a woman, holding a book, surrounded by stars.

21

She'd slept fitfully the night before, so of course Lili had chosen that day to wake up early and bounce on her bed from around 6 a.m. Groaning, she turned over and pulled what she could of the duvet over her. 'Lili, it's early,' she said. 'Mummy needs a rest.'

But Mummy clearly wasn't going to get a rest. Lili stopped bouncing, but wriggled and fidgeted so much, Adeline realised that there was no point at all trying to cling onto sleep. Instead, she shifted herself up so she was half sitting, and looked at her inquisitive daughter.

'You're awake!' Lili said delightedly, as if she'd had absolutely no part in this.

'Yes,' Adeline replied, unable to stop herself smiling at the tousled, excited girl in front of her.

'It's the holidays!'

'Yes, it is!' Adeline said, trying to inject a similar excited tone into her own voice. She felt a little guilty, as Lili would be spending at least some of the holidays in the local playscheme, and some 'helping' her and Monique in the bookshop. Still, she supposed it would be exciting for her – probably more exciting than spending every day at home with her mum.

Today, she'd planned to visit the swimming lake 15 kilometres from St Vianne. The weather was warm enough to spend a little time on the sandy beach she'd been told was there, and maybe if they were feeling particularly brave, they could dip their toes into the edges of the water and have a little paddle. The taxi would cost them forty euros each way and she'd baulked at the expense, but with the majority of Lili's holiday being taken up following her mum to work, she'd decided to splash out.

If she stayed, if she decided to make St Vianne her home, then she'd have to invest in a car – something small, modest, in keeping with the little cars people seemed to drive around here. But right now, with so few journeys and so much uncertainty hanging over her, it made more sense to pay the one-off taxi fare.

Two hours later, they'd washed, packed – ambitiously, she'd added her and Lili's swimming costumes, but doubted she'd be brave enough to actually go in – and they were standing outside waiting for the taxi. Sunday morning started slowly in St Vianne, but the warmth had driven walkers and their dogs out for a morning stroll. She nodded to familiar faces and exchanged a few pleasantries with one of the regular bookshop customers.

Then their taxi arrived – a slightly dented white vehicle with a yellow light on top. They slipped into the back and, as Lili chatted to the driver, Adeline looked out of the window and watched the final houses of St Vianne slip past her and the countryside begin to take over. Views stretched over lower ground on either side, and a slight mist hung over the river that snaked forwards out of sight. The sky was a brilliant blue and the sunlight bright; although the air was still on the cool side, the forecast had promised highs in the low 20s – practically summer in Adeline's book.

Her eyes glazed as she took in the view, and then she was back in the shop, handing that book to Claude, feeling again that sense of purpose – an urgent need to pair him with the book she felt could heal him. A few bumps in the road startled her out of the daydream, and she realised they'd turned down a small track; probably the route to the lake. They passed a closed restaurant and bar, a couple of holiday chalets with darkened windows, a children's playpark that had Lili pressing her face against the glass to see a slightly wonky see-saw and swing set. And finally, the road opened out into a car park.

It was half past ten, and Adeline was surprised to see the car park almost empty, other than two camper-vans and a motor-bike leaning casually on its stand. She'd thought the beach would be busy today – the hottest of the year so far, and a Sunday to boot.

She paid the driver, thanked him, and asked him to pick them up at four in the afternoon. Then she and Lili exited into air that whilst still on the cool side, held the promise of later warmth every time the sun's rays exited from behind the cluster of white clouds that had formed en route.

'Come on!' she said to Lili with enthusiasm she didn't yet feel. 'Let's find somewhere great to set up.' The little girl raced ahead, infected by Adeline's apparent excitement, and she felt a pang of guilt that she wasn't as into the idea as she'd pretended to be. Her mind was cast back to a beachside holiday in Cornwall, splashing in the shallows with Mum, eating fresh crab sandwiches and ready-salted crisps, drinking hot tea from a flask after a soaking by the sea. Her mother's laughing face, delighted at everything Adeline had done.

Had her mother been feeling as weary as she did as she fixed on a smile and pulled a plastic spade from her backpack? Had the outward display of reckless abandon been a carefully orchestrated show for her and Kevin? Each stage of motherhood Adeline entered made her feel closer to her mum somehow; she'd slipped behind the curtain of childhood and was seeing how everything worked backstage. She wished Mum were here so she could answer the questions that Adeline hadn't known to ask back then.

'What's the matter?' Lili asked.

Adeline jumped a little. 'Sorry. Mummy was just dreaming for a moment.'

Lili seemed satisfied with this response and pointed to the spot on the sand she'd chosen. 'Here!' she said proudly as if she'd discovered something unique and amazing at the random little patch of sand.

'Perfect,' said Adeline, unfurling a towel and laying it down for them to sit on. She set the backpack at one end, and slipped off her shoes and set them at the other in case the breeze got any ideas about whipping the towel away. 'You start,' she said to her daughter, handing over the spade. 'I'll just a have a little rest, then I'll join you.'

Lili didn't need telling twice. She was soon drawing out shapes in the sand with the corner of the spade, mapping out the ambitious design of a castle that was clearly going to take all of their construction skills combined to create.

Looking across the scene, Adeline watched a small dog at the lakeside, trotting and dancing in front of a man who'd occasionally throw a ball into the shallows for the dog to splashily retrieve. To the side, a couple sat on a picnic blanket, sipping something warm from a flask. There were a couple of older children – possibly around ten years old or so – kicking up sand at the water's edge. Otherwise, the beach was empty.

Perhaps everyone was waiting until the afternoon, she thought. Lunch, she knew, was sacrosanct in France – probably people would be in the restaurants or at home with family, then hit the beach later on. She wasn't too disappointed. It would be nice to see a few more faces, have a few more sights and sounds to add to the atmosphere, but in some ways, it was nice to have this privacy, a little slice of paradise just for the two of them.

She pulled the flask of coffee she'd made before setting off from her bag and poured herself a tiny serving in the small cup that served both as a lid and a receptacle. Sipping the hot liquid, she hoped it would give her the impetus she needed to build what by now looked like the plan for an entire medieval village.

'I see Monique has given you a holiday at last!'

The voice made her jump. She opened her eyes and saw the face of someone standing behind her, looking over, his face stretched into an enormous smile.

'Michel!' she said.

'*Oui, c'est moi,*' he said, moving around to face them. Lili looked up briefly from her digging then went back to work, clearly too busy to be interrupted.

'What are you doing here?' she asked, almost clapping her hand over her mouth after the question escaped it.

He laughed, clearly amused, and rocked back on his heels slightly. 'Ah, even professors get weekends. I am here to paint.' He nodded to a leather case under his arm which apparently contained his art materials. 'The light is perfect here,' he added, looking across the sun-dappled water; 'I often come at weekends.'

'Oh. Monique didn't mention that when she recommended this spot to me.'

They looked at each other for a moment, sizing up the situation. Another engineered meeting?

'Well, hope it goes well!' she said. 'Unless you want a cup of coffee?' She waved the tiny flask and laughed.

He stepped forward, and she was sure he was about to move off, then realised that he was actually moving to the spare piece of towel. Before she'd had time to say anything – although honestly, what would she have said? – he'd plonked himself down next to her, so close that they were almost touching. 'Thank you, that is very kind.'

A British person probably would have known Adeline's offer had been a friendly rebuff – an offer made in the certainty of polite rejection. Only the nuance was lost on Michel.

She tried to calm the slight annoyance she felt at his presumption – because she'd actually offered, she had to remind herself – and instead tipped the last drops of coffee from her cup and rinsed it out using water from Lili's bottle, before pouring him a fresh cup.

'*Merci*,' he said, blowing steam from the top of the black liquid. 'This is exactly what I need.'

'No problem.'

They settled into silence, Adeline still feeling a little out of sorts at the thought that Monique might have recommended the beach to her for a very specific reason. She'd have to have words with her boss – but how?

'Ah, so Lili is now on holiday,' Michel said, his voice close to her ear.

'Yes.'

A silence fell over them.

'I am sorry, I'm interrupting,' he said, sensing the atmosphere.

She felt suddenly guilty. 'No, not really. I just…'

He looked at her, his eyes so intelligent, it felt as if he were reading her. She sighed; there was no point in beating around the bush. 'It's just Monique. Do you think she's trying to – I don't know... *work her magic* with us?'

Michel let out a small bark of laughter. 'Possibly. You never quite know with her. But no matter. We are friends, right? It's good to bump into each other.'

Adeline felt herself relax. 'Yes,' she said.

'And I did want to talk to you a little,' he admitted. 'About the fight I had with Monique. I don't want you to think I'm a monster!'

'Goodness, no. Not at all!'

He sipped the last of the coffee and set the tiny cup down next to him. 'Did she tell you what we fought about?'

Suddenly her cheeks were hot. 'Oh, no. She hasn't really said anything. It was just... well, I was only downstairs when it happened. It was... pretty obvious something was up.'

He gave a half-smile. 'The platter?'

She nodded. 'The platter.' They exchanged a grin.

'It nearly took my bloody head off,' he said, but he was grinning. 'Don't worry, I have fast reflexes. Like a panther!'

She laughed as he held his hands up to resemble claws.

'Look, I am Monique's friend,' he continued. 'Her family, almost. And I don't want to betray her. But I think perhaps it is important I tell you what we were fighting about.'

She turned towards him, eyes wide. 'Oh, no. Don't. It's fine. It's none of my business, I—'

'*Mais* it is your business I think, Adeline. We were fighting about you.'

'About me?' Her voice came out louder than expected and Lili looked up with a frown. She smiled at her daughter to reassure her that everything was all right. 'It's looking great, darling! I'll help in a minute.'

'*Oui*. About you.' Michel repeated.

She looked at him and gave a little, almost imperceptible nod, permission to continue.

He sighed. 'You know already of course that Monique had a baby. Well, when I was there, staying, she confessed to me that she thinks you might be her daughter. That she can feel it.' He tapped his chest and rolled his eyes as if it were a ridiculous notion.

Everything in Adeline's body suddenly felt as if it were on high alert. 'She does?' Adeline's heart began to thunder. Because if she was honest, she'd started to have her suspicions too. Had felt something; a connection that seemed to go deeper than she could explain.

He looked at her, his gaze steady.

'It's just...' she said, aware now that she was gabbling a little. 'I know it's far-fetched, but I was actually adopted. I don't know if Monique told you that? And I know that my mother – my birth mum – was French, and very young. And that Monique—'

'*Non*,' he said. The word was so cold and stark that it cut her off mid-flow and she found herself looking at his face, the clouded expression; his knitted brow. 'It is not possible. Monique, she is deluding herself. It is a fantasy.'

'But you don't know everything!' she said. 'Yes, maybe it was too long ago; maybe her baby was born years before I was. But even you must see that there's a possibility. She's very vague on the dates. And people have remarked that we're similar. I... well, I felt something in the shop. A connection. And there's...' she stopped abruptly, not quite sure how to explain what had happened with Claude, and how she might share Monique's strange gift. She wasn't ready to acknowledge that yet.

He was shaking his head at her and she almost had the urge to shove him. Perhaps Monique's platter-throwing had been justified after all. What made him the authority on this? It barely concerned him.

He put his hand on her arm and she flinched a little but let it stay. 'Adeline, I was afraid this might happen. Afraid for you.'

'Afraid?'

'Yes. That you might start to hope. That Monique might make you wonder...' he shook his head. 'Adeline, I am sorry but even if the timing were right with your age – and it isn't – I can say with certainty that Monique is not your mother.'

'How can you be so sure?'

He looked at her, his brown eyes deep pools of sadness, full of pity and honesty. 'Because, yes, Monique had a baby,' he said. 'But Adeline, her baby died.'

22

A couple of days later, halfway through Lili's holiday week, Adeline was in the shop trying to simultaneously search for books on the Internet and keep an eye on Lili who was drawing at the tiny desk with crayons that could easily ruin a book or a wall if the urge occurred, when her phone pinged with a new email. It was from Kevin.

Dear Addy,

Hope your week is going well! Just thought I'd drop a note to say thanks again for putting me up (and putting up with me) on my impromptu visit. I'm already looking at tickets for the summer, so watch this space.

Also, I wanted to say that I've taken a leaf out of your book. No, I'm not moving abroad to take a job in a tiny village. But I am putting myself out there. Kind of. What I mean is – I've downloaded a dating app. Not the one I was on before, but one (and don't laugh) that's for professionals looking for that special someone.

I've decided it's time to look at my own life rather than

trying to boss you around. Although, as your big brother, I still reserve the right to do that, obviously.

I've been thinking about Mum too. I mean, obviously – right? I think about her all the time. What I mean is, I've been thinking about what life was like those last months. How tired we both were. How she took up every waking hour we had outside of work. And for you, in those final weeks when you got leave from work, every moment you had.

I'm proud of us. I think Dad would have been proud of us too. We looked after Mum to the best of our abilities and gave her the best possible care. And I don't regret it for a minute. BUT I guess I've started to realise the impact all of that had on my life. On our lives.

It's hard, going from 24/7 caring to nothing at all. And it's not just grief, is it? It's that kind of vacancy of time – not knowing what to do with ourselves. All the things I used to do before have sort of fallen away. And I think I've been a bit lonely.

So there, this is me getting out of my slump. Dipping my toe into the dating pool and hoping for the best.

And I wanted to thank you. Because I came to persuade you to come home, but instead you kind of showed me that I needed to make a change.

Don't get a big head though. You're still wrong about most things.

Love

KEV x

'What's that?' Lili's voice made her jump. Adeline turned her face away from her phone to see Lili standing at her side, peering towards the screen. 'Just a message from Uncle Kevin.'

'For me?'

'No sweetheart, for me. But he said to send his love,' she replied, knowing that despite the fact it wasn't explicitly stated, it was definitely what he meant in his sign off.

'OK.' Lili didn't seem too bothered about it. She scuffed her shoe on the edge of the counter, kicking at a bit of wood that had splintered slightly.

'Leave that, Lili, you'll get a splinter.'

'Lili, why don't you help me with something,' Monique said, appearing as if from nowhere. 'I have some new children's books and I'd like you to help me choose which one to put in the window. Do you think you could do that?'

Lili nodded, eyes wide at the prospect, and Monique gave Adeline a little wink over her shoulder as she led the child to a box of books. This afternoon, Lili was booked into the playscheme, but she'd chosen to have her in the store this morning as Tuesday mornings – their first proper open morning of the week – were often quiet.

Adeline tucked her phone away and got back on with the job in hand – Monique had given her a list of titles to find, some vintage, some current – and she was searching on second-hand selling sites to try to locate decent copies. As she was typing in a particularly complicated title, the bell rang on the door and she looked up to see a woman who looked familiar step into the shop.

'Hello,' the woman said, her blonde ponytail swinging as she walked confidently over to the counter. 'Oh, and *bonjour*,' she added, noticing Monique in the corner with a large cardboard box.

'Hi Stacey,' Adeline smiled. 'Back already!'

'Yeah, I'm surprised too,' Stacey grinned. 'But that book you recommended last time, I loved it,' Stacey said. 'Read it in two evenings. And I wanted to know if she'd written any more.'

'The Catherine Cooper?'

'That's the one.'

'Yes,' nodded Adeline. 'One or two. We've got some in stock actually.' She pointed over to a shelf where contemporary novels were organised in alphabetical order.

'Brilliant,' Stacey said, giving her a wink for no apparent reason. Then she went and busied herself at the shelf, looking over the titles and flicking through until she made her selection. Seemingly decided, she came back and paid. 'Probably see you next week. Thanks again!'

'Thank you.' Adeline smiled.

'Don't forget to ring me for a coffee... if you need,' she added.

'Definitely.'

When the door closed, she looked up to see Monique smiling at her. At her feet, Lili had laid the new books out in a line and was carefully inspecting the first one, taking her choice seriously.

'*Ça va?*' Adeline asked, after a beat.

'*Oui*,' Monique smiled. 'It just makes me happy that you are so good with the customers. That you have a gift.'

Adeline shook her head. 'Oh, this wasn't... *that*,' she said, not quite knowing how to put in words the way in which she'd recommended a book to Claude. Instinctive perhaps? Looking back, it seemed bizarre at best, and in all honesty she was trying to forget it had ever happened. 'I just... she's English and we had a good chat – her French isn't good – and I was able to recommend something for her to read, based on her preferences. That's all.' She smiled, tightly, and turned back to her screen.

But she could feel Monique's eyes still on her. And when she looked up again, the woman was still staring at her, the same sliver of a smile gracing her face.

'Monique!' she said.

'I'm sorry.' Her boss shook her head. 'I was dreaming.'

'It's OK.'

Monique walked over to the counter, her floral skirt swishing at her calves. 'I think it's so wonderful you came to work here. Like it was fate, perhaps.'

Adeline had thought the same herself from time to time, but hearing the words aloud, teamed with the look Monique had given her, made her shoulders tense. 'Yes, well, I really enjoy it.'

'And you have a gift! Ah yes, I know that you will say you do not. That you just listen and recommend books like a librarian. But deep inside, I think you know that it is more than that. That you can read people, just like I can.'

'Honestly, it's not...'

'And to have found someone else who has this... instinct, it is a wonderful thing for me.'

Adeline glanced up to see that Monique was once again smiling at her, fingering the moonstone at her neck, her eyes full of emotion. She turned away from the keyboard and looked at her. Because this had to stop. It really had to.

'Monique,' she said slowly. 'I saw Michel on Sunday.'

'Oh, was he well?' she asked. 'Where did you go?'

'We bumped into each other. On the beach.' Adeline watched Monique's face to see if there was a reaction. 'We got to talking.' She dropped her voice to a near whisper, aware of Lili's almost supersonic hearing. 'And we spoke about his argument with you.'

Two spots of colour appeared on Monique's neck. 'But that is all forgotten!' she said, her volume matching Adeline's.

'Yes. Yes, he told me you were both OK now,' Adeline confirmed. She took a breath. 'But he mentioned something that... worried me a bit.'

'*Ah oui*?'

'Yes, Monique.'

A silence descended over them. Lili picked up one of the books and walked decisively to the window. Otherwise, nothing moved; Adeline could feel her heart thundering. Clearly Monique wasn't going to help her out here.

'He told me that he was worried you'd begun to imagine I was your daughter,' she said at last, forcing the words out.

Monique turned her face sharply towards the far wall, as if preoccupied with something there.

'But you know that's not possible, don't you, Monique?' she added gently, feeling horribly cruel.

She watched the woman's face, usually graced with a smile, crumple in front of her. Monique put a hand up to hide her expression, and her shoulders slumped. She made a sound, a tiny almost indistinguishable cry.

'I'm so sorry,' Adeline said. 'I know how hard it is to want to believe something. I know how hard it is to feel that ache for someone. But I needed to say it. Because I think Michel might be right. I think perhaps on some level you were starting to believe it.' She felt suddenly as if she might be sick – a prickle of sweat traced her brow. She put her arm across Monique's shoulders. 'Even *I* had thought... well, imagined I felt something between us before I found out that your baby... About what happened,' she said, trailing off. Monique was standing still, her eyes fixed on a point beyond Adeline's shoulder, at the rows and rows of books, their spines glistening in the light.

'You're right,' Monique agreed eventually, her voice so quiet that Adeline had to lean down to hear her properly. 'It is impossible. I know this. But it seems that my heart does not know. And I suppose just sometimes I allowed myself to dream...'

'Oh, Monique.'

'No. It is stupid. I am a silly old woman.' She batted Adeline's arm away and straightened up. She took a deep breath.

'I thought I had felt the deepest pain possible when I gave my child to another woman and watched her being taken away from me. I didn't sleep for days, I couldn't eat. Even my parents began to worry. I was just sixteen but I was running out of reasons to live.'

Adeline touched Monique's arm and this time she wasn't shrugged away.

'But in time it got better. I began to get up, and go to school and I told myself I would be OK. Because the moment I was old enough I would find her. And we would be together again. Oh, I know, I was young and stupid. I did not realise that sometimes this is impossible; that they make it impossible.' Monique turned her eyes towards Adeline now and they were shining. 'But before I found this out for myself, my mother sat me down and told me that my baby had died. That she had caught a fever and it had been too much for her little body. And this pain, the pain I felt then in my heart, I was worried it might tear me in half.'

Monique paused and took a deep breath. 'That's when I ran. And over time, I learned to live again. Learned to forget. Staying in a new place, breaking ties with my past. It was my way to cope. But every day I find I think of her still – and my heart knows that if the baby had been with me, she would not have died. I would have known she was sick sooner, taken her to the hospital more quickly. Because she was *mine*,' she said, her voice louder now, emphatic. '*My* baby. And I was her mother. And that is why I will never forgive my mother for what she did. Not until the day I die.'

Adeline watched her silently, then, cautious as if approaching an animal that might dart away, she reached out and gave her a hug. They gripped onto each other tightly, both overcome. 'I'm so sorry,' Adeline said. 'I can't even imagine...'

'This is why...' Monique pulled away and flicked the tears from her face as if dismissing her emotions. 'This is why I let myself dream, just a little. This is why I believed my heart knew you when we first met. And I decided that fate had brought us together. That somehow my baby was still alive; my mother had been given the wrong information. It was a delusion. But such a beautiful one, I allowed myself to have it, just for a little while.'

Adeline nodded. 'Of course,' she said, slightly guilty to have forced Monique to bring the dream out in front of them both and expose it to the light. 'I...' she began.

But at that moment, two things happened. Lili raced across the shop, oblivious to the emotional trauma happening just next to the counter, and excitedly showed Monique her choice for the window display. At the same time, the bell jangled as three customers entered the shop, chattering happily. The moment was broken, the heaviness began to dissipate from the air. Adeline took a breath and stepped into her work mode, feeling the weight of everything set aside for now. Looking at Monique, hand in hand with Lili by the window, she could sense the woman had done the same.

23

The park in the local town was a large expanse of grass, with a corner given over to children's playground equipment: a small climbing frame made of metal, a wobbly bridge which stretched over a dip, a slide that descended from the end of the climbing frame and a couple of carved wooden animals set on springs.

While the shop was quiet, Adeline had asked to go and sit at the edge of the space, knowing that Lili would be there playing with some of the children from the holiday playscheme run by the local school. She'd taken a book with her, but had left it closed on her lap as she watched her child, with six others, swarm over the equipment, laughing and running and shouting with complete abandon. It was hard not to smile.

When Adeline had seen Lili, she'd assumed her daughter would run over. But instead, she'd given her a subtle wave and grin before disappearing with the children. Once in a while, she'd look up to make sure Adeline was watching, and they'd exchanged looks and thumbs ups at the end of a particularly brave climb, and after a turn on the swings where she'd gone higher than ever before.

It was pleasant, sitting in the warm air, smelling pollen on the breeze and watching the children play. She took a deep breath of the fresh air and released it, trying to relax her shoulders as she'd been taught during a yoga and meditation class she'd attended back in London. Her practice had lapsed since her move and her muscles felt tight, her shoulders hunched. True, she needed the class less now, away from the relentless stress she'd felt back then – a combination of teaching, caring and single parenting – but she made a mental note to try to find something local to attend before she seized up completely.

Leaning back to stretch out her shoulders, Adeline looked across the grass in the other direction, where a stone building marked the edge of the common ground. There was a pathway stretching from one side of the park to the other, and locals would often use it as a cut-through on their daily walks, sometimes with dogs on a lead or sniffing interestedly in their wake. Today there was a man pushing his bike, the basket straining with groceries, and another with a baguette under his arm – it was a common sight in St Vianne, but one that still felt like something out of a cartoon – then her eyes focused on another man, something familiar in his movements. His face was hidden behind a small paperback he was somehow managing to read as he walked along. She wondered whether it was wise to read and walk, especially so close to the small river that flowed on the far side of the path.

As the man grew closer his features came into focus and she snatched her gaze away, embarrassed; she hadn't expected to see Michel and half hoped he hadn't noticed her. But when she allowed her eyes to wander back to him, she realised that he was crossing the grass towards her, book at his side and a wide smile on his face.

'Hello!' he called out.

'*Bonjour*. What are you doing here?' She hadn't quite meant her words to sound so sharp, so followed them with a grin. 'I mean, you're not usually...'

He laughed. 'I'm making a delivery for Monique. She called and asked me to take an invoice to a customer who lives close to my flat. It is no worry. It was actually her who suggested I walk through the park – it's a nice day. She is always sure that I am working too hard.' He made a mock sad face, then broke into a broad grin.

She glanced at his book. It was a French one she hadn't heard of, *Matin Brun*. 'Any good?'

He smiled. '*Mais oui*. It is one I often recommend to my students. You must try it.'

'I don't know how you do it.'

'What? Teaching? Working in the holidays?'

'No, walk along and read at the same time. Isn't it a bit dangerous?'

He laughed. 'Maybe. But not illegal, like drinking and driving. And better than looking at your phone all the time like my students.'

'True,' she said. She thought of herself in London, always buried in her phone, walking, queueing, sitting on the bus. Somehow being without it for a few weeks had broken the habit and she was trying as much as she could not to slip back into her old ways.

Something occurred to her. 'Sorry, but it was Monique who suggested you walk through the park?'

'And she knew that you would be here,' he said, picking up her train of thought. 'Ah, *merde*. My aunt, she is always meddling!'

'So now you think it might be intentional?'

He nodded. 'Ah, Monique. She cannot understand that I am

176 GILLIAN HARVEY

alone because that is what is right for me at the moment. She thinks I am shy. Or hopeless in love.'

Adeline shook her head. She wasn't sure whether to be amused or angry.

'I hope you won't be too cross with her? I think she means well,' Michel said.

'I'm sure. But even so...'

'Yes. Even so. Well, don't worry. I will be more suspicious next time she makes a suggestion.'

They grinned at each other in their mutual frustration. 'I was going to ask if you wanted to walk back to the store with me – I have had some books delivered I need to collect. But perhaps you want to stay here, especially as it might please Monique too much to think her plan is working?'

'Actually, I probably ought to get back,' she said. 'I'll walk with you. Monique can think what she likes.'

She stood, stretched and gave Lili a little wave as she lifted her bag onto her shoulder and turned to join him on the path.

'I hope I didn't upset you – when I told you about Monique, about her baby, I mean?' he said, as they walked, his eyes fixed on the road ahead.

She shook her head. 'Oh, no. It was better to know. I've spoken to Monique and...' she trailed off, wondering how to put the next part into words. 'Well, everything's OK,' she said.

'*Bon*. Good.'

The silence returned, starting off comfortably but then began to stretch into awkwardness. Next to her Michel shuffled slightly and cleared his throat. 'Do you ever think about finding your own mother?' he asked suddenly, posing the question into the silence. He reddened. 'Sorry, perhaps that is too personal.'

She looked at him briefly. 'It's OK,' she said. 'Yes, I did. I do. I've only known for a few weeks.'

'*Ah oui*?' he seemed surprised by this. 'That must have been a great shock.'

She nodded. 'It was. My mother, the mum who adopted me, died without ever telling me.'

Michel let out a breath at the enormity of what Adeline was going through. 'Wow. I understand it must be incredibly hard.'

'Just a bit.'

'You're actually the first person I've spoken to about this,' she admitted, slightly embarrassed. 'Other than Monique and my brother of course.'

'*C'est vrai*?' He seemed surprised. 'Then I am honoured.'

She laughed, briefly. 'Thanks,' she said, wanting to add that he might not be if she let it all spill out, everything she'd been carrying inside her since her arrival. She'd pushed it down and focused on work and France and, for a while, her suspicions about Monique. But the thoughts and questions had become so big that sometimes they overwhelmed her.

In previous years, she'd have discussed things with her best friend, Chris. They'd worked together at the school and would sit together at lunchtime putting the world to rights over lack-lustre sandwiches. But then Adeline had been swallowed up into the world of caring, which took up every free hour she had. Something had been lost between them.

She could talk to Kevin of course. And she knew he'd listen. But he was Mum's son. He had feelings she didn't want to hurt; might not understand her inner conflict.

Michel was safe – partly because she felt instinctively that he'd understand, but also because it didn't really matter if he didn't. 'I've actually done a DNA test recently,' she admitted. 'I haven't mentioned it because, well, I suppose I'm trying not to think about it too much.'

'But that is exciting!' he exclaimed.

'Yes. I haven't had the results back. And it might lead to nothing. I mean, there's no way of knowing if my birth mum will have done a test too, or any of her relations. But it might be a start to things,' she said, shrugging to convey a nonchalance she didn't feel.

'You must be nervous to wait for the results.'

'Terrified.'

'*Oui, j'imagine.*' He lightly patted her back in a motion of comfort.

'My brother, Kevin, gave me the idea. I'd kind of assumed that if my mother had put me up for adoption it would mean she wouldn't want me to trace her. So when I did the test, I didn't have much hope of making contact, not really. But since sending it off I've spoken to Monique, I've seen her pain. Knowing how she regrets giving up her baby.' She lifted a shoulder. 'It changed me. I realised that maybe my mother was similar – perhaps she hadn't wanted to give me up either. Maybe she would want me to find her.'

He nodded. 'Yes. I hope so for you.'

'Thank you.'

They reached the main high street now and the terraced houses began to merge into stone-fronted shops. Some – a *boucherie*, a small *galerie* – were boarded up, their signs faded. But others had lights on and life inside. At the patisserie, she could see André organising the window display and he gave them a wide smile.

Adeline smiled back, raising her hand in a small wave.

'Did I tell you that André almost hit my brother?' she asked.

'*Non*! Why was this?'

'Apparently he thought he was my boyfriend, and that he was mistreating me!' she said, looking askance at Michel.

Michel laughed, shook his head. 'This is so typical of him.

He grew up just with his mother and he is very protective of women.'

'You've known him a long time then?'

'*Oui*, since school.'

'I was so surprised! He raced out of the cafe after us and practically put Kevin in a chokehold. Is he always like that?'

'Like what?'

'So... dramatic?'

Michel laughed again. 'No, not quite so dramatic. But I think I know why.'

She felt suddenly nervous. 'What do you mean?'

'Well, this didn't come from me. But I know for a fact that he has noticed you.'

'He's... what?' She felt her cheeks get hot. André – St Vianne's answer to Ryan Reynolds – had noticed her? Not that she was interested.

Michel nodded. 'Yes, of course. He has seen that you are new here, and that you are alone.'

'Oh.' She couldn't see herself, but she was pretty sure the tips of her ears had gone pink.

'And I think you probably remind him of his mother.'

'Oh. Right. His mother.'

Michel looked as if he were about to say something else, but then gave his head a tiny shake and stood up a little straighter. 'Ah, and here we are!' he said almost too enthusiastically as the shop came into view.

As she glanced at the shop window, she noticed movement in the flat above and saw a figure quickly retreat from the glass. Monique. Probably seeing whether her meddling had worked. Adeline didn't know whether to be annoyed or amused.

24

The house was silent when she woke, suddenly, at half past five. Her heart was pounding and she could feel her chest and hair damp with sweat. Instinctively she clicked on her bedside light and let the comforting electric glow drive the shadows to the edges of the room. Then she shifted herself back until she was sitting up slightly against her pillow and tried to still her racing thoughts. Whatever it was, it had been in her imagination. There was no need to chase the dream through her subconscious and bring it up again.

She reached for her phone – something she'd vowed not to do on sleepless nights – in an attempt to find some sort of normality to help her fears subside. Perhaps reading the news or checking the weather would get her back into the moment. Her eyes and body felt tired, but she was too full of adrenaline to sleep, at least for now.

Unlocking her phone, she started by flicking through the headlines on her chosen news site, but they were all distressing and depressing; not the best thing for her to be looking at for distraction. Instead, she brought up Facebook and was pleased to see that she had a message from Chris.

So, now you're back online, are you going to update me on all the news? How's France? How's Lili? Any handsome Frenchmen on the horizon? Seriously, we need to catch up x

It was short, sure, but it was nice that someone was thinking of her. She wondered how to get even a fraction of what she was going through into a suitable message. It just wasn't possible. Besides, she wasn't sure her thumbs would survive if she truly updated her friend on everything going on. Perhaps she'd call her at the weekend. It seemed an odd thing to do, making an actual phone call. For a while, she'd barely had time to remember her friend, when Mum and her illness dominated her every waking thought and action. Short messages had been a way to jot down a couple of lines whenever she had the opportunity, their friendship reduced to brief soundbites.

She realised, suddenly, that the last proper phone call she'd made had probably been to Monique, when she'd rung about the job. Yes, she'd called booksellers and the odd customer since, but nothing personal, meaningful.

I'm good thanks. How are you...

She started to write. Then deleted and started again.

So much has happened recently. I can't even begin to write it here! I'm good. But it would be lovely to chat properly. If you have a moment sometime soon?

It would be four thirty in the morning in England. She doubted her friend would be that pleased to speak to her now. And besides, she knew how busy Chris could get. But hopefully they could chat soon – re-establish the kind of closeness they used to have.

She wondered why it had taken her rushing to France and working in a bookstore with a possibly psychic boss to realise that she needed to start reaching out properly and restocking her life with people who cared about her.

With a jolt she realised suddenly that she hadn't replied to Kevin's email yet either. And he'd been so touchingly open about his feelings. She clicked on her email icon and began to scroll through the various spam missives she'd received over the past twenty-four hours, looking for his name.

Only something else caught her eye.

DNA RESULTS IN! the heading read.

Shaking slightly, she tapped the heading and opened the email which congratulated her again on her results, and gave her a link to find out more.

Taking a deep breath and glad, for once, that she was alone and Lili was asleep, she clicked on the link.

After ten feverish minutes of forgetting her password, trying different versions of it, being locked out and finally resetting the whole thing, she was able to bring up her report.

And her life changed the moment she read it. Because the email revealed that she had matches.

Genetic matches.

And there was a link.

It took her a couple of minutes to work up the courage to click on it. Whatever it contained would be a partial answer to the questions she'd had since finding out she'd been adopted. A sibling, a cousin... possibly even a parent. She hadn't known, in the past, but Lili was the only genuine blood relative she had in her life. Now, there might be something new.

Two matches came up.

One, identified as a second cousin.

The other, as a parent.

A parent!

Her initial instinct was to throw her phone across the room – partially out of fear, partially out of shock. But instead, she steadied herself. This is what she'd wanted, wasn't it? That her mother, or possibly her father, had taken a DNA test. Had opted to make their findings available to people who might show up as DNA matches. It was wonderful. But she was utterly terrified.

'Sorry, Mum,' she whispered to the woman who had raised her, as she clicked on the parent icon and waited for the page to appear. And there it was. A woman called Sophia; her mother. And there was more – a photograph and the option to get in touch. Somehow so very ordinary and everyday. Yet earth-shattering too.

Currently her settings meant her results were kept private from matches. Sophia wouldn't yet be aware of her existence. Everything was still in Adeline's hands. She could close the page, pretend nothing had happened; be one of those people who chose not to find out. Or she could enlarge the photograph and see her birth mother's face – right now. And write her an email that perhaps she was longing for.

Sophia wouldn't have taken a DNA test and made the results searchable if she hadn't wanted to be found.

It seemed bizarrely easy, and utterly terrifying all at once.

Shaking, Adeline enlarged the photo.

The woman looked young – much younger than the mother who'd raised her. In her forties perhaps. But it wasn't this that struck her first of all. It was the fact that the face – one she'd never seen in her life – was almost as familiar to her as her own. There were similarities in their features – she could already see they shared the same eyes, the same lips. But it was something else. Something that went beyond the simple matching of facial characteristics. Something inside her, in her heart, a feeling that she'd known this woman her whole life. 'Mum,' she said, touching the woman's face and feeling the tears come.

A sudden thudding made her jump and Lili entered the room, the door banging against the wall as she violently pushed it open. Instinctively, Adeline closed the window she was viewing and put her phone on the bedside table. She tried to smile.

'Why you crying?' Lili asked, more interested than sympathetic.

'Oh, it's nothing,' she lied. 'Just had a bad dream.'

'About dragons?'

'No. About... well, it's complicated,' she said, putting out her arm for Lili to nestle beneath.

It was still only six o'clock. In half an hour her entire life had been rocked on its axis. She had woken up without a mother, but now, suddenly, she had one.

She just wasn't quite sure what to do about it.

* * *

Two hours later, walking a chattering daughter to her playscheme, she made the right faces and noises to demonstrate enthusiasm to Lili and hide the turmoil inside. She'd decided to wait until she was at work, on the PC there, and look at the picture properly. Decide whether to write a note to her mother. Her mother!

She arrived at work early; Monique had just opened the

shop which was empty of customers. 'Would you like a coffee?' her boss offered, and she gladly accepted. With Monique upstairs in the flat, this really was her chance.

She typed in the complicated link from her email and brought it up again. A picture of the woman – bigger now – the familiarity even more striking. Sitting for a moment, studying it, and feeling a rush of unfamiliar feelings – love? Fear? Shock? – she didn't hear Monique's feet on the stairs behind her.

So it was even more of a shock when she heard the coffee cups clatter on the wood behind her, spilling their content onto the shop floor, one breaking, the other rolling across the room and settling under a shelf.

Letting out a little cry, she turned to see Monique on the bottom stair, both hands over her mouth, her face pale and her eyes staring.

'Why do you have that?' Monique asked, her voice full of an emotion it was impossible to place.

'What?'

'*Mon Dieu*, you have a picture of my sister!' Monique rushed to the screen, touching the face that was displayed there.

'Your sister?'

'*Oui*,' she leant forward. 'I have not seen her for years, but I would know her face anywhere. Where did you get this?' she demanded. Then there was a moment of silence. Her fingers traced the outline of the woman's face. Then her shoulders slumped. '*Non*, it is not her,' she said. 'But it looked like... I was so sure...'

'I'm sorry,' Adeline said. 'I shouldn't have been looking at this at work. But Lili...' she trailed off. 'I'm sorry,' she said again.

'But who is this, this woman?' Monique asked. 'Where does this picture come from?'

Adeline looked at Monique's face – still pale from the upset.

She could still smell the coffee, its strong scent mixed with the smell of damp wood as it seeped into the floorboards. She felt a well of sympathy for this woman, whose own baby had been lost not once, but twice; whose questions would never be answered as Adeline's might.

'Well, I think...' she said, 'in fact, I *know* – she's my mother.'

25

They worked quietly in the afternoon; fulfilling their usual roles, talking to customers, organising the shelves, reading the latest books to arrive in store. Monique spent more time in the apartment than usual, and found a few reasons to exit the shop entirely. It was clear that something was bothering her. Adeline suspected it was Monique's own feelings about the baby she'd lost, brought to the fore by the fact that Adeline had found her mother.

During a quiet period, she took a break and, settling down with a cup of coffee, she finally wrote a reply to Kevin.

Dear Kevin,

Thanks for your email. Sorry it's taken me so long to reply (useless as ever!).

It was great to see you too. And please do book more tickets – you are welcome anytime.

Glad to see you're getting out there on the dating scene too.

I have some rather big news myself. You were right about

the DNA test. I've got my results back and have been matched with a woman. Well, not a woman. My birth mother.

I can literally contact her by clicking a link and writing a message. But what do I say? And what will she say in return? I'm terrified.

You definitely think Mum wouldn't have minded? And you don't, do you? You know if Mum were still here, I'd be doing this anyway. This woman, whoever she turns out to be, whatever she's like, she'll never be the mum who brought me up. Just someone new – a new bit of information I guess. Something to piece together my puzzle.

Anyway, there you have it.

Thanks for getting me to do the DNA test.

Love you lots, bro

Addy xx

Adeline was just pressing 'Send' when the door opened and an older man walked in, smartly dressed in chinos and a corduroy jacket. He'd pushed the door quite forcefully and the bell jangled more loudly than usual, making her start and sit up straight.

At first, she didn't recognise him – his hair was brushed and gelled and he was clean-shaven. But as he walked towards the counter, his body language uncharacteristically open, she realised he wasn't a stranger at all.

'Claude!'

'*Bonjour, Madame,*' he said, tipping his head slightly towards her. He smiled and although it wasn't a wide, open smile of happiness, it was different from the sad smile he'd had previously.

Something must have happened.

'You're looking well!'

'*Merci*.' He gave a little nod. 'I thought it might be time to smarten up. Violet, my wife, was always telling me I should make more effort.' His smile, after these words, was tinged with sadness, but somehow his manner was lighter. He'd never mentioned Violet to her so openly before. 'And perhaps it is time that I listened.'

She smiled. 'Well, good for you. You look great.'

'Ha, as Violet would say "better late than never",' he told her and she smiled and nodded her understanding.

He leaned on the counter then, his head tilting in her direction. 'Thank you for the book.' Then lowering his voice added: 'And also for saying what you did about the doctor. I am an old man, a stubborn fool. Too proud to go to the doctor for my head, for my broken heart. But you were right.'

'I'm so glad,' she told him quietly.

'It was always Violet before, who made me go,' he added. 'And now she spoke through you, perhaps.'

Adeline wasn't quite sure how to respond to this – to say that she was simply being sensible, giving him advice she'd give anyone, without a nudge from the spiritual world. But it seemed cruel; it was nice for him to believe Violet had had a hand in things. She smiled and nodded her head.

'*Bonjour*, Monique,' he said, turning and noticing Monique in the far corner, kneeling down next to a pile of books. She gave him a nod and he walked over and crouched down, speaking gently. Adeline watched as he reached out an arm and gave her a small rub on her upper back, as if comforting her.

She straightened, got to her feet with Claude's help and they began to talk. It was hard not to listen and although Adeline busied herself with the order book, she couldn't help but pick up snippets of their conversation.

'I don't know what to do, how to feel,' Monique was saying.

Claude shook his head. 'But I think that you do.'

She looked up at him, 'Then what is it? What is the thing I must do?'

'*Non*, I do not know. But *you* do. Monique, you always know what to do. You are so in touch with instinct, emotion. You need to think what you would tell someone else. If someone came into your shop with this problem, what would you tell them?'

Monique looked at him, shaking her head. 'I am not sure.'

'But it is there,' he insisted. 'It is in your heart if you take a moment to listen.'

She nodded again, raising her face to his. Their eyes met and an understanding seemed to pass between them. Smiling, he turned and walked towards the door, stopping to say goodbye to Adeline before pulling it open. 'I'll be back later in the week for a new book,' he said.

'See you soon,' Adeline called after him as the bell rang, signalling his exit.

Silence settled in his wake, like a blanket covering a birdcage, sending them back into their quiet, reflective state. Adeline busied herself, turning the pages of a new book and trying to get into it. She'd read more books in the weeks since she'd arrived than she had in the months beforehand and was thrilled that reading was now part of her job.

She'd begun to sink into the story of a young girl and her friend, finding entertainment in 1970s Yorkshire, when a voice by her ear made her jump. '...*Un café*?'

'Monique!' she said, turning and touching her heart. 'Sorry, I was miles away. But yes, please. I'd love one.'

Monique seemed to be in no hurry to disappear to the apartment to make it. She remained in place, her hands wringing together, her shoulders still slightly slumped. Then a decisive motion took over her body and she straightened. 'I need to say that I'm sorry.'

'Oh, Monique. What for?'

'Ah, you are kind. But I have not been. I have been lost in my own selfish thoughts.'

'Not at all,' Adeline said, firmly.

'*Mais si*! You have found your mother. It is incredible! And you must have a thousand emotions. You probably need a friend, to talk, and I have disappeared today. But it is because of my own sadness, you understand? I am very happy for you, but...' she trailed off, not sure how to finish.

But she didn't need to. Adeline was only too aware of what she was referring to. 'I know,' she said, softly. 'I'm so sorry, Monique.'

'Pah!' Monique said, flapping her hand and looking much more like herself. 'But your good fortune is not my bad fortune, *n'est-ce pas*? We have similar stories, but they are not the same story. And what is good for you does not change my situation. I am truly, truly thrilled for you,' she said, her eyes shining with emotion.

'Thank you. That means a lot. Really.'

'And have you written to your mother?' she asked.

Adeline shook her head. 'Not yet.'

Monique nodded. 'But you will?'

'I'm just afraid.'

'Of course.'

Adeline felt the words suddenly pour out of her: 'What if she doesn't want me to get in touch? I know the fact that she's on the site in the first place – well, it must mean something, mustn't it? But what if she hasn't even thought about it? What if I'm a bolt out of the blue; someone she'd left firmly in her past? What if—?'

She was stilled by a hand on her shoulder and looked up into Monique's steady, intelligent eyes.

'"Mama never forgets her birds." Your mother will want to hear from you. I know it.'

'You feel it?' A month or two ago, Adeline would have scoffed at the idea someone might sense something, might have an instinct about something without evidential proof. But now, her need for reassurance overwhelmed her scepticism. And perhaps it was more than that, she thought. Perhaps she was starting to believe a little in Monique's ability.

'*Oui*. I do not know her, of course. But I feel it as a mother. In my heart. She will want to hear from you, I promise.'

They smiled at each other for a moment and Adeline was struck with the thought that, in some ways, Monique had become a little like a mother to her. Nobody would ever fill the void left by her adoptive mum, but she'd become a confidante, a trusted friend – one that Adeline had needed more than she'd realised.

'Was that Dickinson? The line you quoted about a Mama and her birds?' Adeline asked, recognising the words but unable to reach them.

'*Oui*, it is a beautiful poem. A mother is always a mother. Whether she is here or elsewhere, or even in heaven. She watches. She loves.'

> *She looks down just as often*
> *And just as tenderly*
> *As when her little mortal nest*
> *With cunning care she wove*

Adeline felt the shudder of grief move through her body like ripples from the impact of a stone splitting the surface of the water. Memories hit her in waves: her mother's hand, pale and thin, squeezing hers for the last time. Her mother, fit and well, laughing at the table. The same mother, her hand younger and plumper, holding Adeline's on the way to school, or walking in town, or through a busy market. At that age, she'd had a feeling of being safely cocooned in her mother's love and when Mum had been there, she'd feared nothing.

As she'd grown, she'd learned that even mums have limitations, but that sense of security, the sense of steadiness her mum had imparted from the start had given her a platform of ease on which to build. When Mum had gone, she'd felt untethered, but the words Monique had spoken resonated. She hoped beyond anything that there was a place in which her mother could look down on her, still be there in a sense in her life. Adeline had never believed in God, had never believed in spirits or ghosts – she'd had no need to; everyone she had ever loved had still been at her side. And it was probably a mixture of wishful thinking and sadness that made her find truth in these words now. But the idea gave her comfort anyway.

'I hope so,' was all she could manage to say. Then, 'And what about you? I heard Claude ask what you would advise someone in your position. Are you OK?'

Monique lifted a shoulder briefly. '*Oui.* I suppose you finding your mother, it has made me think of mine. And to think perhaps if you forgive your mother, I should think about mine too. Because maybe she did what she did because she truly thought it best. I should at least listen, I think. It was not her fault my baby died; she wanted us both to live, and thought this was the best way.'

Adeline nodded. 'That's very brave of you.'

Monique laughed properly then. 'After several decades, I

finally have the courage to confront her! Perhaps that is not so brave.'

It was Adeline's turn to shrug. 'Well, I think it is,' she said with a small smile. 'And I really hope you can find some answers; something to help you.'

A customer entered – a small woman Adeline hadn't seen before – and the moment was broken. But she worked the rest of the afternoon in a dreamlike state – knowing that while nothing had changed in her life yet, perhaps everything was just about to.

26

There was a limited number of times you could refresh an email page without driving yourself mad, she'd realised over the evening, night and morning that followed her tentative message to the woman who'd given birth to her.

She kept running the words she'd written in her head – she'd kept them brief, not knowing how the woman might respond. Her profile details said that she'd been on the site for four years, so this really would be a bolt out of the blue.

Hi, she'd said. I'm Adeline. Your daughter. Can we talk?

She'd spent at least half an hour deliberating whether to end the message with a kiss. It was ridiculous, really, as she sprinkled them liberally in all her other messages and social media posts – so much so that once a colleague had become convinced she had a crush on him and politely reminded her that he was married. To her, a kiss just took the sting out of a difficult conversation, or simply softened the words above. It wasn't a literal *kiss*. If she actually kissed everyone she sent a virtual kiss to, she'd probably have perpetual cold sores.

But she'd left one off this particular missive, not wanting to be overly familiar.

It was horrible, this second-guessing.

The moment she'd sent the email, she'd refreshed her inbox, as if somewhere out there her mum would be sitting and waiting for her and would respond immediately. Then she refreshed ten minutes later, then half an hour.

After this, as she'd left the shop to pick up Lili, she'd told herself she wouldn't look at her emails until the next day – after which she'd proceeded to break the promise she'd made and had kept glancing and refreshing throughout the evening. Even when she'd woken up at 3 a.m. for a wee, she'd quickly touched her phone screen to see if there were any updates.

At this rate, she was going to make herself ill.

Now, at work, she found herself thinking of her phone almost constantly – like a teenager waiting for a text from her crush. It was now sixteen hours since she'd sent the message and nothing had yet arrived, except a special offer from the DNA site she'd used that had almost caused her to hyperventilate when it had pinged in her inbox.

Monique, knowing what was going on, kept giving her sideways glances – the question written on her face. Each time, she'd give a slight shake of the head and they'd both resume whatever they'd been doing before.

In the end, she knew she had to get away from her desk, the computer, her phone. 'Monique,' she said. 'Do you mind if I go for a walk?'

Her boss nodded. 'Of course.'

Exiting into the open, Adeline breathed as if she'd been released from a dungeon, filling her lungs with fresh air and letting the sunlight play on her face. She'd left her phone under the counter, and already her fingers itched to go and pick it up.

But she had to be strong. It could be days. Weeks. The message might never come at all.

This was almost worse than when she'd known nothing, expected nothing.

She began to walk in the bright morning air, concentrating on putting one foot in front of the other, trying to remember advice from her mindfulness classes – about keeping her head in the moment and not letting thoughts draw her away. It helped a bit. She concentrated on the feeling of her shoe hitting the stone underfoot, the sensation of warmth on her skin from the sun and the slight breeze, the sights, sounds and smells of St Vianne on a sunny, May morning.

She'd walk for twenty minutes, as fast as she could in her sundress and sandals, then turn and march back. And if she could help it (and she wasn't entirely confident about this), she'd try not to check her messages until after lunch. Or perhaps just before lunch. Or maybe a quick check when she first returned to the shop, then not until after lunch.

Or maybe... But her thoughts were interrupted as she accidentally stepped on an uneven stone on the kerbside. Her ankle twisted beneath her and she found herself sitting awkwardly on the pavement, her ankle giving a sharp twinge of pain and her hip and leg stinging as if slapped.

Instantly, despite the pain, she felt embarrassed and tried to get to her feet. The one or two people close by began to cross the road towards her as she heaved herself up and tried to smile. 'I'm fine,' she said, 'honestly.'

'Are you sure?' came a familiar voice. 'You took quite a tumble there.'

She looked up and realised that one of the hovering spectators was Michel. Seeing his kind, sympathetic face almost made her burst into tears – she wasn't sure whether this was because of the fall or her state of agonising uncertainty – but she managed to hold it together. Just.

'Yes, it's my own fault. Not concentrating.'

Michel nodded at the other man who'd come over to help as if to say, 'I'll take it from here,' and reached out to hold her arm. 'Allow me?' he said, dropping into English and putting on an upper-class accent.

She laughed – something that surprised her given the circumstances – and let him. 'If you insist, sir,' she returned in her own clipped tones.

They hobbled to a set of steps leading to a house that was clearly locked up and empty – its shutters newly painted, but fastened tightly against the light. She sank onto one of the steps gratefully, rubbing her ankle and her leg with her hand. She longed to rub her bottom too, but seeing as she was in the middle of town, judged that it wouldn't be the seemliest thing to do.

'I'm such an idiot,' she said.

'Not at all. It is the pavement that is the idiot. It has one job – to be smooth and enable us to walk. And it failed.'

She laughed again; Michel seemed to have a natural talent for cheering her up and she was grateful for it. 'I'll be OK,' she told him. 'You can get on if you like.'

'Perhaps in a moment. I'm not in a rush. I am avoiding my desk – I have to mark exams. In fact I was going to the shop – Monique called and asked.'

'Oh,' she said.

Their eyes locked.

'So you just happened to bump into me on the street...'

Michel laughed. 'She is persistent!'

'Yes. Although I don't think even Monique could have engineered my falling over,' she said, grimacing a little as she flexed her ankle.

Michel made a non-committal noise.

'Seriously?'

He shook his head. 'No, but sometimes I do wonder...'

It was hard to know whether he was joking or not.

'So, are you running an errand for Monique too?' he persisted.

'Oh, no. I'm actually just trying to distract myself,' she admitted.

He looked confused.

'It's a long story,' she said.

'Well, I have time,' he offered. 'And I'm sure that Monique won't mind if you are a little longer than planned. We could get a drink; you can tell me this long story. I am sure Monique would be very happy about this.' He rolled his eyes and grinned. 'Let her think her plan is working!'

She smiled. 'That's kind of you.' And she realised that she absolutely needed to tell someone. She couldn't talk to Monique, not pour salt on her friend's wounds over and over. And Chris would take hours to update, when she finally managed to get her on the phone. Kevin was also out. But she couldn't dump all of this on Michel either. She barely knew him.

'I...' she began, her mind racing. 'I just think it's probably best...'

'Ah, you do not have to tell me everything if you don't want,' he said. 'But if I am honest, you look as if you need a friend perhaps?'

To her horror, she felt the prickle of tears again. What was wrong with her? It was the kind of thing people said all the time. Only this time it hit hard. Because she really did. And she was realising more and more that she didn't have many people she could talk to. Caring for Mum had pushed friendships out of her life, had taken away thoughts of anything else. Now all she had was the void that was left; the space where her life used to be. And she was lonely.

'Perhaps a quick coffee...'

They began to walk together, Michel's hand on her elbow supporting her, braced, she could feel, in case she fell again on her weakened ankle.

Finally, they reached the cafe, and Michel pushed the door open and helped her into a chair, sinking into the one opposite with a sigh.

'Are you OK?' she asked.

He laughed. 'Yes, I'm fine. It is a new thing, this sighing when I sit. Perhaps I am getting old.'

She laughed. 'I doubt that very much.'

They ordered coffees then sat and sipped, and Adeline felt herself telling him all about her turmoil – how she'd dipped her toe into the pool of possibilities but wasn't sure if she was ready to take the plunge. And how she was both terrified her mother would reach out, and terrified that she wouldn't.

'Basically, I seem to spend half my life being terrified at the moment,' she said with a self-conscious grin.

He smiled back. 'I understand. I think anyone in your situation would feel this way.' He leaned forward slightly. 'But as I tell my pupils, remember that the times that are the most frightening can also be the most wonderful. When we change, we grow, we learn and we become more the person we were meant to be. And I think there is very little difference between being afraid and being excited.'

Adeline thought of the phone tucked under the counter at work, the photo online of her birth mother. The fact that at any moment she could make contact. It was terrifying.

But Michel was right. It was exciting too.

'Thank you,' she said.

They were just finishing up when the door opened and André came in, laden with white boxes from the patisserie. He walked to the counter and set them down, exchanging a few words with the manager, then turned to leave. Catching sight of the pair of them for the first time, he smiled and walked over. Michel rose to greet him, then gestured to Adeline. 'You already know each other, I think.'

'A little,' André said, smiling in Adeline's direction but not quite making eye contact.

'Yes. Not always in great circumstances,' Adeline admitted. 'I'm sorry I knocked into you that time.'

He made a flicking gesture with his hand. 'It is nothing.'

'But I was so rude! I was rushing, because...'

'You don't need to explain,' he said, although now he was looking at her directly. 'I also need to apologise for almost punching your brother!'

Adeline laughed. 'Oh well, he probably deserved it,' she joked.

There was a pause and Adeline found herself forming words in her mind. *Let me buy you a coffee to make up for it!* The sort of thing that someone more socially competent might say to a potential friend. But the words died before they reached her tongue.

André was just turning to go when Michel shot out a hand and put it on his forearm. 'Wait,' he said.

André looked at the hand quizzically.

'I have an idea,' Michel said, his eyes sparkling with mischief.

27

'Are you sure this is OK?' Adeline said as she leant heavily on his arm. Her ankle pain was ebbing away a little but it was still quite painful to walk. Later she'd ice it and it would hopefully feel better.

'Of course,' André said, supporting her weight effortlessly with his – ridiculously muscular, now she could see it up close – arm. He was wearing a T-shirt, and feeling his skin against hers as she hobbled felt strangely intimate.

As they rounded the corner she could see the bookshop, the light reflecting slightly on the glass, making it impossible to see beyond the book display in any detail. But she hoped that Monique might be there, peering out and hoping to witness the result of the engineered 'meet cute' between her and Michel.

'How about,' Michel had suggested in the cafe, 'André takes you back to the shop. Perhaps you can look a little romantic together? Perhaps, at last, this will show Monique that she may be able to control some things, but she cannot force two people together if they are not right for one another.'

'Oh, no,' Adeline had protested. 'We can't ask André to do that.'

But André was smiling. 'I am happy to help,' he'd said, offering an arm. 'It will be a pleasure.'

She wondered now, feeling the heat of his body close to hers, whether he'd meant it would be a pleasure to help send a message to Monique, or perhaps a pleasure to help his friend, Michel. Or was there any part of him that had meant it would be a pleasure to help her in this way?

And was it her imagination, or the fact that she'd spent too long in Monique's company, or did she really feel some sort of connection between them where their arms touched? A sort of tingle of recognition, as if he was both a brand-new acquaintance and someone she'd known for a very long time.

She looked up at his face, his jaw strong and set from this angle, his long-lashed eyes and tousled hair, and – perhaps sensing that she was looking – he glanced down at her.

She felt suddenly silly, hanging on to the arm of a man she barely knew, imagining all sorts of things. Could he sense it? She dropped his arm.

'I think I'll be OK from here,' she said, gesturing to the door of the bookshop just a few metres ahead.

'Are you sure?'

'Yes. Don't worry. And thanks for... you know, helping.'

'It was a pleasure.'

Which bit? she wanted to ask.

'I hope Monique will have got the message that she shouldn't meddle with matters of the heart,' André said. 'I hope she has seen us together.'

'Yes,' Adeline agreed.

'But perhaps...' he stepped forward so his body was just inches from hers again, his face leaning in towards her, his voice quiet. 'Perhaps we should make sure she definitely knows there is no chance for you and Michel.'

She looked at him, his earnest eyes hard to read. 'And how would we—' she began.

He gently leaned down and put a hand under her chin, tilting her face towards him. Then slightly hesitantly, he brought his lips to hers and kissed her carefully.

There it was again, that feeling of this being both a first kiss and something timeless. Before she had time to question herself, she found herself leaning into him, kissing him back.

* * *

Lili was finally asleep and, barely daring to breathe, Adeline stood and made her way out of her little girl's bedroom, closing the door softly behind her. She felt a flood of tiredness as her body finally acknowledged that she was exhausted – and still aching a little from her fall earlier.

Thinking of the fall made her think of André. The softness of his lips on hers. How, suddenly, he'd gone from being a virtual stranger to someone quite different. He'd pulled back. 'Do you think Monique has got the message?' he'd asked.

So it had all been for Monique. 'Yes, I think so,' she'd said, suddenly shy. 'Thank you.'

'And have you?' he'd added, his tone slightly faltering.

'What do you mean?'

He had stepped back slightly, his eyes glancing at her face then over her shoulder, avoiding eye contact. 'I like you, Adeline,' he had said.

She touched her lips now, feeling a mixture of pleasure and anxiety. He'd asked for her number and had already sent a message asking her out for a drink that week. And she'd found that although she was checking her phone for messages from Sophia, she was also now hoping to see messages from André too. She couldn't seem to help it.

She'd resolved not to get involved with anyone. Not to complicate her life when the pieces it had fractured into weren't yet set into place. But when his name flashed up on her phone, her reason seemed to go out of the window.

Downstairs in the living room, she sank into the chair and picked up her notebook from a side table. Using the Emily Dickinson book as a rest, and feeling slightly guilty about it, she turned over a new leaf and began to make a list.

Things I've lost:

- *Connection with friends – especially Chris*
- *Sense of purpose?*
- *Sense of home/family*

She chewed the end of her pen thoughtfully, thinking of the things that had fallen away from her life in recent months – friends, colleagues, even her sense of what she wanted, where she wanted to be...

Her relationship with Kevin had been damaged over the last year: they'd stopped joking, stopped talking about trivialities and instead spoken almost exclusively about Mum's care, the finances, how they would split their time; then the will and funeral arrangements.

Their argument and Adeline's subsequent escape to France had severed their bond completely for a while. Now, it was time to rebuild. Try to find the kind of playful, supportive relationship they'd had before. Something both old and brand new.

Before finding the papers, she'd had a sense of where she

belonged; she'd grown up in London and had lived there all her life. But finding her true birth certificate had thrown even that into question. She'd raced to France, convinced she was getting in touch with a piece of herself, but looking back, she'd been running away.

Michel was right; it had been a devastating time, but she could see that there were opportunities on the horizon too. To find a home that was right for her and Lili, to reconnect perhaps with her birth mother. To make new friends and rediscover old ones.

The sudden trill of her mobile phone sent her pen scuttering across the pad. She reached into her handbag and brought it out, convinced for a moment that it must be her birth mother – although of course she hadn't given out her number. Instead, the screen read 'Monique.'

'Hello?' she said, answering.

'Hello, Adeline. I'm sorry to call you in the evening.'

'It's OK. How can I help?'

There was a silence for a moment, the sound of breathing. Adeline realised suddenly that Monique was crying.

'Are you OK?' she asked.

'Everything is fine, but I need you to mind the shop tomorrow. Will that be OK? You have your key.'

'Of course!'

'Because I have to take a trip.' A pause. 'I have decided to go visit my mother.'

'Oh my God. Monique! I mean, that's wonderful,' she said, hoping this was the right response. 'Terrifying' might have been a better word.

'*Oui*, it is perhaps. I have called. I spoke to my sister. She was a little cold. But I understand. And my mother, she is quite old now. Almost ninety. A little frail. But she has her mind. It was only when I came to call that I wondered whether it might be too late, that I might have lost my chance.'

'Oh, Monique! What did she say?'

'Ah, nothing. I did not speak with her. She was in bed. But my sister told me I should come. That she would talk better in person. And I am sure she is right. I cannot wait now that I have decided. So I will take the train to Paris, early. And be back, I hope, by the evening.'

'That's fine. Of course. Longer if you need.'

'Thank you.'

'I can...' Adeline began.

'*Pardon*?'

'I can come with you, if you need,' she offered.

There was a short silence. Then, '*Non*,' Monique said. 'But thank you. That is a kind offer.'

'It's fine. Just take care, OK?'

* * *

The next morning, the shop felt odd without Monique's presence. Although Adeline had been left in it alone many times previously, Monique had never been far away – either busying herself in the apartment above or out running errands and calling in and out as she did so.

Today it was as if something was missing from the small space – an energy that was usually there. Adeline smiled, greeted customers and tried as best she could to watch Lili who was alternating between being wonderful, reading or colouring at her small table, or racing around the shop to expend excess energy and occasionally having a near miss with an unsuspecting browser.

There was a steady stream of customers, once in a while a

queue would form at the counter which was almost unheard of when Adeline and Monique were both in position. Once, Adeline lost sight of Lili for a moment and worried she'd taken the opportunity to exit through the open door and onto the sunny street outside. But then she'd spotted a little blonde head behind one of the stacked tables and felt her insides relax.

When lunchtime arrived, she was relieved to be able to turn the little sign in the window to 'Closed' and lock the door on any customer who might try the handle just in case. With Lili in tow and the shop busy, she hadn't felt able to go up to the flat and make herself a coffee; her throat felt dry and her whole body heavy and tired. It wasn't just the busyness of the shop, or the need to look after her child – or at least keep half an eye on her – while working. It was the thought of Monique, too, some-where on a train or walking towards her childhood home, her head full of questions, that weighed on Adeline's mind.

'Come on, Lili, Monique said we could use the apartment for lunch. Shall we go up?'

Lili – clearly delighted – raced up the stairs and through the door before Adeline got her shoe on the bottom step. Once Adeline reached the top, she'd already flung herself on Monique's special chaise longue, a piece of furniture that Monique guarded fiercely and had only let Lili sit on once, after removing her shoes and making sure that her hands weren't sticky.

'Off that,' Adeline said.

Lili acquiesced sulkily and plonked herself in her usual chair at the table, slumped. It was at times like this, when defi-ance broke through her daughter's happy exterior, that Adeline wondered exactly what might be waiting for her when puberty hit.

Luckily, at five, the mood didn't last long and was cured by the offer of baguette with Nutella and a glass of milk.

Adeline watched her child dig into her rather unhealthy lunch and sipped from her own cup of tea. She'd cook something proper for dinner, but right now she just wanted to take a weight off.

She dug out her phone and unlocked the screen for the first time since she'd opened the shop, seeing several notifications flash up. A sale at one of the stores she'd frequented back in London, an offer for virus protection for a laptop she no longer owned, a newsletter from an IT specialist she couldn't remember signing up to, and a message about a book she'd enquired about online.

A text pinged in from André and she opened it with a smile. He asked her to call past the patisserie on the way home. He had a cake he'd saved for her and Lili.

And then she saw the last message in her inbox. A notification from the DNA site.

In all the chaos and busyness, she'd forgotten her usual email refreshing. And of course that had been the moment when her birth mother had decided to get in touch. She felt suddenly cold as she tapped the link and entered her password to get onto the site. And finally read the words, written in French.

Adeline, my baby girl. I am so glad to hear from you. Of course I would like to get to know you.

* * *

It was impossible to eat. To drink. To do any more than act as normal as possible on the surface and get through the rest of the day.

Her fingers itched to write a response, but she didn't want to fire something off without thinking about it – and had no time to think about it as Lili, newly energised from her sugar intake, rushed around the shop, the customers flowed in and out and time seemed to move at a frustratingly stilted pace.

By six o'clock, things had quietened down. Lili was in the apartment watching YouTube on her mother's phone – a rare treat but much needed – and Adeline was tidying and stacking and making the final checks on the shop before closing time, when the bell at the door tinkled.

She straightened from where she'd been reorganising a low shelf, ready to serve yet another customer and determined to – this time – stay focused enough to at least hand them the right book.

Except it wasn't a customer.

Standing just inside the door was a woman she recognised, but who didn't look quite like herself. Her skin was paler, eyes seemed larger, their shadows deeper and more ingrained into the skin. Her hair was tied up but strands escaped to wildly frame the face. Her cheeks and eyes were tinged pink, her dress rumpled. The bag she was carrying dropped from her hand.

'Monique!' Adeline exclaimed, alarmed at her friend's appearance. She rushed forward to support her, picking up the bag and guiding her to a chair. 'Are you OK?'

'*Oui*.' Monique's voice was flat, monotone.

'But you seem... Have you been crying? Was it OK? Was it awful? Did your mother—'

'It was incredible.'

'It was? Oh, I'm so pleased. Did you... your mother – did she answer your questions? Did she...' Adeline realised she was babbling. She took a breath, steadied herself. Part of her longed to blurt out the fact that she'd heard from her own mother. But it wasn't the right time, clearly. 'Did you get some answers?' she asked at last, her tone carefully controlled, more measured.

'*Oui*. But Adeline, I did not expect the answers I received,' Monique said, her expression unreadable.

'Oh.' Adeline was trying to phrase a question correctly – forming the words in her head before blurting them out. She wanted to ask whether that was a good or bad thing, whether Monique's mother and sister had been friendly or hostile. Whether she had more information about what had happened all those years ago. But she didn't want to overstep the mark. This was Monique's story, Monique's private business. She didn't want to push her before she was ready.

But Monique suddenly turned to her, clutched at her hands, making her jump. 'I found out that my mother lied to me,' she said, her eyes filled with an indefinable emotion.

Adeline nodded, seeing that there was more to come.

Carefully, her voice trembling slightly, Monique looked her in the eye. 'Adeline, my baby. My little girl. She is not dead. She didn't die.'

28

Adeline dialled Stacey's number, then after the phone began to ring she almost wished she hadn't. But too late, Stacey answered the phone with a friendly 'Hi!'

'Hi, it's Adeline from the shop,' she said, feeling suddenly shy. 'I thought I might take you up on that offer of a coffee, if you've got time?'

'Sounds good to me!' Stacey said, instantly friendly. 'Everything all right?'

'Yes. Well, kind of. There's a couple of things...'

'Long story?'

'Long story.'

Once they'd agreed on the venue and time and ended the call, Adeline wondered whether she'd made a mistake. It was one thing to get to know a new person, quite another to dump what was proving to be a rather complicated dilemma in their lap. But something about Stacey – her openness, friendliness and the fact that she wasn't part of the story herself – made her seem like the best option Adeline had when it came to unburdening herself and seeking advice.

Over the past few days, since Monique's visit to Paris and her life-changing discovery, her friend had been quiet and withdrawn. It was hardly surprising; but Adeline was worried about her all the same. The combination of the revelation and Monique's obvious shock had also meant she'd felt unable to tell Monique that her own mother had responded; it seemed the wrong time to ask advice about the meeting they were planning, wrong to offload her fears and hopes onto someone who had so much to process.

On the day that Monique had returned, pale-faced, to the shop, carrying the news that she'd never dared hope she'd receive, they'd sat up late into the night in the apartment, Lili fast asleep in Monique's bed and excited to be having a 'sleepover' at her *Mamie*'s.

Monique had told her how her mother – with misguided but loving intentions – had told her that her baby had died, in the hope that it would give her some sort of closure; free her from the idea that her child was out there somewhere and needed her. 'She thought she was saving me from a lifetime of wondering, that I would grieve properly, deeply, but be able to move on with my life without the shadow of what had happened hanging over me.'

'But what about when she realised how much it had affected you?' Adeline had asked, incredulous.

'Ah, she was trapped,' Monique had said, pouring them both another glass of red wine. 'She knew I was angry, that I blamed her first for the adoption and then for the fact that my baby had died – because I was convinced it would not have happened if she had been left with me. She wanted to mend things with me and was afraid that confessing would simply make things worse. And I think she still hoped that I would eventually be able to build a new life after my grief.'

'But you couldn't...'

Monique, calmer after a couple of glasses of wine, had shrugged. 'Well, I did in a fashion. Just not the kind of life my mother imagined I'd have. No husband. No more babies.'

Adeline had nodded. 'And have you... will you be able to forgive her?' she asked.

Monique had fixed her eyes on Adeline then. '*Oui*,' she said. 'I have already done it.'

This seemed incredible after decades of no contact and Adeline's face had obviously registered surprise.

'My mother is old,' Monique explained. 'I have punished her with years of silence, I see that now. And before, when I ran away, I was a child. I saw only what a child would see. That my mother had stolen my baby and did not understand my pain. And I carried that vision of my mother for so many years; something I had constructed in childhood. But now I am a woman, and I have known pain, known life. And I looked in my mother's eyes and I saw that I had hurt her perhaps just as much as she had hurt me. I understood that her decision had not been easy as I had imagined, but done with love. Because I was young, and times were different. And she hoped so much for me.'

'Well, that's really generous of you.'

Monique shrugged. 'Perhaps the child inside me will never fully forgive her, but the woman I am now can build something new with what time we have left. My sister,' she added, taking a big sip of wine, 'is another matter.'

'Oh dear.'

'*Oui*, because she has watched the pain I have inflicted on my mother for all these years and she blames me for that. And of course she has petitioned me over and over again to visit to forgive, and I was stubborn and wouldn't communicate. I understand. It will take time. But we are not so old. There will be time.'

'And the baby...' Adeline had hardly dared mention this fact. 'What are you going to do? Are you going to try to find her?'

Monique sighed. 'It is hard to imagine her after all this time. For so many years, I imagined her as a baby who had her life taken so young. It is hard to imagine her as a woman. As someone I might meet, perhaps. Yes, I want to find her. But like you, I am afraid.'

The days that had followed had been strange. Monique had seemed shaken and exhausted, and while they'd spoken about books and the weather and their customers, they hadn't broached the subject of the baby again. And Adeline had not been able to say anything to Monique about her mother's message, or the fact that she'd responded; that she'd found her mother lived in Toulouse, just a few hours away on the train.

But she needed to tell someone. Someone who knew both her and Monique, both of their stories.

* * *

School had resumed the day before, and Lili had reluctantly sloped into the playground before seeming to remember that she actually loved her time in the little stone building with the other children, and rushing forward to see her friends.

By the time Stacey arrived in the cafe, hanging her coat on the hat stand and looking around before breaking into a smile as their eyes met, Adeline was almost jittery with a combination of nerves and over-caffeination. She'd taken the morning off work with Monique's permission to 'meet a friend' but had felt so restless at home she'd decided to sit in the cafe with a book until Stacey arrived.

Stacey plonked herself down unceremoniously in the chair opposite and grinned. 'How's things?' she said. Then, before Adeline could respond, 'Actually, hold that thought. Can I get you another coffee?' She gestured to Adeline's empty cup. 'I'm gasping.'

'I think I'd probably better get something less... stimulating,' Adeline admitted. 'I've managed to get through three of these things already.'

'Orange juice?'

'Perfect.'

Stacey made her way to the counter to place their order and returned with a tray, bearing an enormous latte and a tall glass of orange juice, complete with paper straw.

'Right,' she said, propping her elbows on the table and lifting her cup to her lips. 'Spill.'

'Are you sure you don't mind? We hardly know each other. I feel a bit... it's just I didn't know who else to call.'

'Course I'm sure,' Stacey said, smiling. 'Believe me, I'm settled here now, but it was tough at first. And I had Matt and the kids to offload to. So! Out with it!'

'OK.' Adeline prepared herself, taking a brief sip through her straw and feeling her taste buds fizz as the tangy orange broke through their coffee coating. 'Here we go.'

She relayed her story, as far as she knew it, and saw Stacey's eyes grow wider with every revelation.

'Bloody hell, it's like an episode of *Coronation Street*!'

'Ha. I suppose it is. *Coronation Street, en France*.'

'Sorry, I don't mean to make light of it. It must be tough. Losing your mum like that, then finding out... and your boss having all that going on too.' Stacey puffed out her cheeks in an expression of disbelief and expelled a noisy breath. 'It is A LOT. I'm not surprised you needed to talk to someone.'

'Yes. And, you know... Thank you, for listening.'

'So you're going to see your mum?'

'My birth mum, yes. Soon, actually.'

'Bloody hell. And you're dating André?'

'I don't know. No. I mean... We're meeting for a drink. It's just... I'm not sure I really want all that...'

'All that? What – Provence's most eligible bachelor, you mean?'

'Provence's?'

'Oh OK, St Vianne's at least.'

They smiled. Then Adeline shook her head. 'I don't know, Stacey. It just... I like him, obviously. But the last thing I need – Lili needs – is another man to let us down.'

'Who says he'd do that?'

'Bitter experience,' Adeline said, making a face.

Stacey shook her head. 'I hear you. But you know, maybe give him a chance. He really seems to like you.'

'Yeah,' Adeline agreed. 'Quite a surprise after everything... I was sure he couldn't stand me at one point.'

'Very *Pride and Prejudice,* isn't it? All the glowering and simmering tension, then whipping you up in his arms.'

'I thought it was *Coronation Street.*'

'*Coronation Street* meets Jane Austen.'

They laughed, then gradually this died away as Adeline thought again about her mother, what might happen going forward. Stacey was right. It was A LOT. But having said it all out loud had given her a release. She felt more relaxed, more able to smile at it all.

Stacey shook her head. 'Well, for what it's worth, I think you're pretty amazing.'

'Really?'

'Yeah. Course. Coming here by yourself. Doing that test. Writing to your mum – your birth mum, I mean.'

'Thank you.'

'Plus bagging our resident hunk in the process.'

Adeline smiled. 'One kiss,' she said. 'That's all.'

'So far,' Stacey said, her eyes twinkling. 'But seriously, your whole life has been blown apart but you're... I dunno. You're kind of working through it, and fixing it. I'd probably still be in the denial phase if it were me.'

'Denial would definitely be easier.'

'Wine helps,' Stacey said with a wink.

They slipped into silence for a moment, both finishing the last of their drinks.

'Thank you.'

'Don't be daft, it's just an orange juice.'

'No. For coming. For listening.'

Stacey reached a hand over and gave Adeline's a squeeze. 'You're welcome, my love. And look – if it makes you feel any better, I've enjoyed it. It's nice to feel like I'm helping. My kids are all far too big and self-sufficient for me these days. Nice to feel a bit like a mum again. Well, not a mum – you've got enough of those – but...' she trailed off.

'I know what you mean.'

'Plus,' Stacey added with a wicked grin, 'I've always been a big fan of *Coronation Street*.'

29

'Stand still!' Adeline told wriggling Lili as she tried to tie the ribbon on her dress into a bow. She stood back and Lili twirled gleefully.

'Ah, but you are beautiful!' Monique said, smiling.

It was eight o'clock, and after work, Monique had made Adeline and Lili dinner in the flat – a boeuf bourguignon that she'd had in the slow cooker for most of the day – and was now helping Adeline prepare Lili's costume for the upcoming *spectacle* at the school. Lili's only instructions had been to be as colourful as possible, so the brief was an open one. Adeline had brought over one of Lili's dresses and Monique had helped her fasten ribbons and bows to the costume until it glowed with the colours of the rainbow. Lili walked over to the mirror they'd propped against a wall for the purpose and admired herself, her face glowing.

It was probably time to ask, Adeline thought.

She looked at Monique, who'd seemed to come back into herself over the last few days. Michel had come to see her a couple of times; clearly talking it through with him had helped

Monique to come to terms with everything. Adeline still hadn't felt able to bring the subject up again though, and because of that had also been reluctant to mention her own potential reunion. But it was time.

'I'm going to need a day off on Monday, if that's possible?' she asked.

Monique looked up from where she was winding ribbons around her fingers to store back in the empty biscuit tin she kept odds and ends in, a question in her face. 'Of course. I hope everything is OK?'

'Yes. Actually, I'm going to Toulouse. On Sunday, and staying over.' She paused. 'I've arranged to see Sophia, my – well – my birth mother.' Her hands felt hot and she found herself fidgeting uncomfortably.

Monique turned quickly to look at her, her eyes unreadable. 'Well, that is wonderful! Why didn't you mention this before?'

'It just didn't seem the right time,' she admitted, looking down.

Monique nodded, taking it in. 'Well of course you can have all the time you need.'

'Thank you.'

There was a silence. 'I will come with you, if you want? The shop does not open on Mondays in any case,' said Monique abruptly.

'Oh, no. It's fine. I'll be – we'll be fine.'

'But I think it would be helpful. I can mind Lili while you speak to your mother. And perhaps help you in the evenings with her. And besides, I have a feeling... I think it might be important that I come with you.'

Adeline considered. 'You're sure you wouldn't mind?'

Monique smiled. 'It is about time I left St Vianne for a holiday. And Toulouse is a nice place. Why not?'

'Well, that's really kind of you!'

Monique shrugged. '*C'est normal*. Friends support each other, *non*?'

'Yes. Yes, they do,' Adeline smiled. The question bubbled up in her before she had time to overthink it. 'And you?'

'Me?'

'Have you thought any more about your... well, your baby?'

Monique gave a single nod. '*Oui*, it is constant.'

'And?'

'And I have some feelings about it. But I cannot share them yet. Not until I am sure.'

'Sorry, I didn't mean to pry.'

'Not at all. It is nice to have someone who cares enough to ask.'

Adeline nodded, her attention drawn to the window as a bird swooped past.

Outside, it was bright and light; the day still had all the trappings of early summer – warmth, birdsong, people calling to each other or walking by. There was an energy in the air – as if the world had been paused on its axis for a time but had now started to move once more. Everything was changing, but the change was positive.

Lili turned from the mirror and began trying to pull the dress down over her arms. 'Finished,' she said.

'Oh, don't rip it!' Adeline cried. 'Come here, sweetheart.'

Lili came over obediently and raised her arms to help Adeline slip off her dress. As soon as she was back in her former outfit of leggings and a T-shirt, she sat on the chaise longue and started bouncing slightly.

'Lili! Don't!' Adeline found herself shouting.

But Monique shook her head. 'Ah, let her,' she said. 'It is only furniture. It's not important.'

To hear Monique say this about her precious chaise longue was more than a shock. Lili's face cracked open with a smile and she continued to jiggle, delighted that her behaviour had been endorsed.

'Still, you don't want it ruined,' Adeline said.

'Right now, I could not care less about it.' She turned to Adeline, her eyes shining, the smile on her face full and genuine. 'Because the thing I hoped for more than anything has happened. My baby is alive. The furniture, it really doesn't matter.'

Adeline smiled, their eyes locking. She wondered what had led to this sudden optimism, but perhaps it was the fact that she was meeting Sophia – perhaps she'd inspired Monique to hope. Whatever it was, it could not be a bad thing.

* * *

After reading the message from her birth mother, Adeline had found herself closing her email screen and putting away her phone. It was hard to know exactly what to do, what to say. What exactly she wanted to happen next. Then, before she'd had time to form a proper reply, another message had arrived.

Adeline, I know this must be difficult for you. I imagine you might have complicated feelings towards me. Perhaps my earlier message didn't acknowledge that. I realise we have a lot to learn about each other, that things might not be easy. It is just that I have waited so long to find you that it was impossible not to be filled with joy at your message. Then I thought about it and realised that you don't know your story. You don't know why I had to give you up. Perhaps you hate me for this? I understand if you are not sure whether you want to see me. But I would love the opportunity to talk, to explain. To at least put to rest some of the things that I've carried with me for so long. I hope we can find a way. Sophia.

She'd replied at last:

Hi Sophia, thank you for understanding. It is difficult. My lovely adoptive mum died recently, and I only just learned about my adoption. So it's all very new. I would like to see you though. Shall I come to Toulouse?

She'd forced herself to press 'Send' before she changed her mind. And, although it would involve some travelling, she'd chosen to go to her mother rather than the other way around, as it gave her more control. She didn't have to reveal her exact whereabouts to this stranger if it turned out she didn't want to know her. She could control the length of time she stayed, when she arrived, when she left. It seemed better this way.

Afterwards, she'd tried to compose an email to Kevin. It had felt confessional. As if she'd done something to hurt them both and had to apologise for it. Every time she'd composed a sentence, a stumbling paragraph, she'd deleted it almost immediately. She simply couldn't find the words. Maybe it was better to tell him afterwards, when she knew exactly what her situation was.

The two days that had passed between then and now had been a blur. Thankfully the shop had been busy – there were more and more tourists locally, many flocking to the shop for English language titles. Their book recommendations had become more ordinary – based on a person's potential enjoyment rather than anything more therapeutic.

Still, whenever the shop had grown quiet and she'd looked at Monique, feeling that this could be the moment to tell her boss about the trip she planned to make, it had felt like the wrong time. She'd talked about benign things such as the weather, or books, or the fact that Claude – who'd been back to the shop several times – was looking so much better.

She still hadn't thought what she might tell Lili about it all. Her daughter was oblivious to her recent discoveries – she hadn't wanted to upset or confuse her. Now, thinking about Monique's offer to babysit, she realised how important it would be to have some time alone with Sophia to talk properly. And to have the option, if things didn't go well, to choose not to introduce her child to this complicated part of their history.

She looked again at Lili who had now slumped on the chaise longue, passing from full energy to almost unconsciousness in the way only little children can.

'Think I'd better get this one home,' she said, nodding at her daughter.

Monique looked and smiled. 'Yes, perhaps.'

'Thank you. You know, for the costume. For everything, really.'

'It is OK.' Monique paused. 'That is what family is for.'

30

It was raining. Adeline felt a little guilty as she rushed along the road with Lili who, even wrapped in her shiny yellow raincoat, was getting her face and exposed legs soaked. They passed the market, its usually colourful awnings dripping with relentless moisture – a few sad, soggy people with baskets and raincoats, or clutching umbrellas, perused the stands behind which stall-holders shivered and hugged themselves.

Hopefully at least, she thought, rounding the bend and finally coming to a halt in front of the shop, it would be a quiet morning – she'd have time to collect her thoughts and speak to Monique about their trip tomorrow.

An hour later, she was kicking herself for having tempted fate. While the rain had driven people away from the open-air stalls, it seemed to have driven more people than ever into the bookshop. Some browsed, sheltering from the rain and with no intention of buying, others looked more seriously. The window at the front became thick with condensation, the umbrella stand by the door heaving with damp nylon.

Lili was restless, bored of the books, wanting to go outside and splash in puddles and resisting any inducement to go up to the flat and play with something there. She clung to Adeline, whinging and complaining, and Adeline found herself being short with her, then feeling guilty – after all, who really wanted to spend Saturday morning at their mum's workplace?

In the end, Monique managed to prise Lili from Adeline's leg and entice her up to the flat with the promise of some cartoons on her laptop and – the clincher – some of Monique's patisserie-bought madeleines. Adeline smiled as the woman took Lili's hand and walked with her up the wooden staircase, disappearing from view. She turned back to the customer in front of her, determined to give her full attention and feeling some of the stress she'd experienced draining away.

She even managed to recommend a book for Claude, who popped in and expressed a desire for detective fiction, and sold a collection of short stories to a woman with a stern face who wanted a light read.

It was close to midday when the post arrived. Usually, the postwoman would deliver to the box just outside, but today she brought the letters into the shop, already peppered with raindrops. 'Your box has a leak,' she explained. 'They would have been ruined.'

'Oh, thanks. I'll tell Monique,' Adeline said, taking the pile of letters from her.

She sorted out the bills, letters addressed to the shop, and put a couple of leaflets into the recycling box. Then she placed the pile next to the computer, nudging the mouse.

The screen lit up with Monique's email inbox – she must have forgotten to log out. Leaning in, she grabbed the mouse and moved the cursor to the 'x' at the edge of the screen to close it for her. Then stopped when her eye caught a familiar company name in the list of new emails received. It was the

DNA company, and the heading read 'Thank you for your enquiry.'

Had Monique decided to do a test too?

Adeline resolved not to say anything, unless Monique mentioned it herself. But it was hard not to feel her heart fill with hope for her friend. If Monique's baby was still out there, if she was able to make contact, it would be truly wonderful.

She was smiling at the thought when the bell rang and André walked into the shop carrying a white cardboard box emblazoned with the name of the patisserie. '*Bonjour*,' he smiled.

'*Salut*.' She felt herself prickle with energy, as she always did when he was close. A kind of electrical charge. Something magical.

He lay the box on the counter. 'Something sweet for you,' he said grinning.

'Thank you.' She peeped in to see the glisten of a strawberry tart – her favourite.

'And later? We can have a glass of wine?' he asked.

She nodded. In truth it wasn't the ideal timing, with her trip booked for tomorrow. But she was loathe to put it off – she was tired of putting things on hold, wanted to embrace this forward motion that had suddenly come into her life.

By now the rain had cleared, but the saturated streets still glistened with moisture. André gently touched the top of her arm and nodded. '*À tout à l'heure*,' he said. 'See you later.'

The shop was silent once he'd left. It was ten to twelve so, rather than sit and overthink things, she decided to turn the sign to 'Closed' and make her way up to the apartment to see whether Monique was all right, or whether she needed rescuing from Lili. She resolved to look into other childcare options if they decided to stay here beyond her trial period. What had seemed simple in principle – Lili sitting and reading or drawing in the shop when not at school – was in practice becoming a bit more complicated.

She knocked lightly on the half-open door then made her way into the hallway. She saw Lili, sitting on the chaise longue, shoes still on, watching Monique's laptop which was balanced on a small table, transfixed by the colourful cartoons that played out their make-believe on screen. Monique was nowhere to be seen.

Walking further, Adeline peered into the little kitchenette, its surface cluttered with coffee cups and a half-filled pot. But nothing.

'Monique?' she said softly, walking forward and pushing open the door that led to her bedroom. She found her friend sitting on the bed, her shoes slipped off, her legs crossed in their long floral skirt. When Adeline entered, Monique jumped to her feet almost guiltily. She was holding her phone and a piece of paper, her mouth a straight line, her brow furrowed.

'Sorry!' Adeline apologised. 'I didn't mean to interrupt. Do you have a headache?'

'*Oui,*' she said, putting her hand to her head as if to demonstrate. 'It is too much coffee, perhaps. Or maybe too little.' She tried to smile, but her face was pinched.

'Is everything... else OK?'

'I just have a lot in my own head right now, but sometimes it is not the right time to talk.'

Adeline nodded. 'I know what you mean. It can be overwhelming, can't it?' She thought again of Sophia's email, of the address she now had recorded in her phone. Of the tickets she'd printed out for tomorrow's journey. 'If you do want to though,' she added, 'I'm always here.'

'Ah, thank you.' Monique said. This time when their eyes

met, Adeline noticed that Monique's were swimming with tears. 'You are truly a godsend. I will talk. I will. Just, when I know what the words are.'

Adeline nodded. '"Saying nothing sometimes says the most",' she found herself saying.

Monique barked out a single laugh. 'Dickinson?'

'Yes,' Adeline grinned.

She walked a few more steps into the room and tentatively touched Monique's shoulders, then pulled her into a hug. To her surprise, Monique pulled her arms around Adeline's back and held her tightly for a moment. There was that energy, the fizz she remembered from last time. As if every part of Monique were magic, as if there were something flowing from her that connected with Adeline in some inexplicable way.

The sun outside the window, already becoming stronger as it freed itself from behind the tangle of clouds, began to shine in earnest, rays escaping from their waterlogged prison and beginning the work of drying the cobbled street, the shop awnings, the cars and people soaked by the morning's rain. It was nature, coincidence, not magic; yet there was something magical about it, as if the weather had decided to send her a message – that no matter what storms life threw at her, the sun would always emerge eventually from its hiding place.

Adeline hadn't met her birth mother yet, so had no idea what feelings that meeting might evoke in her, but right now, at this moment, she realised that even if things fell apart in Toulouse, she'd found someone – not a mother, exactly, but someone who was becoming part of the family she was creating for herself.

She thought back to when Michel had described Monique as 'family, but not my blood family' and realised it was true. Kevin, Monique, and even the mother who'd raised her – none of these people were connected to her via DNA. Yet all of them were as important to her as any family could be.

Even if tomorrow didn't work out the way she hoped, she had already begun to anchor herself, to find the missing pieces of herself and put them back together.

31

She looked in the mirror again. The woman who looked back was wearing a red summer dress, patterned with white flowers. It was something she'd ordered online, inspired by Monique's unabashed love of bright colours – and she had to admit it looked pretty good on. But was it her?

She'd straightened her hair a little and used a bit of volumizing mousse on the roots; then brushed everything out and simply tucked it behind her ears, the way that felt comfortable to her. Then added earrings – something she hadn't bothered with for a while.

And although she wasn't always comfortable with the way she looked, even she had to admit that she'd scrubbed up quite well.

Even so, on André's arm, she knew she'd feel nervous. As if she were simply waiting for it all to fall apart.

'Can I come?' A little voice in the background made her turn and there was Lili in her rumpled unicorn pyjamas, wearing a scowl.

'Oh, baby. Next time. We're going to a grown-up place,' Adeline said, turning and leaning down for a hug.

Lili slipped out of her grasp, refusing to acquiesce.

'Anyway, Monique's coming round tonight!' Adeline said, keeping her voice as bright as possible. 'She's going to play some games with you.'

Lili's face brightened at the thought, before she remembered that she was angry with her mum and scowled again, with slightly less conviction.

Adeline laughed and ruffled her daughter's hair. 'I won't be out for long anyway. We're off on a train tomorrow, remember?'

Half an hour later, Lili was happily curled on the sofa with Monique, looking at the first of quite a pile of books Monique had brought over from the shop. Watching the pair of them snuggled together gave Adeline a sudden pang – remembering how her mum and Lili had often sat together, watching cartoons or playing snap or cuddling and reading just like this. Her stomach gave a guilty somersault as she thought about what she was going to do tomorrow. But it wasn't a betrayal, she reminded herself. Mum would always be Mum – how could she not be?

Then there was a knock on the door and her stomach gave another kind of somersault – more from excitement this time, although she wished her innards wouldn't react to every emotion she had and simply do their job of digesting the hurried meal of savoury crêpes she'd made for herself and Lili an hour earlier.

She felt both Monique's and Lili's eyes on her as she opened the door to André, who was grinning self-consciously on the front step. He handed her a flower, plucked en route by the looks of things, and she thanked him and laid it on the bureau before turning to Monique and Lili. 'Be good,' she said to Lili.

'Ah, we will,' Monique joked. 'Go have fun!' Then, 'And look after her, André,' she called as the two of them exited.

Adeline pulled the door behind her and grimaced slightly. 'Sorry about that,' she said to a grinning André. 'I guess she's quite protective of her staff.'

'Don't worry, it's nice. And in any case, she has nothing to worry about.'

They walked in silence for a few moments; Adeline racking her brain about what to say. 'How was work?' she asked eventually.

André laughed. 'Yes, very good – and yours?'

'Yes. Good.'

He laughed again. 'What?' she asked.

'Ah, nothing. I'm not laughing at you, don't worry. But perhaps at us. Because we are so desperate to speak to each other properly, but it is hard to know what to say at first, *non*?'

And she laughed too. 'Yes,' she said. Then, 'Sorry.'

André's hand nudged at hers, finding its way in between her fingers until they were holding hands. His grip was warm, firm, comforting. 'I do not think you are responsible for this,' he said. 'I think it is normal when you get to know someone new. But don't worry. We have plenty of time to learn about each other. To find things to say. And sometimes, too, it is fine to say nothing at all.' He squeezed her hand gently.

And she felt herself relax as she realised the truth in his words. This wasn't a job interview, or the kind of date where you had to get everything right or risk rejection. It didn't actually have to be a date, officially. Just an evening out; a drink. They had all the time in the world.

* * *

Later, when Adeline let herself into the house, Monique was alone on the sofa, curled up with a well-thumbed copy of *Chocolat*. Adeline realised it was her book, the one she'd brought with her when she came. Monique, hearing her, laid the book down, carefully marking the page with a bookmark and smiled at her.

'So was it good?' she asked.

Adeline smiled. 'It was lovely, thank you.'

André appeared from the front doorstep behind her. 'Good evening, Monique. I wanted to say goodnight. And thank you for helping Adeline.'

Monique looked at him, not quite smiling. 'It was my pleasure,' she said. She began to get to her feet.

'Oh, no, don't rush off,' Adeline said. 'André's not staying.'

She walked up to the man whom she'd spent the last two hours opening up to. Saying so many things that she hadn't expected to, things that might ordinarily be too much for a first date. But it had felt so comfortable, so familiar once they had finally begun to talk, and her carefully constructed guard had crumbled under the warmth of his gaze, the squeeze of his hand over the table. And the couple of glasses of Pinot Grigio had helped enormously too, of course.

She stepped just outside the front door to see him off. 'Thanks again. I had a lovely time.'

'Me too.' He kissed her, softly, moving his hand to the small of her back and holding her to him.

'Thank you.'

'And I'll see you again?' His was a question rather than a statement.

'When I get back,' she smiled.

'Good luck tomorrow,' he said as he turned to leave.

'Thank you.' She realised that although she'd spoken about

everything with André tonight, her feelings of worry and anxiety and stress at the impending meeting had disappeared during the time they were together.

Inside, Monique looked at her quizzically. 'So he behaved himself?'

'Monique! Of course he did!'

'Ah, he is a good boy,' Monique nodded. 'A little wild, perhaps, when he was growing up. But I think he is becoming a good man. Perhaps not good enough for you,' she added, pointedly. 'But a good man nonetheless.'

Adeline laughed. 'Glad to hear it,' she said, wondering whether Monique still harboured secret hopes for her and Michel.

They faced each other. 'Well, I will go,' Monique said. 'We must get some rest before tomorrow.'

'Yes,' Adeline agreed. And there it was, the feeling in her stomach back again. 'Or try at least.'

Monique leaned and kissed her forehead – a gentle, motherly gesture. 'Yes, *ma belle*, we will try.'

'Monique,' Adeline said, her voice sounding small, uncertain, as her friend opened the front door into the warm night air.

Monique turned, her eyes deep and dark in the shadows. 'Yes?'

'Will it... Will it be OK?' she asked. 'Do you feel that things are going to work out?'

Monique pressed a hand to her chest. 'With all my heart, Adeline,' she said. 'With all my heart.'

As she shut the door, Adeline felt a little embarrassed at having asked. She didn't fully believe Monique could feel such things, predict the future. Know things that were unknowable.

But she had to admit that hearing Monique's confidence

sent a flood of calmness through her. As if, on some level, she could feel it too.

32

'Is it a castle, Mummy?'

Adeline smiled as she crossed the road towards the station building. It was an impressive sight – stone-built, with an enormous clock tower at one end, and a roof that was tinted green. Cars lined the three taxi lanes outside and swarms of people disappeared through the more modern sliding doors of the entrance.

Stepping inside was a little like travelling forward in time – the clean, tiled floor, glass-fronted ticket offices, digital ticket machines and shiny-signed cafes seemed initially out of place in such a beautiful old building. The modernity reminded Adeline of home – of rushing for a train in London, grabbing a takeaway coffee, buying a ticket on a digital screen, taking an escalator to the correct platform. After seven weeks in St Vianne, she'd become used to a gentler pace of life, of scenery that had barely changed for decades.

It felt odd, too, to have Monique at her side – the woman who'd seemed to belong to St Vianne, whose style and way of life seemed to belong to a simpler time, now somehow out of place in this contemporary setting.

Being here awoke something in Adeline, a strange home-sickness for things that she'd known all her life. Her time back in London, her friends, even her apartment. The Petite Librairie felt a million miles away, and when she allowed her mind briefly to drift over recent events – the tingle in her fingers when she'd chosen the book for Claude, the connection she'd felt with the Dickinson poetry, even the date with André – it seemed odd, as if it were something she'd dreamt rather than experienced.

They soon found the right platform and, ten minutes later, an eight-carriage train trundled to a stop in front of them. The speaker loudly proclaimed the stations they'd stop at between here and Toulouse, and then they were on board, walking down aisles with digital numbers displayed above, trying to find their seats.

Once they'd settled and Adeline had handed Lili a colouring pad and a new pack of pencils, she drew a book from her bag and tried to lose herself in its pages. But it was impossible; her mind kept pulling her back to the present – the purpose of their trip, the number of hours left between now and the moment she'd meet Sophia. Opposite, Monique also held a book, but when Adeline glanced at her, her eyes didn't seem to be following the words but remained fixed, as if Monique's mind were elsewhere.

Monique had been strangely quiet in the taxi, listening and nodding to Lili as she prattled away, but barely meeting Adeline's eye. Adeline wondered whether she was thinking of her own prospective meeting, of whether she'd come any closer to finding the baby she'd given up for lost; or perhaps Monique was thinking of what would happen later, worrying on Adeline's behalf about how it would go.

With Lili there, it was impossible to ask, and something about Monique's manner made her sure she wouldn't get a straight answer even if she was to enquire. She popped her bookmark in between the pages of *Tant que le café est encore chaud* and lay it on the table between them, then, leaning her head back against the headrest, watched the scenery flash by – predominantly green, peppered with the odd fields of cows, stone barns, or the shock of a vibrant field of sunflowers. Every little while, the houses would build slightly as they passed a village and she'd see streets and cars and lights on in windows, then they'd emerge back into the countryside. She'd watch as the land dipped away to reveal a river, then rose gently again, the sunlight playing on the fields, making the scenery sparkle.

Eventually her attention was broken by a man trundling past with a drinks trolley, and twenty minutes after that, she felt a heavy head rest against her arm and realised that Lili had fallen asleep. Gently, she prised the pencil from the little girl's hand and slipped the colouring pad back into her bag. As she did so, she noticed that Monique had set her own book down and was looking at her, an expression on her face that Adeline couldn't read.

'Seems a long way, doesn't it?' she said, smiling.

The journey was set to be three hours and they were less than halfway into it. She hoped Monique wasn't thinking about the shop, regretting her offer to join Adeline on this quest. Hoped, too, that Monique wasn't sensing that things wouldn't go well once they reached their destination.

'*Oui,*' Monique said, her voice slightly distracted. She smoothed her black skirt – a neater, more fitted style than the one she'd ordinarily wear. Adeline noticed, as if for the first time, that she was wearing a little more make-up than usual, that her nails had been polished in a gentle pink colour. She reached into her bag and drew out a small bottle, its inside a mixture of powders in burnt orange and beige, a green dried leaf, some moisture or oil. Green candle wax formed a seal around its glass throat and as she passed it to Adeline, there was a scent of ginger and cinnamon, and another scent she didn't recognise.

'What is this?' Adeline said, holding the tiny bottle and turning it in her hands.

'It is for good luck.'

Adeline nodded. 'Thank you.'

'Keep it on you. If you want.'

Adeline slipped it into her bag.

'And this, too,' Monique said, sliding something into her hand. It was a crystal, this time in a dark red.

'For luck?'

Monique shook her head. 'No, this is for strength, resilience. To help you be strong for what is to come.'

Adeline felt a shiver. 'Thanks,' she said, her voice cracking a little.

'Ah, do not worry. There is nothing terrible ahead. But these times are difficult, it is good to be strong.'

'Thank you.'

Monique smiled. 'Once, I would have been afraid to give you this.'

'Afraid?'

'Yes, when you came from England, I think you disliked the idea of magic. Of charms and crystals. The stone I gave Lili. But now, perhaps you feel differently.'

Adeline turned the stone over in her hands. 'To be honest, I don't know how I feel. About anything.'

Monique leaned forward, held the hand with the crystal

within her own. 'But that is good. It is good not to know. Not to be fixed. To be open to possibilities.'

They looked at one another for a moment. Adeline gave a brief nod. 'OK,' she said.

It was enough. Monique smiled, leaned back in her seat. 'And I am very open to the possibility of coffee,' she chuckled as they heard the rattle of the refreshment cart. 'Would you like one?'

Adeline grinned. 'You read my mind.'

After they'd had something to drink, Adeline tried to distract herself with the scenery again, watching the fields and houses and roads and small industrial areas whip past the window. She wondered whether Sophia would look as she did in her photo – glamorous and well put-together – or whether, like most people, her social media portrait showed the glossiest version of a more normal reality. What would Sophia think of *her*? She'd brought a white blouse and some cotton trousers to wear for their meeting, but had chosen a more casual outfit for the train – her familiar jeans and T-shirt ensemble, with trainers. Would she be a disappointment to her mother? What had Sophia thought of the photo she'd displayed on the DNA site – an ordinary selfie she'd snapped quickly with her phone? She leaned slightly against the window, feeling it cool against her forehead.

There was a jolt and, sitting up, she realised she must have drifted into sleep. Her neck ached and her back felt sticky. Monique was leaning forward saying something. Feeling her consciousness return, finding her bearings, she looked out of the window and realised the station sign read 'Toulouse.' Abruptly, her senses flooded back and she heard Monique's sharp 'Quick!' and got up from her seat, almost banging her head in the process.

Lili was rubbing her eyes, still a little out of it too, so instead of trying to rally her, Adeline picked her backpack up, then grabbed her child, lifting her out of her seat and rushing towards the open door.

They needn't have hurried. Once they emerged, dazed, onto the platform, she remembered that was the last stop on the journey. People poured from the carriages and others waited patiently to step aboard. She put Lili down, holding onto her a little in case her legs were wobbly, and took a moment to centre herself.

'Wow,' she said. 'So, we're really here.'

'*Oui*,' Monique said.

'Are we at the hotel?' Lili asked, still not quite with them.

'Soon, baby.'

Luckily, the train had arrived on time, as she'd booked a taxi on an app to meet them outside the station. Once they'd clambered up the steps and found the right exit point, they emerged into strong sunlight and throngs of people, a road heavy with cars and a taxi rank with several silver vehicles lined up in a neat row.

Almost immediately her phone began to ring. Drawing it from her pocket, she checked the screen – an unknown number flashed up. 'Hello?' she said.

It was the taxi driver. 'I'm here,' he told her.

Almost simultaneously, a black car with a slightly dented back door made its way around the curve of the drop-off area. Adeline recognised the number plate, which had been sent in her confirmation text, and they hurried towards the car, opened the door and sank into the grey leather seats in the back.

'Grand Hôtel de l'Opéra?' he asked for confirmation, looking a little confused – as if it were an odd choice of hotel.

'*Oui, merci, Monsieur*,' she said, leaning back in the seat and settling in for the ride.

Two minutes later the taxi pulled up outside a hotel that was an easily walkable distance from the station. '*Voilà*,' he said.

'Oh. Is that...' She saw the signage and her question was answered. She felt herself get hot. She'd thought the taxi ride – quoted at eight euros – had seemed very affordable. But that was because, apparently, they'd booked a taxi for a journey that was less than a mile.

Monique let out a small laugh. '*Mon dieu*! I know I am old, but I think even I could have managed to walk here.'

Adeline felt her own laughter bubble up. 'I know. I don't think I investigated it properly.'

Lili, looking at the two women laughing, giggled delightedly too. 'Silly taxi,' she said.

They stumbled out of the cab, thanking the driver and stood, still smiling, in front of the enormous red and white brick building. Something about the grandeur of the ancient hotel made Adeline's humour dry up. Its seriousness, or perhaps simply the reminder that they were here and that the next few hours – however they went – would be life-changing.

33

It took her a moment to realise where she was. She sat up in bed, letting the sleep finally filter from her mind, and took in the lush red carpet, the floral scrolled wallpaper, the soft but unfamiliar bed. She checked the time on her phone: 2.58 a.m. Much too early to get up.

Shifting down under the covers again, she snuggled into Lili's sleeping form and tried to switch her mind off. Tomorrow morning, at 11 a.m., she was due to meet her mother. She had to get some sleep or she'd be completely wrecked for that important moment.

They'd spent the remaining hours of yesterday finding somewhere to eat and settling into their rooms; she'd tried to read her book, watch the enormous TV, but had felt every minute stretch before her unbearably. She'd longed for sleep, and it had come. But sadly, it had been short-lived.

Unfortunately, her brain seemed not to care much about whether she was tired or out of sorts tomorrow, filtering images and ideas through her mind at alarming speed. What if they didn't get on? What if they did? What would they talk about?

What would she feel like when she walked into the lounge and saw her mother sitting at a table? Would she recognise her? Would they recognise each other? Would there be a bond, something beyond understanding, or the kind of formality you feel when you meet a stranger?

It didn't matter. None of it mattered right now in this silent room with blackout heavy curtains and luxurious fittings. All that mattered was that she slept, rested for what was to come. She listened to Lili's regular breathing with envy – her daughter, once asleep, was usually out for the count in a way she could never remember being herself. Sleep came, for her, with a restlessness at the best of times. She doubted she'd be able to drop off again.

She climbed out of bed and went over to the window and quietly pulled the curtain back, allowing a sliver of artificial light to fall into the room. Outside, the road was still busy: cars purred along, people walked in small groups or alone, perhaps coming home from nights out or starting an early shift at work. There was a sense of purpose in the air, similar to that she'd felt in London – as if everyone had somewhere to go, something to do, somewhere to be.

In St Vianne, the houses would be in darkness by now, the inhabitants nestling under a blanket of sleep for a few more hours. Then André would emerge from the flat above the patisserie and begin work, preparing fresh bread and pastries for the day ahead. Gradually lights would appear in windows and, as the sun rose, doors would begin to open and houses would spill their inhabitants into the street for another day.

She wasn't sure which type of place she most belonged in – the quiet backwater where all was peaceful and people had time to stop and pass the time of day with one another; or the

purposeful city where lights, action and energy seemed to pulse
at all times.

Turning, leaving the curtain slightly ajar so that a little light
remained in the room, she caught sight of a painting on the
wall. A simple oil sketch of a woman in a cafe, her eyes downturned, a coffee cup cradled in her hand. Her face beautiful; sad.

She felt suddenly weary, as if even her chattering brain
wouldn't be able to prevent sleep from coming. Pulling the
curtain into place, allowing darkness to plunge into the room,
she made her way gingerly to the bed, feeling her way, and
climbed under the covers, their warmth making her aware for
the first time that she was cold, dressed only in a long T-shirt.
She snuggled up to her daughter who turned, moaning slightly,
and tucked her little body expertly against her mother's. At last,
Adeline felt her eyelids grow heavy.

* * *

'Mummy! We're on holidays!' The little voice made her start and
she was aware that the mattress she was on was wobbling wildly.
She opened her eyes to find the room light – despite the thick
curtains, daylight had found a way around the edges of the
material and morning had made its way into their room. She
looked up and saw Lili's excited face and her stomach dipped.

'Yes,' she said. 'How exciting!'

Monique had told her she'd take Lili for a walk this morning
to look at the river, then to pop into a couple of shops and stop
for a pastry somewhere. All the little girl knew was that Mummy
was meeting a friend and Monique was taking her for a treat. No
wonder she was excited.

Adeline shifted up on her elbows and eyed her phone. It was

8.30 a.m. Flinging the covers back she made her way to the little en suite and stepped into the shower, feeling the warm water cascade down her body. It made a change from the rather less decadent bathroom facilities in her tiny cottage, where she'd taken to having baths, as the water barely dripped from the showerhead.

Dressed, she went to knock on Monique's door, Lili in tow, and the three of them went down to breakfast.

They didn't speak in the lift, except to give Lili permission to press the buttons, but made their way to the breakfast room in silence. There, they were greeted by a light, airy room with modern tables, set on a carpet that was a riot of colour in contrast. Adeline selected a croissant and a tiny pot of jam and ordered a coffee, but found she couldn't stomach any of her food. She looked up during the meal to see Monique regarding her, her brow furrowed. 'Can't eat,' she said with a shrug.

'*Non*, nor can I,' came the reply, and she noticed that Monique's food was also untouched. She was quite surprised that Monique was feeling so nervous on her behalf and gave her friend a small smile.

Lili seemed to have no such problems with her appetite and managed to work her way through two pains au chocolat and an orange juice, chattering all the while into the near silence. Adeline wondered whether, even if Lili knew what was going to happen today, she'd realise its significance to their lives. She was so in the moment, so accepting of new things in the way that children can be, taking whatever happens to them as simply a sign of the way things are – never realising how their life differs from that of their friends'.

Then it was 10 a.m. and she was back in the room, carefully changing her clothes and brushing her hair. Monique had taken

Lili off straight after breakfast, giving her a hug before they left that almost squeezed the air out of Adeline's lungs.

Away from her two travelling companions, Adeline had felt time slow to a painful speed. She took her time on her hair, noticing that it had grown since her arrival in St Vianne and quite liking the slightly softer look it gave her. She applied her mascara, curling her eyelashes first, more out of a need to kill time than any sort of vanity. Spritzing herself with Coco by Chanel, she stood in front of the mirror and concluded that this was as good as it was going to get. It was only twenty past ten; forty minutes to go and far too early to make her way down to the hotel bar.

Instead, she flicked on the TV in the room and watched mindlessly as scrolling headlines ran across on the screen on which a woman was talking. Her eye kept being drawn to the digital clock in the corner, torturing her every time a minute passed.

Eventually, she snapped off the TV and told herself enough was enough. It was 10.45 a.m., and although she'd resolved not to be first, not to risk sitting there and scanning the room and trying to recognise someone she'd never met, she felt that if she stayed in her bedroom any longer, she'd go mad. She straightened, grabbed her purse and keycard and made her way along the carpeted corridor to the lift.

Inside, as the lift dipped, she turned away from the mirrored wall, not wanting to see herself, see the fear that was no doubt in her eyes. A couple got into the space with her, chatting about their day ahead, and she moved to the corner to accommodate them. Then they all spilled out into the foyer, into bright light and movement and, beyond, the double glass doors of the exit.

She felt sick as she made her way to the bar entrance and

stood just outside the door, checking the tables within. Most were empty, but a few were occupied with people on their own, reading or checking their phones. A couple sipped from espresso cups in the corner. A woman was sitting close to a pillar, her hair swept up with just a few strands escaping. Adeline stepped in and the woman, perhaps sensing some shift in the atmosphere, turned.

When asked about it later, she'd tell people she'd recognised Sophia instantly. And not because of the photo, but because something inside her tugged the minute their eyes locked onto each other. And suddenly it didn't seem to matter why her mother had had to give her up, or that she'd grown up not knowing that she was adopted, or that she wasn't quite sure how to fit this new information about who she was into her life, her sense of self.

She found herself walking quickly, not caring what she looked like, or what Sophia might be thinking, but just carrying herself as fast as she could towards a woman she both did and didn't know.

Sophia, stepping forward, her face already crumpling slightly with emotion, then rushed to meet her. And although Adeline was not a natural hugger, she fell into her mother's outstretched arms without a thought. As they locked together in this strange place with its smell of coffee and carpet cleaner, the quiet chatter, the squeal of the cappuccino machine, with the unfamiliar sounds from the street outside, the only thing that Adeline could think was that she was home at last; that here was somewhere she truly belonged.

They stepped back after a moment and looked at each other, Adeline feeling her face stretch into a smile and seeing her own happiness reflected in her birth mother's features. '*Maman,*' she said, feeling a pang of guilt at using the word so freely with this stranger when the woman who raised her had earned the title each day of her childhood.

'Adeline,' Sophia said, her own voice choked with emotion. 'Thank God. Thank God.'

34

———

'You're back!' Adeline exclaimed the minute Monique entered her room with a tired, but sugar-energised five-year-old some two hours later.

'*Oui*, and you are too!' Monique smiled, letting Lili run forward and leap into her mother's arms. 'Was it OK?'

'We had ice cream!' Lili shouted.

'That's wonderful, darling. And yes, it was OK. More than OK. And I know we thought we might go out this afternoon before the train. But would it be OK if I saw her again? We barely touched the edges of what we need to say. And I didn't think I would – but I really want Sophia to meet Lili.'

Lili looked up, interested for the first time at the mention of her name. 'Who?' she said, her lips, coated with sugar, glistening slightly in the light that streamed through the open curtains.

They'd sat together for two hours, talking incessantly, barely remembering to order coffee until a waiter started hovering by their table, coughing slightly. It had been absolutely effortless. And wonderful. And she hadn't wanted it to end. But she'd

promised Lili she'd be back in the room when she returned, and
hadn't wanted to spring the whole thing on her daughter out of
nowhere; she'd need to prepare her.

'But of course,' Monique said gently. 'We can stay another
night, also, or take a later train. So that you have enough time;
so you don't have to worry.'

'But the shop?'

'Ah, it is just one day. What is the point of having your own
business if you become a bad boss to yourself!' Monique told
her. 'I will have Michel put a note in the window and people will
have to come back on Wednesday, that is all.'

'It's so kind of you.'

'Ah, it is not so kind.' She seemed about to say more, but a
shadow crossed her face and she closed her mouth.

Lili was now camped on the bed. 'Can I watch SpongeBob?'
she asked. She'd become a big fan of the yellow cartoon sponge
in the moments when Monique let her watch cartoons on her
laptop.

'I'll find something for you,' Adeline said, nearly bursting
with all the things she had to tell Monique, but unable to do so
properly in front of her daughter. She found the remote control
and selected a Disney film. Lili was soon transfixed, her eyes
looking set to close at any minute.

'She looks exhausted,' Adeline said, smiling at Monique. 'I
bet you are too?'

'A little,' Monique shrugged. 'But I am excited to hear what
you discovered from Sophia. If you wish to share.'

'Of course, of course I do.' Adeline inclined her head and
they moved to the two small chairs set against a table at the edge
of the room. With Lili engaged, they could probably talk
without her eavesdropping if they kept their voices low, the tone
even.

'She never wanted to give me up!' Adeline said, triumphantly. 'She was a little like you. Her mother thought it would be best. She got pregnant at sixteen, and had her education, her life to think of.'

'Ah, so she was forced into the adoption?'

'No, not quite. I found out something else too,' Adeline said, barely able to form coherent sentences. 'Monique, Sophia was adopted too. And she had a wonderful childhood – like mine, I suppose. One of the reasons she agreed with her mother that having me adopted would be best was because her mum had always said how much happiness she'd brought to her parents' lives when they'd adopted *her*, and how she could pass a wonderful gift to a family. And her mum said, too, that I would be better off being raised by a couple who were ready for the responsibility than by a sixteen-year-old who might have regrets down the line and was in no place to raise me properly.'

Monique's eyes were glistening a little. 'And was she right?'

'Yes. Yes, she was.' Adeline replied. 'I mean, I felt a connection to her instantly. Something I've rarely felt before. But I had a wonderful mum and dad. A great childhood. I can't say I'd necessarily change things now. Obviously, I wish I'd known the truth about myself growing up, but I would have wanted to stay with my parents, I think.' She felt something lurch inside her at the thought of Mum and Dad; she wished she'd had a chance to talk to them about all this. They were out of her life now, and there was no way to reach them, but even though she knew it was irrational, she couldn't help feeling guilty at seeing Sophia.

Monique was quiet for a moment. 'That is good. And she said her childhood was good too? Even though she was adopted?'

Adeline nodded.

'Has she ever tried to find her mother, did she say?'

'She tried a few times over the years. But there was no information available. Then a couple of years ago a cousin of hers who's really into family trees suggested she try the DNA site. She thought she might find me or her mother, or at least some relative. All she knew was that I was in England; that my birth father came from there. But she wasn't in touch with him any more and didn't know where else to start with me. Then suddenly she got a notification, then my email, and it all joined up!'

Monique smiled. 'That's wonderful. That she found you, and that she forgives her mother too.'

'Yes,' said Adeline. 'But then she's so nice. She's kind. She works as a teacher in a high school, like Michel. And she's got children too. Much younger than me. One in his teens, another in his early twenties. But I'm her only daughter – and I think it made her more desperate to find me somehow.'

'So you have this enormous family now!' Monique said, her jollity sounding a little false.

'Yes. Well, one day at a time, but yes, I've suddenly got all these people. People I might get to know and who might become, well, really important. And did I tell you I also have a niece? About Lili's age?' She shook her head, unable to contain her excitement at how much her life had changed in a single morning.

'And she is coming here again later?'

'Yes. I hope that's OK. She's actually still here. Well, nearby. I just wanted to come and see if you guys were OK. And talk to Lili. Sophia, my... my mum has gone for a walk to give me time to talk to Lili.' Adeline could sense that she was babbling, but didn't feel able to stop.

'*Mon dieu*,' said Monique softly, almost to herself. 'She is still here.'

'And you'll join us?'

'Oh!' Monique seemed shocked at being asked. '*Non*. It is not my place. This is your special time.'

'Honestly, she'd love to meet you. I've told her about my job, about you. About what brought me to France.'

Monique shook her head, just once. '*Non*. Perhaps another time. Perhaps when I have had time to... it is hard to explain.'

'OK,' Adeline said, knowing when she was beaten and – if she was honest – too excited about it all to stay in one emotional state too long. 'So! This afternoon then!' She hugged Monique. 'Thanks for not minding!' she said, and felt Monique's arms squeeze her almost too tightly.

It was easier than Adeline had thought it would be trying to explain to her five-year-old that she was going to meet her grandmother. Lili had only known one grandmother in her life and didn't know much about biology, but was quite happy to accept who Sophia was. 'So I have two grandmothers?' she asked.

Technically, she had another blood grandmother too, and possibly a grandpa, on her father's side. Colin's parents. One day, perhaps, they'd find that other woman – a woman who had a granddaughter and perhaps wasn't even aware of her. But for today, it was simply important to help Lili understand Sophia's place in her complicated family tree.

'Yes,' Adeline said, feeling a little guilty for the half-truth. 'Yes. She's another grandmother.'

This, it seemed, was enough for Lili, who bounced with excitement on the bed.

Eventually she was coaxed down; they ordered a room service snack for all of them, changed Lili's clothes, brushed her hair and wiped her sticky face and hands.

The time passed in a flash and soon Adeline was gripping

Lili's hand, feeling a mixture of excitement and nervousness – it had been wonderful meeting Sophia, but already she was starting to lose that feeling of ease she'd developed in this new mother's presence.

They made their way to the lift, Lili dancing and pulling on Adeline's arm in her excitement, babbling about how she would tell her new *mamie* all about school and her friends and the concert that was coming up, and did Adeline think that she'd give her a gift, and would she come and live with them one day? In the end, Adeline stopped trying to answer Lili's questions and let her babble away – realising it was her own version of excitement prompting the interrogation rather than any real need to know the answers to the torrent of questions.

This time, Sophia had taken a seat near the window on one of the red, plush chairs that flanked a mahogany table. She stood when they walked in, her eyes locking with Adeline then moving down to see Lili. This time, she didn't rush towards them but stood waiting for them to reach her.

She crouched down to Lili's level and looked into her eyes. '*Bonjour,* Lili,' she said. 'I am Sophia. Your grandmother.' Only an adult could have detected the wobble of emotion in her voice.

Lili, suddenly shy, gave a small *bonjour* and then hid behind Adeline's legs. But after she'd been lifted into one of the velvet chairs, and offered an orange juice with a straw, she began to gain confidence and chattered away to Sophia with an ease that was almost astounding. Was it blood that led to a near-instant connection like this? Adeline wondered. Or simply the fact that she knew this woman was a grandmother, and that she understood this meant she was more important to her than some other grown-ups?

She sat back and sipped her coffee, watching with pleasure

as Sophia leaned forward and nodded her head as Lili talked. Once in a while, her mother would glance up and their eyes would lock and they'd exchange a look of pleasure – a shared joy at a sweet story or expression or simply an acknowledgement of how special this moment was – before returning her gaze to her brand-new granddaughter.

Across the room, past the other customers sipping their drinks or standing at the bar or reading books on solitary tables, nobody saw the woman with dark hair tied in a neat chignon, whose mid-length skirt swung a little when she moved. Nobody saw the expression on her face as she gazed at the three generations of women who were both strangers and closely connected, finding out about one another for the first time. Nobody noticed the glistening in her eyes and the fact that once in a while she'd take a step forward as if to join them, before shrinking back, a look of fear skittering across her features.

Everyone was too engaged, too busy, too taken with their own conversations or drinks or newspapers or books to see Monique hovering in the doorway, her gaze fixed on the three of them as they talked.

35

'Hi, are you OK?' Adeline said when Monique answered her call. 'I'm sorry we were so long.'

All in all, it had gone well. Sophia had been completely taken by Lili, apart from the moment when her new grand-daughter had sprayed a little orange juice on her when talking too enthusiastically. She'd stiffened a little, tutted and mopped her dress. Lili had looked at Adeline wide-eyed. But the moment had passed, Sophia had apologised – *'Sorry, it is a favourite of mine, but please, it's OK'* – and they'd relaxed into conversation again.

Eventually, Adeline had said she had to go and Sophia had given them both a hug and promised to stay in touch. She still felt as if Sophia was somehow a stranger – she knew so little about her. But they'd see each other again. So, while there were still things unsaid, questions unanswered, there was a lightness too. Because something that was broken had begun to heal. Adeline was convinced that they could all feel it – even Lili – that sense of belonging and rightness that had washed over them all as they sat and bonded over coffee and orange juice and – in Lili's case – probably too many madeleines.

When she'd glanced at her phone and realised the time, she'd felt terrible. She'd told Monique they'd probably be an hour – but hadn't banked on their talking for two. She knew her friend would understand, but it seemed a bit remiss all the same to have stayed away so long and not contacted her or encouraged her, once again, to come down and join them.

She'd knocked on the door of Monique's room on the way past, but there'd been no answer. Her own room was also silent and empty when she'd slipped the keycard through the sensor to let them both in. So instead she'd called, wanting to know if Monique was OK.

'*Oui*, I just went for a walk,' came the response.

'Well, we're back,' Adeline said. 'Let me buy you some tea perhaps? Dinner? There are some lovely restaurants.'

There was a deep sigh. 'Perhaps. Or we can order to the room, *peut-être*? I am feeling quite tired. And our train will be early tomorrow.'

'Of course, whatever you want.' Adeline slipped off her shoes and felt her socked feet sink into the soft carpet.

Lili had already flung herself on the bed, so she picked up the remote and was about to flick through to find a cartoon or film when she realised that her daughter's eyes had already closed. The excitement of both the morning and the afternoon had wiped her out, and she lay curled into herself and completely unconscious. Usually, if she fell asleep at this time, she'd try to gently wake her – to make sure she had something sensible to eat, a bath, got changed into her pyjamas before settling down. Today, just this once, it didn't seem that important.

'I will come back.' Monique's voice was still rather flat. 'Perhaps I will be half an hour.'

'OK, see you soon,' Adeline said softly, sitting on the edge of the bed and ending the call. Instinctively she checked her emails and found one from Kevin that he must have sent this morning.

Hi sis,

Well, I've done it! I've been on a date. And you know what? It didn't go too badly.

How are you? Have you found out more about your birth mother? I want to hear everything.

I'm sorry I haven't been in touch for a few days – it's been manic at work and time's just flown by. But I'm looking at flights for June – I'd love to pop out and see you again, and that little rascal of a niece. If that's OK?

I'll give you a call at the weekend if you're around?

See you soon.

Kev x

She smiled reading his message and resolved to reply tomorrow on the train, when things seemed a little less fraught and she knew how to put into words everything that had changed since she'd last updated him.

On Facebook, there was a message from Chris.

Hey you. Sorry I've been crap. We've heard we're getting inspected this term, so everyone is crazy at work. Stressful! But we need to catch up properly. I feel like I've been a bit of a crap friend since you left work. You must update me on ALL YOUR NEWS. And I've spoken to Dave; reckon we might manage to take a little trip to France at some point soon – maybe half-term?

It was followed with a GIF of a cat wearing dark glasses with the words "How You Doin'" written across the bottom.

Adeline smiled and returned her own cat GIF, resolving again to write a longer message tomorrow.

For now, she felt exhausted. Happy, but tired to her bones; the tension of the last couple of days had ebbed away and she realised for the first time how much the anticipation of meeting Sophia and the travel to get here – not to mention her sleepless night – had taken its toll.

Before she had time to lay back on the bed and close her eyes for a moment or two, there was a soft knock on the door. It opened and Monique was there, her eyes red, a big smile forced across her face as if to try to distract from the fact that she'd obviously been crying.

'What's wrong?' Adeline said, all tiredness forgotten.

'But nothing is wrong!' Monique said in a voice she clearly intended to be upbeat, yet sounded anything but.

'You've been crying,' Adeline said, looking at her steadily until she glanced away, like a child who'd finally had to acknowledge a crayoned wall or an empty biscuit tin. She wrapped her arm around Monique and led her to the chairs and small table by the window, nodding in Lili's direction en route to confirm that they were effectively alone and could talk about proper, adult things if they needed to.

Monique slumped into the chair and Adeline reached for one of the bottles of water that sat on the dresser and passed it to her. She opened it and drank from it gratefully.

'Now,' Adeline said firmly when the bottle had been set on the table. 'Tell me what's the matter.'

Monique shook her head. 'It is too difficult.'

'Did something happen while we were with Sophia? On your walk perhaps? Did you get a call? Some news?' Adeline's eyes searched Monique's face, but other than the evident upset written on it, she couldn't read her.

Monique shook her head again. 'It is too much to explain for now. "The truth must dazzle gradually".' She met Adeline's gaze.

If she thought she was going to get out of telling Adeline whatever it was that was bothering her – that had clearly been bothering her over the past few days – by quoting Dickinson, then she had another think coming. 'Monique,' she said. 'Please. I can handle it. Honestly.'

Monique remained silent.

'Look,' she said. 'I know what you're saying. There is something wrong and you don't want to burden me with it, or for it to be too much. But I've realised over the past few months how important truth is. It might not always be perfect, might not be what people want to hear. But it's still the truth. People shouldn't be afraid of it.'

Monique nodded softly.

Adeline reached for Monique's hand. 'So tell me. What is it? Is it the shop? Michel? Something else?' She remembered the letter from the DNA company. 'Something about your daughter?' she found herself asking.

Monique flinched slightly at her words. Then her features softened as if she were at last releasing something, some sort of barrier between them. '*Oui*,' she said softly. 'I think I know who my daughter is.' Her hand reached up to the moonstone at her neck.

'Oh my God, that's wonderful! Why didn't you say?' Adeline began before realising that her own reunion had probably taken precedence in all their conversations. Monique probably hadn't known how to raise it with all of this going on. 'Anyway, no matter. It's brilliant news! You've found her? You know who she is? Did you do a DNA test?'

Monique shook her head. '*Non*. I considered it. But in the end I didn't need it. Because I found my daughter quite by accident, and it is sure.'

'You know – truly?'

'*Oui*,' Monique said softly.

'But that's wonderful! Oh Monique, I'm so happy for you!' She pushed back her chair and wrapped her arms around Monique, squeezing her tight. She felt Monique stiffen slightly, so released her and sat back down. Clearly, something was wrong.

'It is wonderful, isn't it?' Adeline repeated. A thought occurred to her. 'Oh. Did you make contact? Was she not... Did she not want to...'

'*Non*. It is not that. It is just... well, complicated I suppose.' Monique fixed a steady look on Adeline, this time neither happy nor sad. As if she were trying to communicate something with her eyes.

'OK...' Adeline said slowly. 'But what kind of complicated? I mean, life is complicated... so I'm sure whatever it is, we can find a way to... to...' She trailed off as something stirred inside her.

'Adeline,' Monique said, her gaze not wavering. 'My beautiful girl. You already know.'

'I... what?'

'You already know.'

A shiver ran through her. Adeline raised her eyes and met Monique's. She felt the months fall away, back to that first contact between them. The fizz she'd felt when Monique had touched her. The way she'd settled so quickly into the shop. Lili's closeness with Monique.

Monique's deep brown eyes, her hair. That expression when she laughed. The way she touched her cheek when she was thinking. Her mouth, the set of her teeth. Even her skin. But something, too, beyond all of that. Something that might be science or might be magic. A connection that was almost inexplicable.

'Your daughter...' she said after a moment. 'She's Sophia, isn't she?'

36

'I don't understand,' Adeline said. 'How can you know?'

Monique smiled kindly. 'I know you are afraid of intuition, perhaps of magic. But you looked into my eyes and felt it too. You cannot deny it.'

Adeline opened her mouth to say something about wishful thinking, or imagining or dreaming, but closed it again. 'But a feeling. It isn't...' She wasn't sure how she felt about Monique's revelation. Surely it couldn't be true.

'Ah, you are worried because it is not science,' Monique said. She smiled fondly, as if Adeline were a child.

Adeline felt herself stiffen. 'Well, yes. I mean, science is the only way of really knowing, isn't it?' She was trying to keep her voice level. 'I'm sorry, but it's true.'

'Perhaps to some people,' Monique said, somewhat dismissively.

'And also, if you do really believe this, why didn't you come and meet her earlier? Surely you must have been curious?'

Monique's shoulders slumped. 'I tried to come, but I could not make myself. I couldn't say everything I needed to in that moment. And it seemed dishonest to just come to see her as a friend of yours when the truth is a little more complex.'

'Possibly.' Adeline said carefully. Not wanting to get Monique's hopes up, but not wanting to break her either. Hope was a fragile thing, a rare thing. 'But Monique,' she persisted, 'you realise what you're saying is... quite far-fetched. It would make me your granddaughter, Lili your great-granddaughter. Isn't it a bit...' she trailed off.

'A bit what?' Monique said, tilting her chin slightly. 'A bit wonderful?'

Adeline couldn't help but smile. 'True,' she said. 'It would be wonderful. I mean, really, *really* wonderful. But it's so unlikely, Monique. The kind of thing that happens in dreams, perhaps. In books, even. But not in real life. It's too neat. Too unlikely.'

'*Mais non!*' Monique said. 'Things like this happen all the time. But people are afraid. They say there is coincidence, or try to find an explanation that they can cope with. But it doesn't make them any less real. It is not impossible for Sophia to be my daughter.'

Then Adeline reached out a hand, covered Monique's. 'You're right. It's not impossible. It's a wonderful thought. And the dates seem to add up. But we mustn't get ahead of ourselves. We mustn't assume. I mean, the coincidence of my finding your advert alone is just...' She blew out a puff of incredulous air.

Monique smiled. 'Perhaps it was not such a coincidence.'

'What do you mean?'

'Because Adeline, I made it happen. With a charm. I cast a spell for family, an end to loneliness. And then suddenly the phone rings and it is you.'

'Oh.'

It seemed cruel to unleash any scepticism on Monique right

now. Cruel to point out the flaws in her logic. Cruel to suggest a DNA test. Instead, Adeline tried to smile.

Monique nodded, her eyes on Adeline's face. And Adeline could feel that she wanted her to join her in her thinking, to share this sweet but ultimately flawed delusion.

'I should have taken the chance to see her,' she said sadly. 'I think if we could meet, we would both know.'

Adeline couldn't say it, but she was relieved Monique hadn't had that chance. Surely it could break the fragile link she'd made with Sophia – scare her off entirely? Surely, too, it could be upsetting for Monique.

'Perhaps it wasn't meant to be this time,' she said softly.

'Maybe it will still happen. If we wish for it. Sophia will come into my life if it is meant to be.'

'Maybe.'

'And I wish it,' she said.

Almost instantly, Adeline's phone began to ring.

Sophia. She snatched the phone up, but not before Monique had seen the name flash up on her screen.

'Hello?' she said, lifting the device to her ear.

'Adeline,' Sophia said. 'I forgot to give you something. I am turning back – is it OK if we meet quickly?'

'Yes, of course.'

When she ended the call, Adeline saw Monique looking at her expectantly and felt her heart sink.

'It was Sophia?'

'Yes.'

'Then it is a sign!'

Adeline gave a weak smile. 'She's just popping back to give me something. Could you mind Lili while I...' She gestured to the door.

Monique shook her head. 'No, I must come too. You were right. I was afraid before, but I should be brave, just as you are.'

Adeline felt herself stiffen. 'Monique, I'm not sure that it's...'

'You think that she won't want to see me?'

'Monique,' Adeline reached out a hand to her friend. 'I just think she might not be able to understand exactly why you think... what you think. It might be better to prepare her. Or even do the test! We know she's on the DNA site. It'd be better to have it confirmed, surely?' *And I don't want you to drive my mother away.*

'Pah! DNA!' Monique scoffed.

'Monique. It's pretty conclusive.'

'Yes. I understand. But not everyone needs this kind of proof.'

'But it might make it easier.'

'*Non*. She will know. If she is mine. She will know.'

Adeline's phone flashed with a message. Sophia was already in the hotel foyer. 'Perhaps let me go down at first, at least,' she said. 'She might want to talk to me privately.'

Monique nodded. 'OK. But then I will come. I will wake Lili and we can come together. The whole family, *non*?'

Adeline smiled weakly. 'Well, I'll call you when we're done.'

As the lift descended, she saw her expression in the glass. Not the nervousness from earlier, or the elation she'd seen in her expression when she'd travelled up to the room again. But a fear. A guilt. She wasn't sure what Sophia would make of Monique. Wasn't sure whether there might be something plausible in what Monique was claiming. But she felt strongly that she oughtn't to let Monique see Sophia. Not today, this first time. Not yet.

She exited into the bustling foyer, her shoes sinking slightly into the soft pile of the carpet, and there was Sophia, standing just inside the door, looking at her watch. Adeline raised a hand and Sophia glanced up and raised hers in return.

Hopefully they could make this quick.

'Sophia,' she said, smiling.

'Adeline. I'm sorry to disturb you. It's just that I meant to give you this, and with all the excitement, I forgot.' Sophia said. She drew a small square item from her handbag and handed it to Adeline. It was a small double frame, with two photos displayed side by side – one black and white, the other a colour, slightly faded with age. Two pictures of young mothers, each holding a baby.

'Oh,' Adeline said. 'Is that us?' She pointed to the picture on the right where a younger, dazzlingly beautiful Sophia was holding a white-blanketed bundle, her slight smile doing little to hide the grief written on her face. 'And this?' she asked, pointing to the other.

'It is my photo. It is me with my mother. My natural mother,' said Sophia. 'See how the photos look alike.'

'Yes,' Adeline agreed. 'They really do.' She felt the buzz of her phone in her pocket and felt again a pang of guilt and fear about what Monique wanted to do and what she herself hoped to prevent. She looked at the woman in the second photo, her face slightly turned for the camera. Was she Monique? She had the look of her, but it was hard to say. The photo was old, its resolution limited, and it had been taken so long ago.

Sophia smiled. 'I have my own copy, so this one is yours.'

'And your mother?' Adeline asked, unable to stop herself. 'Do you think you might find her one day?'

'Yes. Yes, I hope so,' Sophia said.

'Me too.'

They smiled at each other. There was a pause in which Sophia looked as if she were wrestling with something.

'In fact, I know I will,' Sophia added.

'You've found her?'

'Not yet. But I know I will because I feel it. I feel it in here,' she said tapping her chest emphatically so that the crystal on her necklace wobbled. 'Do you believe in this? This... intuition.'

'I—' Adeline began.

Then two things happened almost simultaneously.

A small, whirlwind of energy and animation slammed into Sophia's legs with a 'Granny!' of delight. And behind Adeline, someone gasped loudly.

'Come here, Lili,' Adeline said. 'You'll knock her over! Are you all right, Sophia?'

But Sophia didn't react. Her features were fixed as she looked over Adeline's shoulder. Adeline followed her gaze and saw Monique standing, frozen in just the same way.

'*Mon dieu*,' said Sophia. 'My God.' As both women raised a hand to their chests, both touched the crystal at their neck.

Adeline looked from one to the other. And she could feel it; an energy. The sense that something momentous was happening.

And she felt suddenly that everything was going to be all right. That everything was going just as it was meant to.

37

Adeline felt a wave of exhaustion wash over her as she finally sat back into her allocated seat early the following morning. Moments later, the train began to pull out of the station and along the almost invisible track that snaked away in the grey light of the early morning. Lights, people, the platform and the scenery appeared to move away from them as they began their journey back; it had all happened in less than forty-eight hours, yet all of their lives had changed in ways they could barely have imagined.

After the two women had met, Adeline had taken herself off with Lili to give them time to talk.

When she'd finally seen Monique emerge through the doors, she'd stood up and almost called across the wide reception area. But Monique had seen her and walked quickly to her, taking both her hands. Lili had looked up interestedly before returning to the picture of a school she was colouring in on a low table.

'Are you OK? Did it...? Was it...?' Adeline asked.

Monique nodded. 'We have said many things, and we have many more things to say. But things are good. We are happy.'

They'd all said goodbye shortly afterwards, as Sophia – the person who bound them together – left to return home. But it wouldn't be forever. In fact, plans had already been mooted. They'd come to her here, she'd go to them there.

As soon as Sophia had gone, Adeline had finally felt how much her legs ached, how tired her body was, how heavy her eyelids had become. She'd lived several years in those two days, but the excitement and fear and turmoil of it all had kept her mind buzzing. Then it was as if a rug had been pulled from under her and all she wanted to do was sleep. Yet they were four hours from home, and hadn't even booked their journey.

She'd slept fitfully, getting up earlier even than her alarm. Then after a hurried breakfast, they'd taken the short walk to the station, and were en route to Avignon, after which a taxi would pick them up. Adeline stared at her reflection in the glass of the train window – a rough outline of her face, a ghost floating over the scenery. But there was a lightness there too, and she felt it – a kind of release that perhaps she'd been waiting for all her life.

She turned to Monique suddenly; her grandmother – and it was going to take a long while to think of her this way – looked equally tired, her expression distant, her eyelids heavy. 'Monique,' she said. 'Do you mind if I ask you something?'

'*Mais oui*, of course.'

'What I don't understand is how... how I ended up working at your shop in the first place? I applied for one job in France, on a whim, and it happened to be in my grandmother's shop. It's just too...' she tried to find a word to fit, 'unlikely.'

Monique smiled, kindly, as if to someone much younger. 'Ah

mon coeur, I have wondered this too, many times. I posted the advert many months before, but couldn't find anyone suitable. But I felt it – that someone important was coming. That I had to wait. And perhaps there was a little magic too, a little manifestation. I knew I wanted to find family, to make connections, but I did not know how. I know you do not like this – but I tied a knot of finding in cloth and buried it, and asked the universe to answer my prayers. Then you came.'

'I'm sorry, I just can't...' Adeline shook her head. 'It makes me feel strange, uncomfortable.'

'Then don't think of it. Think of it as a wish, a prayer that was answered.'

'But what were the chances of me even seeing that advert? Of it being that particular week when I decided to google the area, just to see what it was like?'

Monique nodded. 'I had never sought my daughter, I believed she was dead long ago. But when you arrived, I had this strong pull. I cannot explain it. I started to believe that perhaps *you* were my daughter – or perhaps I let myself believe this delusion because for the first time when I was with you, I didn't think so often about the baby I had lost. That is why Michel and I argued. He thought I was crazy. And perhaps I was.'

'Do you think it's something scientific? That kind of primitive recognising that a person is connected to us through blood? Something we don't understand, but is there anyway?' Adeline mused.

Monique leaned forward and took her hand. 'We cannot understand everything. I do not really understand what it is that draws me to people, that helps me to read their pain, to find a solution sometimes. But I know that this is something I can do. You can too, I think. Some people might call it science – want to study it and work out the way in which it all works. Other people would call it magic.'

'And what do you call it?'

Monique smiled. 'Ah, I think you know. And Adeline, it is not something you should fear. There are always things we can't quite explain. We think we see something. We sense something about another person. We take a remedy not because the doctor says we should, but because our grandmother swears by it. We seek to understand, but I have learned that sometimes you can just accept. That maybe it is science, this connection, this pull between us. Or maybe it is magic. Or maybe there is something else. But whatever it is, it is a good thing. And we can embrace it, even if we can't give it a name.'

Adeline nodded.

All her life, she'd tried to find ways to make sense of her world. But as she'd grown, more and more things had happened that she didn't understand. Lili's father not wanting to know her. Her own father dying. Her mother's illness. Then finding the papers. Now, her journey to France and a brand-new family to get to know.

Life was messy. It didn't fit neatly into a box. And nor did she, she realised. Perhaps she would never find a place where she felt she truly belonged, because there were several places where she could live and be happy and find connection. Perhaps the problem wasn't as she'd thought – she had questions, but perhaps it wasn't always necessary to have all the answers.

'Thanks, Monique,' she said.

'For what?'

'For all of it. For being my friend, my support, and now my family. For what it's worth, and although I don't believe in it, really, I do feel that all this was meant to be.'

Monique smiled, a little like a teacher at a pupil who'd finally figured out algebra. 'Well, I am glad,' she said.

Their smiles softened as they both relaxed and began to let sleep take over. Beside them, Lili was still snuggled up, oblivious to the world. And while they all slept, Adeline felt a sense of peace that she hadn't experienced for a long time.

38

'So let me get this straight,' Stacey said, leaning forward over her glass of wine. 'Sophia's your birth mum, but turns out she's also Monique's long-lost daughter. Which means Monique's your nan, and Sophia's Lili's nan, and you've suddenly got four generations of relatives when you barely had one before.'

'That's about the size of it,' said Adeline, taking a long sip from her glass.

'Bloody hell.' Stacey let out an incredulous laugh.

'Yep.'

Stacey shook her head. 'But Monique doesn't want to take a DNA test even though it would confirm everything, make it, like, official?'

Adeline shook her head. She gave a little eyeroll then felt a bit guilty. 'I mean, I get it. She's seen the photo, although... well, it's not that clear. But she and Sophia feel a connection. They are quite alike.'

'Seems a bit weird,' Stacey said. 'Sorry. I don't mean to sound rude.' She made an apologetic face. 'Just... you know.'

'It does seem a bit weird. Talking to you now, hearing it all out loud...' Adeline admitted. 'But when I'm with Monique, I'll be honest, I find myself believing it all.'

'But if she's that certain, why not take a test?'

'I know. I definitely would, in her situation. But whenever I speak to her, she says she's completely certain and she feels that to take the test might be to question her good fortune, to say that she doesn't have enough faith.' Adeline smiled.

'OK. I suppose that's kind of sweet.'

'It is.'

'Odd though. She has her little ways, doesn't she!'

Adeline laughed. 'She does at that. Mind you, don't we all. I mean, since meeting Monique I've realised how many things I'm superstitious about or have faith in. You know, like walking under ladders – I know it's nonsense but I still can't do it. And Friday thirteenths always freak me out.'

Stacey nodded. 'I do keep this on me all the time,' she said, drawing a battered, tiny toy tortoise from her handbag. 'It's like a mascot, I suppose. I've had him since I was about twelve; he came to the labour ward when I had the kids. My lucky charm.'

'Aw!' Adeline said. 'And I have this,' she fingered the tiny silver heart she wore on a chain. 'Mum – my adoptive mum – gave it to me when I was a kid. And I found it when I was clearing out her stuff. I'd obviously abandoned it when I moved out. But I put it on and now I sort of... I can't take it off. It's as if she's with me.' She felt a spike of grief and took a deep breath, forcing out a smile. 'I guess it's no different in some ways from believing that we can manifest things, create a charm, use crystals...'

Stacey nodded. 'Maybe it's just that we're a bit more private about it.'

'Maybe.'

'Still, I'd also get the DNA test if it were me.'

Adeline nodded, wrinkling her nose. 'Yeah.'

'But I suppose it's not up to us.'

'No. And I've started to wonder how much it matters. I mean, finding my natural mum, I suppose that was important to me. So biology counts for something. But the family I grew up with – Mum, Dad, Kevin, they'll always feel like my real family too, blood or no blood. Maybe Monique's right. Maybe sometimes it's better to be happy and have faith.'

Stacey took another sip of wine, her face thoughtful. 'Yeah, I get that. Plus, those DNA tests are pricey, right?'

Adeline laughed. 'True. She's saving herself a fortune!'

They both sipped from their wine and leaned back into their chairs. The day was warm and Adeline had placed a little table just outside the front door on the pavement, to make the most of its rays. It was good putting the world to rights with her friend; she was glad she'd taken a chance on Stacey.

'What about André?' Stacey asked. 'Anything happening there?'

Adeline touched her hand to her lips, feeling them stretch into a smile. 'Well, I think there could be. If I wanted it to.'

'You don't want him?'

She shook her head vehemently. 'No, I do of course! He's... well he seems nice. Great even, but...'

Stacey was looking at her incredulously.

'I've thought about it a lot,' Adeline said. 'I just... it's too much right now, you know?'

'Because he might let you down?'

'Not exactly. It's just hard to know how I feel. So much has changed for me. I'm not sure whether I'm staying or going, whether I've finally answered the questions that were driving me mad about my mum, my story, or whether I've just added even more questions to the list.'

Stacey nodded.

'It's too much. Embarking on something new with André too,' she said, feeling a slight shiver run through her. 'It's not that I never want to... it's just...'

'I get it,' Stacey said. 'I mean, it's sensible, I suppose.'

Adeline nodded. 'Yes. Sensible. And you know, with all the odd stuff, coincidences... magic. Well, maybe I need a bit of sensible. Just for a while.'

Stacey shook her head. 'Well, I'm impressed with your resolve. Not tempted to, you know... have a little fling?'

Adeline shook her head. 'It wouldn't be fair on him. Or me. Or Lili.'

They sipped their drinks. Stacey paused and looked up at her and, for a moment, Adeline wondered whether she might be about to try to change her mind about André. But instead, Stacey shook her head slightly and took another sip from her glass.

'Thanks,' Stacey said at last. 'For trusting me with all this.'

'God. Thanks for letting me waffle on about it.'

'It's fine.' She narrowed her eyes and looked at Adeline. 'This better not be the point when you ask me to take a DNA test to see if we're long-lost sisters or something.'

Adeline snorted. 'Ha. No, friends is fine.'

'Glad to hear it!'

'And you still think it sounds like something from *Coronation Street*?'

'Nah,' Stacey flapped a hand. 'This story actually has a happy ending!'

_____

39

Dear Kevin,

Thank you for your email. Please do come! I have a lot to talk to you about. So much has happened since I last saw you, but I think it would be better if we spoke in person about everything.

I wanted to let you know that I've decided to stay in St Vianne. For a year. Then I can see where Lili and I are, and what we need. But I don't want you to think we're abandoning you. You're my big brother and Lili's uncle and we will be over to visit all the time (if you can bear it). And of course, you are always welcome to come here for a break – even bring a partner, if you want.

I've got a lot of things to process and adjust to. If I'm honest, I don't think I'm over Mum's death. Perhaps we never get over things like that. There's so much I wish I could ask her. But I'm learning to accept that we can never know everything – and it's helpful to let go of some of those questions and just accept the way things are sometimes.

Anyway, that's enough philosophy from me! Write back soon with your news.

Love you bro,

Addy xxx

Stretching, Adeline rose from her chair and checked the time. It was eight o'clock. Time to get Lili ready for school and then make her way to the bookshop. It seemed surreal that life was falling into its familiar pattern after so much had happened. But there was something nice, soothing about it too.

Half an hour later, with Lili walking next to her – refusing her hand for the first time – she made her way towards the school in the early morning sunlight. She'd worn a dress; she'd often felt self-conscious doing this in the past, but had decided it was time for a change. Besides, it was due to be thirty degrees later – she'd be grateful for it.

At the edge of the playground, she bent down and gave Lili a little kiss – which was promptly wiped off – and smiled as her daughter disappeared into a crowd of friends. Nothing stayed still for long, and she could already sense the ways in which her daughter had changed since their arrival.

'*Bonjour*,' said a voice behind her.

She turned, straightened and came face to face with André. Almost instantly, she felt her cheeks get hot. The last few days had been so fraught that she'd barely had time to think of him. But she felt a surge of happiness at seeing him. 'Oh. *Bonjour!*' she said. 'Shouldn't you be at work?'

'No, I have some free time,' he said. 'Do you want to go for a coffee?'

'Sounds perfect.'

Rather than have an intimate conversation surrounded by

locals sipping espresso, André suggested they grab a takeaway and sit on one of the benches close to the square.

'So,' he said, watching her as she took a sip of coffee.

'So,' she replied.

'You enjoyed your trip?'

'Oh. Yes. Well, it was quite something.'

'A good something?'

'A very good something.' She took another sip. 'I'll tell you all about it, I promise. It's just... I've got a lot to think about.'

'But you met your mother.'

'I met my birth mother, yes.'

'And she was nice.'

'She was lovely.'

He sipped his coffee and nodded. 'Do you want me to come around tonight, perhaps?'

She took a breath. It was something she'd been thinking about almost constantly since the train ride home. Whether it was all a little too much. Whether she really knew enough about who she really was to give herself to someone else completely. Whether she could trust this situation she found herself in, where the pieces of her life were suddenly slotting together almost too easily.

'André,' she said. 'You're lovely. Truly. But I think it might be too soon. I think maybe I have so much going on, that it wouldn't be fair on you to...'

His features clouded a little. 'But...'

'Perhaps in a few months. If you still want to.'

He nodded, not saying anything.

'Sometimes you just have to stand still a little. So much has happened.'

'I understand. A little. I think,' he said with a sigh.

A few minutes later, they walked quietly to the shop and she said goodbye, taking her familiar position behind the counter and trying not to watch his expression as he walked away.

It was hard to settle back into work after seeing him, but eventually the rhythms of her day returned and she lost herself in the process of getting orders in, sorting stock and dealing with a steady stream of customers.

Claude made an appearance, looking smart, and asked if they had any books on gardening. Another woman was looking for English reading books for her young child.

At around ten o'clock, the door opened and a small woman came in. She looked to be about thirty years old, with short brown hair and large green eyes. Despite the fact that she was wearing a bright red coat, what struck Adeline most about her was the worry etched across her face.

She came timidly up to the counter and looked at Adeline. 'Are you Monique?' she asked.

'No. I'm Adeline. Can I help you?'

'I'm not sure,' she said. 'I'm just... I suppose I wanted to ask if you can recommend a book. Something that might... well, help me.'

Adeline was about to turn and call Monique; to tell the woman to wait. But something began to stir within her. 'I um... perhaps,' she said, studying the woman's face. Their eyes locked and perhaps she was imagining it, but a title swam into her mind. 'Just a second.'

She pulled the book off the shelf. It had only come in a couple of weeks ago and she'd read it curiously. Perhaps she was wrong, but it seemed as if the woman might at least connect with it.

She passed it to her. The woman studied the title, read the back and nodded. 'OK,' she said. 'I'll take it.'

'And you know,' Adeline said, starting to doubt herself as she rang up the total, 'if it doesn't work... you can come back. I'll find something else.'

The woman nodded. 'That's kind, thank you.'

Once the door had closed, she thought again of what had happened. Was it instinct? Magic? Was she deluded and imagining things? It was impossible to tell. But perhaps it was better not to question it. Perhaps this too fell into the unknown place between magic and science where so many things stirred that defied explanation.

At lunch, she excused herself and decided to pop home for a sandwich. Ordinarily she'd taken to eating with Monique or going to the cafe, but today she felt exhausted and wanted to take a moment to sit and not have to talk to anyone at all.

She was in the armchair, cup of tea in hand after eating, when she decided to reach for her Dickinson book. She'd read a little, then make her way back to work along the sunlit road, she decided.

Turning the page, she read the words:

> *If your Nerve, deny you—*
> *Go above your Nerve.*

And smiled at the wisdom in the tiny verse.

Some people would probably think she was brave, moving to France to a place where she knew nobody. But it hadn't been bravery, really. If anything, it had been fear that had driven her. Fear and shock and grief that had propelled her to this place where she'd thought she might hide from the world and work out what to do next. Instead, her journey had opened up her life.

She *had* been brave though, she realised. It had taken bravery to contact her mother, to take the trip to Toulouse.

She'd had to 'go above her nerve' just to get on the train and face such an enormous challenge.

Sometimes reading was a distraction for her, but sometimes it made her focus on herself anew. To see new things in her actions. She wondered whether she'd have got on with Emily Dickinson in real life, with her sharp observations and whip-smart humour. She liked the way that the woman she'd been lived on through her words, that she – Adeline – could bring Emily back to life at any moment. It was bizarre, and she'd never say it out loud, but in some ways this poet had become a friend to her, ever since Monique had thrust the book into her hands.

Slipping it back onto the small table, she straightened up and took her cup to the kitchen. Once it was washed, she set it on the counter, grabbed her bag and began the walk back to work. She thought about André again as she walked. She hadn't been very brave when it came to him, hadn't gone 'above her nerve'. But it was OK. He was giving her space and time, and that was what she needed.

She smiled at a few people, exchanged *bonjour*s en route. The faces were becoming more familiar now – she knew a few names from the shop, and recognised so many others she'd seen around St Vianne. There was a sense of community and belonging that had been absent in London and right now, that was what she needed. Maybe, one day, she'd start yearning for the pace, the excitement, the purpose of a bigger city. But for now, she was where she needed to be.

Unlocking the door, she changed the sign in the shop window to 'Open' and after stowing her bag behind the counter, began slicing the tape on a box of books they'd had delivered this morning. She was going to create a display in the window – the colourful, contemporary covers would really draw people in.

Once she'd removed the books, she flat-packed the box and

went to put it in the cupboard, ready to be taken to the recycling.

Only she almost didn't make it. Her foot came into contact with something hard, thin, which skidded on the wooden floor. She found herself sliding then falling hard onto her bottom.

'Ow!' Feeling under her leg she realised that the object she'd stumbled over had been a book. It was open on a page, but even without closing it she recognised its size, its shape, even the slight discolouration of the pages. Only she'd left the book at home, surely, on the table?

She looked at the open page:

> *To wait an Hour—is long*
> *To wait an Hour—is long—*
> *If Love be just beyond—*
> *To wait Eternity—is short—*
> *If Love reward the end—*

> — EMILY DICKINSON

'For God's sake, Emily,' she said, feeling her fear give way to frustration. 'Do you have to be right about everything?'

How ever had the book got there? Perhaps it had got caught on her bag and tumbled to the floor once she entered the shop? Maybe this was a copy left out by Monique and not her edition at all? But there was no misreading the message in the pages. That she shouldn't wait for love; that she shouldn't let the time stretch between her and potential happiness.

A rational person wouldn't read anything into the poem she'd stumbled over. A rational person would shake their head and file the book back on the shelf. A rational person would know that there was no way a poet from the nineteenth century could be giving her relationship advice here in the 2020s.

Perhaps someone who was more interested in magic, more likely to give implausible, far-fetched explanations for things might say that the book had come to her, on Monique's or even Emily's orders. To give her a message.

Well, she didn't believe that either.

What she did believe in was herself. Her feelings. And her sudden realisation that she was once again getting things wrong. She didn't need to know everything to find herself in order to move forward. Life would move forward anyway, and opportunities and changes didn't always wait.

'Monique – I'm just popping out for a moment!' she called out, then she ran into the street, suddenly knowing exactly where she was meant to be.

40

It took her a while to find him. He wasn't in the patisserie or the cafe. In the end, she tracked him down to the park – close to the bench where she'd sat to watch Lili play a few weeks ago – what seemed a lifetime ago now. He was sitting with his back to her, reading a volume she recognised as coming from the shop. Monique must have sold it to him. Something about the curve of his neck, the way he seemed totally absorbed in his thoughts made her heart swell. She crossed the grass, feeling more nervous now, and quietly slipped next to him on the wooden slats.

He looked up. 'Adeline?'

'Yep,' she said, grinning.

'You are on lunch break?'

She shook her head. 'Actually—' she said, wondering how, as a lover of words, she often found that they failed her in moments like this. 'Actually, I came to see you.'

He turned his book over so the splayed pages rested on his upper legs and gave her his full attention. ''You did?' He looked at her, his eyes full of something she couldn't define.

'Yes,' she said, decisively. 'Yes. I wanted to say that I was wrong. I'm not going to be ready in a few months.'

The smile vanished. 'Oh.'

'No! No,' she said, shuffling closer, taking his hand. 'Because I've realised I've been stupid. What was I waiting for? The stars to align? Everything to be figured out? Because that will never happen.'

He nodded.

She took a deep breath. 'Look, André. I'll be honest with you. I'm afraid. I'm afraid of letting someone in. Of... well, getting hurt. Let down.'

'But I would never...'

She raised a finger to indicate she hadn't finished. 'None of us know what we might or might not do. But I think I've got to learn to be OK with that. If I want anything... worthwhile.' She stopped short of saying 'love.'

He sat for a moment, absorbing her words. Then smiled and leaned in. 'So what you mean is, we need to make the most of how things are right now,' he said, his lips close to hers.

As he reached his arms out to hold her and they gently kissed, his book slipped to the floor.

But neither of them noticed.

EPILOGUE

It always surprised her just how many people lived in St Vianne. Every time the villagers came out in force, gathered for an event, it seemed there were more of them than could possibly fit into the rows of tiny houses, the clusters of stone farmhouses in outlying hamlets.

Tonight, it seemed, everyone had decided to attend. The air was warm, a breeze blew pleasantly. Around the square, stalls sold beer and wine and candyfloss. Children ran through the crowds, sticky and energised and full of excitement for what was to come.

'Here you are,' André said, handing her a glass of wine.

'Thank you!' she smiled, kissing him gently on the lips.

Across the square, some people had started to dance to the music being played from a loudspeaker. Others huddled in groups, chatting and laughing.

Lili came running up and flung herself at Adeline's legs, almost spilling her wine. She held an enormous cloud of candyfloss on a stick and her eyes were sparkling.

'Ooh. Careful!' Adeline laughed. She looked over at Kevin

who was standing just behind his niece. 'How did she convince you to buy *that*?' she asked.

'She promised we'd share it,' he said, making a face to indicate he wasn't banking on having a taste any time soon.

'When are the fireworks, Mummy?' Lili said from behind the pink sugary mess on a stick.

'Shouldn't be long now.'

The firework show took place every 14 July to celebrate Bastille Day. Shops were closed, and the square opened to anyone who wanted to join in with the evening's festivities. Monique was there, chatting with Claude. The atmosphere was one of togetherness and excitement.

'Thank you for coming,' Adeline said to Sophia who walked over now, hand in hand with her husband, Theo.

'Of course,' Sophia beamed. 'I had to be here for Lili's first Bastille Day. And yours too,' she added.

It had taken an age to make the arrangements. Sophia had been determined that they watch the fireworks in Toulouse 'because they are the best,' but Adeline had convinced her that, this year at least, she wanted to see what 14 July was like in her new home. Eventually Sophia had acquiesced.

Adeline laughed. 'Well, it's appreciated,' she said, feeling André's arm on her back as they moved along with the other attendees to the edge of the square, where the buildings fell away and they could see across to the hills beyond.

The first firework made the ground tremble. Lili let out a scream, then laughed delightedly. Then another and another. Sparkling and fizzing and hissing and squealing into the sky.

Adeline looked at the faces of the people around her, lit abruptly by each spark, then falling into darkness again. Their expressions, their eyes, their smiles visible for a moment before melting into shadow.

She was part of something. A family that didn't quite conform to the usual pattern, but was loving and supportive and everything you could want a family to be. Her mother, her grandmother, her daughter, her boyfriend, her brother; they were all connected to her in different ways, and she valued each and every one of them.

As she watched a rocket speed into the sky, she thought of Mum and wished that she could be here now too, to join this family. Because nobody could ever replace her. She was part of Adeline too, and always would be.

Nothing about her childhood had been a lie, she realised that now. Her parents had been her parents, Kevin, her brother. And now she had a new mother, a new grandmother. Not replacements, but additions.

She leaned against André and gently touched the top of Lili's head with her hand as her little girl watched the skies, mesmerised.

And for a moment she realised that however sceptical she might be, she really was starting to believe in magic.

ACKNOWLEDGEMENTS

As always, I am indebted to the brilliant team at Boldwood Books for their hard work and support. My editor, Isobel Akenhead, who has helped to find the magic in this story, the brilliant publicity team including Nia, Jenna and Issy as well as everyone else who's helped make this book a reality.

Huge thanks too to my agent, Ger, who never makes me feel the nuisance I almost certainly am.

To authors who have championed my work including Nicola Gill, Isabelle Broom, Jessica Redland, Kate Frost, Heidi Swain, Ian Moore, Nancy Peach, Natalie Jenner, Beth Morrey, Louise Fein, Kirsten Hesketh and so many others, including all the 'D20 Authors', without whom I'd definitely have lost the plot years ago – a heartfelt thank you to you all.

Thanks to Emilie and Marie at Emma's Bookshop in Clermont-Ferrand who helped me with some of the French titles (and who run a brilliant book club).

I'm so grateful to the online book community on Facebook, Instagram and TikTok who raise the profile of books and reading, and make this solitary pastime something to shout about. Especially to 'The Bookload', 'The Fiction Café Book Club', 'Chick Lit and Prosecco' groups.

And thank you to France, the place I called my home for fourteen years and which has provided so much inspiration for my writing.

ABOUT THE AUTHOR

Gillian Harvey is a freelance writer and bestselling author who lives in France. She writes escapist fiction set in France, including bestsellers *A Year at the French Farmhouse* and *A Month in Provence*.

Sign up to Gillian Harvey's mailing list for news, competitions and updates on future books.

Visit Gillian's website: www.gillianharvey.com

Follow Gillian on social media here:

facebook.com/gharveyauthor

x.com/GillPlusFive

instagram.com/gillplusfive

bookbub.com/profile/gillian-harvey

ALSO BY GILLIAN HARVEY

A Year at the French Farmhouse

One French Summer

A Month in Provence

The French Chateau Escape

The Bordeaux Book Club

The Riviera House Swap

The Little Provence Bookshop

WHERE ALL YOUR ROMANCE
DREAMS COME TRUE!

THE HOME OF BESTSELLING
ROMANCE AND WOMEN'S
FICTION

 WARNING:
MAY CONTAIN SPICE

SIGN UP TO OUR
NEWSLETTER

https://bit.ly/Lovenotesnews

Boldwood

Boldwood Books is an award-winning fiction publishing company seeking out the best stories from around the world.

Find out more at www.boldwoodbooks.com

Join our reader community for brilliant books, competitions and offers!

Follow us
@BoldwoodBooks
@TheBoldBookClub

Sign up to our weekly deals newsletter

https://bit.ly/BoldwoodBNewsletter

www.ingramcontent.com/pod-product-compliance
Ingram Content Group UK Ltd.
Pitfield, Milton Keynes, MK11 3LW, UK
UKHW040625030325
4827UKWH00028B/261

9 781805 499688